POETRY'S APPEAL

MERIDIAN

Crossing Aesthetics

Werner Hamacher

& David E. Wellbery

Editors

Stanford
University
Press

———————

Stanford
California
1999

POETRY'S APPEAL

*Nineteenth-Century French Lyric
and the Political Space*

E. S. Burt

Stanford University Press
Stanford, California

© 1999 by the Board of Trustees of the
Leland Stanford Junior University

Printed in the United States of America

CIP data are at the end of the book

For Nathanael

Acknowledgments

A leave spent at Cornell University, under the friendly auspices of the Society for the Humanities, gave me a precious year's start on this book. The Dean's Office at the University of California, Irvine, working with my department, made accepting that leave affordable.

More than to any institution, my thanks go to individuals. Over the years it has taken to bring the project to completion, these colleagues and friends were especially generous with comments, criticism, suggestions, or—where those did not avail—support: Cathy Caruth, Cynthia Chase, Elizabeth Constable, Jonathan Culler, Neil Hertz, Peggy Kamuf, Richard Klein, J. Hillis Miller, P. Adams Sitney, George Van den Abbeele, Samuel Weber. To a few friends, unstinting throughout, I am particularly grateful. They have made the improbable survival of the book possible, and the life of its author pleasant: Kevin Newmark, Barbara Spackman, Janie Vanpée, Andrzej Warminski.

I owe much to the students in graduate seminars at Irvine and Cornell to whom most of this material has been presented in one form or another. Their lively comments, sometimes even their intelligent silences, alerted me to obscurities or to questions begging treatment. Without their participation, this book would have been a thing far duller and more incomplete.

On the score of encouragement and warm, unflagging support, I owe an incalculable debt to others: to my father, David Burt; to my siblings and their families, John, Terry, and Emily; Emily and Larry; Sarah and Mario; Walter and Annah; Nathan, Lynda, Craig, and David; to my friends Pat, Carl, Billie, and George. It has taken a near village to produce this book; my neighbors have lent almost daily assistance in my single parenthood. I thank especially Katharine and Derek, Gaby and Paul, Erica and Armağan.

The one who has kept me going is my son, Nathanael.

Versions of several chapters have previously appeared in print: "Cracking the Code: The Poetical and Political Legacy of André Chénier," *Yale French Studies*, No. 77 (1990); "Hallucinatory History: Hugo's *Révolution*," *MLN*, 105 (1990); "'An Immoderate Taste for Truth': Censoring History in Baudelaire's 'Les Bijoux,'" in *Censorship and Silencing*, ed. Robert C. Post (Los Angeles: The Getty Research Institute, 1997). I gratefully acknowledge permission to use this material. I am also thankful to Holly Caldwell for her help in turning the manuscript into a book.

E. S. B.

Contents

POETRY'S APPEAL

Modification in the Status
of the Ivory Tower

What seems particularly odd is that while retaining habits thus
derived from books, we have almost completely lost our former
love of literature. In the course of my public career I have often
been struck by the fact that those who reproduce most faithfully
some of the chief defects of the literary style prevailing in the previous
generation are men who rarely, if ever, read our eighteenth-century
books or, for that matter, any books at all.
—Tocqueville, *The Old Régime and the French Revolution*

In 1933 Paul Valéry wrote a brief response to a survey on the relation of
literature and the political. In that response, where he comments on the
open possibility of defining literature and the political so as to exclude or
to agree with one another (and so on the impossibility of closure on the
debate over their relation), he states that various circumstances "can
modify more or less abruptly the status of the 'Ivory Tower.'"[1] By "status
of the Ivory Tower" Valéry means something other than its prestige or social standing.[2] He means the legalities regulating the state and capacities
of the Ivory Tower from without (subjective genitive), and those that affect it from within (objective genitive), that as it were strive to maintain it
standing. Valéry's statement is general but concise: when a modification
occurs, it affects the context, the way it regulates, evaluates, and sets up
literature as an institution, and also the text, the modes and economies
regulating its writing and reading.

Valéry's phrase formulates succinctly the point of departure of the essays that follow. My starting hypothesis was that with the French Revolution, modifications occurred in France in the status of the Ivory Tower,
modifications that have affected—besides the view on and the view from
the tower—the mapping of the boundaries and overlaps between the literary and the political space. In at least one definition the problem of the
political is that of the polis, as the "historical place, the there *in* which,
out of which, and *for* which history happens."[3] As for literature, it concerns itself with place and place-holders—in the *locus amoenus* and the
topos of poetry, the conflicts the novel stages between its topicality as

work tied to a context and its a-topicality, the no-place of fictional utopias, and so forth. It seemed reasonable to think that a study of the changes in the way these sites are mapped onto one another, the topology showing where they intersect or overlay or exclude one another, would be revelatory for both literary and political arenas. The French Revolution and the renascent lyric seemed promising vantage points from which to consider modifications affecting text and context. As just one indication, during the period when the lyric poet is invested with unprecedented centrality, the metaphor of the Ivory Tower undergoes an abrupt and significant extension. As far back as the Song of Solomon, the beloved's neck was likened in color, smoothness, and columnar shape to a tower of ivory. But it was not until Sainte-Beuve commented in a poem on Alfred de Vigny's retreat from the world that the tower, by then having the connotations of falseness associated with the Gates of Ivory through which false dreams issued for Homer, opens to reveal an inner space, and gets an elevation sufficient to shelter an aristocratic poet disdainfully withdrawing from the crowd.[4]

I say, these seemed promising vantage points, putting things in the past tense, because the original project of this book has undergone changes, for reasons to which the resultant collection testifies. A discussion of the transformations that have taken place in the hypothesis about the place poetry allots itself in the planned-for Republic can help introduce the project as it finally coalesced.

In some respects, to say that a modification in the place of the literary occurred around the Revolution is to repeat a banality. Numerous studies have concerned themselves with transformations in the value of *la chose littéraire* over the course of the nineteenth century. Be it in terms of the commodity fetishism of bourgeois ideology and the rise of capitalism; be it in terms of the slow, steady institutionalization of literature or of the laws regulating authorship, copyrights, or censorship; be it in terms of the way texts, genres, or literary movements reflect, reflect on, or intervene in the debate—the transformed relations between the postrevolutionary public space and the literary space have in one way or another occupied studies of nineteenth-century texts. Still, some room seemed to be left to consider the testimony of the poetical texts of nineteenth-century France concerning this modified status, texts that, in an enigmatic inversion of the Platonic philosopher's gesture exiling poetry from the polis, publicize the Ivory Tower as an edifice in the midst of the city into which the poet dramatically and deliberately retreats. With the notable exception of Baudelaire's *Tableaux parisiens*, the poetic texts of post-Revolutionary France have been little consulted for what they have to say about this retreat as it speaks to and impinges on the public space and history.

Poetry as Aesthetic Object: The Appealing Retreat

A first hypothesis presented itself for review. The hypothesis was that, by means of a suspension of the referential function in favor of formalism, poetry allots itself a place in the Ivory Tower in a gesture of aristocratic retreat from the democratic crowds of the post-Revolution. In the midst of emergent industrialization and bourgeois capitalism, with the rise of the political culture analyzed by Lynn Hunt and with the rapid spread of slogans and symbols manufactured or borrowed to represent (or foment) the nation in upheaval, small wonder if a few should seek flight.[5] The lyric poem, I conjectured, can be construed as a place of refuge from the messy immediacies and compromises of practical politics. Its expressive language, with its ties to the pastoral, seems to express a nostalgic wish for simpler times, and the well-chiseled metaphors, the distilled thoughts and concern with poetic form might attest to the disdainful attention of the artist-ocrat to mere form over content, to politeness over the polity. The emergence of the lyric might be nothing more than a symptomatic reaction to overpoliticized times, if not an outright reactionary scurry back to a prepolitical stance.

I found empirical grounds for suspecting this hypothesis forthwith. The poems often credited with providing the first sign of lyric resurgence are those of André Chénier. If we look even cursorily at the work of Chénier, we find that what was published in the poet's lifetime were a few political essays and two poems on overtly political themes. As for the posthumous essays and poems, many show thematic links to the long tradition of considering the role and fate of the mimetic arts in terms of the polis.[6] The poems dating from the Revolution could be cited in easy rebuttal of the theory that Chénier conceived of poetry as a place of refuge from political questions.[7] He wrote quite a number of odes, hymns, and iambs on political themes, some of them violently anti-Jacobin, and some of them equally strong appeals for freedom. If the work of Chénier is at all indicative of what follows, the charge of formalism and nostalgic naturalism cannot be made to stick.

Another reason could be cited for doubting that poetry's concern with symbolic language speaks to its desire for a simple severing of all connection with the referential world. The Revolution brought with it a heightened awareness of form, not only of the symbols and representations for the Revolution that have been the focus of much recent work,[8] but also of the constitution, the forms of law, the order and administration of the state, and so on. In such a context, the acute formal sense of poets was more likely to lead them to style themselves legislators à la Shelley than to an apolitical stance (witness Hugo's term as *pair de France* or Chénier's vision of Orpheus as the singer of laws to princes).[9] Where Chénier and his ilk compose eclogues (as in Baudelaire's "Paysage"), they invariably frame the retreat by a city scene, or stage it as motivated by a desire to take stock of the city.[10] As one example, we could mention Chénier's ode "Versailles," which shows the poet withdrawn from the center of political agitation in Paris, wandering in the forests and dreaming of love. But the poem meditates on a politically symbolic spot—Versailles resonates as the seat of the ruined monarchy dramatically emptied of its king— and it concludes with an abrupt return to a problem of justice:

> tes frais asiles
> Tout à coup à mes yeux s'enveloppent de deuil.
>   J'y vois errer l'ombre livide
> D'un peuple d'innocents, qu'un tribunal perfide
> Précipite dans le cercueil.

> your fresh asylums
> Suddenly appear enveloped in mourning.
>   I see wandering there the livid shadow
> Of a people of innocents that a perfidious tribunal
> Precipitates into its grave.[11]

At the very least, such dramatized retreats mean that the lyric is a more complex mode where the poet withdraws strategically, so as to investigate the relation of public to private space.

Moreover, the poet's special involvement with symbolic language makes the poem in its splendid isolation into a sort of laboratory for testing symbols and the claims of symbolic language. In one poem Chénier dated from 1789, "Heureux qui, se livrant aux sages disciplines" (Happy the one who, devoted to wise disciplines) (p. 58), the poet even sets up this retreat into autarkic solitude as a condition, at once impossible to attain and necessary, for speaking in a poetic language that is not one of dissimulation or fawning policy. The poet wants to speak a language that is free from certain constraints and, if not precisely truthful, yet consistent with truth. The poet wants to provide symbols for readers to mull over that are not, or not only, the stale ones in circulation of the already known and already thought, displayed for vanity's sake. He states a desire for a tasty language, one worthy of being served up at a "banquet of friends," and distinct from the puffed-up language of a rhymster, a "buffoon among buffoons" (*sot parmi les sots*). The phrase "banquet of friends," with its allusion to the Platonic dialogues and to classical writings on friendship, tells us that, in keeping with the period's search for symbols by which to represent new assemblies, Chénier considers the writing of a poem to have a political dimension.[12] Poetry can be seen as engaged in a political struggle not where it expresses Jacobin or anti-Jacobin sentiments, but where it evidences a struggle between a certain tendency of literary language, a tendency to appear as a representation that—because it imitates what is—helps circulate the *doxa*, and a tendency to provide shapes undreamt of, to present itself as an operation of representing that represents nothing, that "imitates nothing that in any way pre-exists its operation."[13] In a word, my first hypothesis fell apart in the face of a language whose power to posit and knowingly to undo forms of and for "banquets of friends" had to be taken into account.

In the passage from Valéry's *Réponse à une enquête* mentioned above, hints can be found to suggest that the areas of convergence and divergence between the political and the literary are best approached from the angle of a literature that, like Chénier's, is at odds with itself. In Valéry's precise vocabulary, circumstances can modify the status of literature. "To modify" is to effect a change in mode or manner, in what used to be called the accidents affecting a thing and not in its essence or nature. Mode refers to the stuff of literature, not only the term for its stylishness, but also for what concerns it. By claiming that the status of the tower is *modified*, Valéry identifies the transformation in the legalities of the tower as one of the sort that literature knows about. This is not to say that Valéry considers the modifications in topography and standing to be just a passing fad in an age-old struggle concerning the status of the poetic arts, a change in style that does not affect the essence. Nor does it mean that Valéry is inordinately privileging art. With characteristic balance, he weighs a suspicion—that a modishness to political structures might be owed to the importation of aesthetic categories into the political realm—against the possibility that literature reserves knowledge about fashion and fashioning, and so could possibly inform about such importation. Literature, he says, is a thinking person's sport, a discipline "which requires the exercise of almost all the faculties of the mind," and by means of which one can meet the "singular need to develop in oneself the relations of thought and sensibility with language" (1: 1148).

Now Valéry's choice to practice this sport, a choice to which his essay with its careful review of definitions testifies, is again not that of an aristocrat exercising in solitude for his pleasure. His choice is dictated by a double concern. First, he wants to bring out, in the midst of a host of possible definitions, what he sees as a sort of vanishing point where disappear any criteria allowing us to draw a line once and for all between the two areas of politics and literature, so that reason cannot direct us in our choice of a definition: "in short, no solution that can be applied to everybody; but individual decisions that depend on character and circumstance, for here reason does not govern [*car ici la raison ne peut rien commander*]" (1: 1149). Having pointed out both the necessity and the impossibility of choosing where reason gives no guidance, Valéry then says that as a result of this vanishing point we enter an area of risk (of chance and its loss) where historical determination becomes inevitable. Why this should be so is perhaps apparent. The point where the distinction between the literary condition (defined as *"writing so as to make think or imagine"* [1: 1149]) and the political condition (defined as *"writing [or speaking] so as to make act"* [1: 1149]) gets lost is the point where aesthetic categories take over in the political arena, for instance in the use of persuasive formulas or *mots d'ordre* borrowed from past writers, irrespective of the context, to argue for a certain shape of the future. Valéry quotes a whole list of examples: Fichte, Hegel, Marx, Gobineau, Nietzsche, Darwin—all loaded examples in the context of the racist arguments and burgeoning German nationalism of 1933. When aesthetic categories take over, though, this is also the point at which the writer has a chance to "do" something, to critique ideologization and to posit a new object for literature. In short, the choice at the point of risk, where we cannot perceive any difference between the literary and the political, is not a choice between doing and thinking, between politics and literature. Instead, it is a choice between two ways of having to do with literature and politics. In Valéry's text, the political and the literary are not in the last analysis opposed. It is always a matter of mode and timing, of how and when one engages oneself, and not whether one engages oneself, in both.

Where one is speaking of "la chose littéraire" and "la chose pratique" (one of Valéry's names for politics in this essay), a modal change is thus a change in the thing itself. In mode is manifested a change in the way the sign system is seized, installed, held as and for representation. That change can consist in an instant evacuation, an emptying out of a whole meaning system that seems simultaneously accompanied by its elevation and enshrinement as formalism. At the end of *Père Goriot*, we find a nice allegory for such modification: the apotheosis, death, and entombment in the heights of the Père Lachaise cemetery of the paternal figure who has literally presided over Mme Vauquer's bourgeois boardinghouse coincides with the abrupt evacuation of that house. But the modification can also involve a sweeping reenergizing, by way of the positing of a new figure capable of resignifying evacuated forms. Where what is to be represented is the possibility that representation might be undergoing modification in one or both of these two senses—the case in the Revolution, but also, differently, in 1933—a privilege will be attached to such texts as attempt, by making readable the vanishing point where the literary and the political are no longer perceptibly different, to enable the risk to be grasped and confronted. Modification in status makes the political and the literary converge, but it also divides and isolates literature, makes it the much-guarded guardian of some secret about the political, about its modishness, which is to say, about it as a place where history happens.

Poetizing as the Producing of a World: The Appeal for Reserves

My second hypothesis was that around the Revolution there was introduced what Peggy Kamuf has analyzed under the title of *The Division of Literature*, namely, a split in literature itself.[14] Literature divides itself: in a single gesture it sets itself up and suspects itself as aesthetic object. So far as poetry is concerned, that means it publicly *stages* its retreat, so as to establish a reserve where its critical, theoretical side can emerge. Only by means of a feint can it address such questions as cannot be addressed so long as one is obliged to respond to the demands of the day, to take sides on an issue, to engage in the affairs of the marketplace, and in every way to assume the priority of literal, proper language. Some questions that affect the very constitution of the political space as itself involving figures cannot be addressed directly without taking for granted the stability of categories that in epochal shifts may be up for grabs. For instance, it would be nearsighted to ask literature to weigh in with its voice for or against the Jacobins or the Communards, if it is asking itself—as lyric poetry does—what constitutes a voice and what is left unrepresented by it. An essay of Chénier's provides an example of this splitting within the poetic text that shows it to be in struggle with itself about its function with respect to the public space. Chénier satirizes the poet at the courtier's table as the flatterer's flatterer who, by holding up a mirror to the court, helps naturalize relations of power and violence.[15] The order and harmony of the work of art, he suggests, get taken as seductively mirroring the order and harmony in the polis. The retreat of the poet from the court then amounts to a strategic withdrawal undertaken the better to combat the interpretation of poetic language as mirror of whatever ideology is in vogue. It is the first step to clearing the poetic stage for a representing of language itself as productive. I supposed it would be possible, through the examination of the verbal act by which the poem does away with its narrow representational function and posits a world having a theoretical existence, to approach the self-grounding performatives characteristic of the fundamental texts of the French and American Revolutions.[16]

This second hypothesis is attractive in the light of some recent important work by Philippe Lacoue-Labarthe on Heidegger, which considers the question of poetic language and the political in terms of mimesis defined not as imitation but as a mode of production. In *Heidegger, Art and Politics* (1987), Lacoue-Labarthe holds his most elaborate discussion with Heidegger over the latter's "brief but decisive" alignment with National Socialism, an alignment that brings Lacoue-Labarthe to "think *with* Heidegger *against* Heidegger" on the question of the political and of poetry.[17] *With* Heidegger because, for Lacoue-Labarthe, Heidegger lets us think the break with Platonic idealism in terms of the function and place of art; in doing so he marks what Lacoue-Labarthe calls the "abyss" that separates his philosophy as a whole from the dream of National Socialism.[18] *Against* Heidegger, because Heidegger's break with idealism was in fact incomplete; in a certain area his philosophy comes into close enough proximity with Nazism that Heidegger could momentarily think they were compatible. In "Poétique et politique," Lacoue-

Labarthe underlines *mimèsis* as a seminal motif in his discussion with Heidegger. He translates *mimèsis* not as the literary category of *imitation* (as in Book Three of the *Republic*) but in ontological terms, as a *mode of production* of existing things (as in Book Ten of the *Republic*).

Lacoue-Labarthe begins by arguing *with* Heidegger. He shows that in the texts and seminars on art and poetry immediately following Heidegger's retreat from public life in 1934, the latter is concerned with what the title of one seminar phrased as "The overcoming of the aesthetic in the question of art," in a reckoning that constitutes an important disagreement with National Socialism over the function of art. Art understood in aesthetic terms, art withdrawn from the world to allow its empty form to scintillate, is art compatible with the crude aestheticization of politics that, for Brecht and Benjamin, characterized the Nazi régime. Lacoue-Labarthe states National Socialism's compatibility with such an aesthetics as follows: "The Nazi project is incomprehensible unless it is referred, beyond Wagnero-Nietzschism, to the great German mimetic dream of Greece and of the possibility of reconstituting that 'living' work of art that was the City" ("Poétique," p. 188). The stakes are high that Heidegger should have applied himself in this period to developing an interpretation of art aimed at "removing art from any aesthetic determination, beginning with the taking into account of beauty," ("Poétique," p. 190) and withdrawing it from the place where it cohabits easily with totalitarian politics as formal harmony, to make it political in another sense, as a *work*, a producing without a subject that by placing us in language brings forth the *possibility* of the political space: "the installation of the world and . . . the possibility of history" ("Poétique," p. 192).

Not coincidentally, Valéry's previously cited 1933 article opens by pushing the *production* of ideas as what brings together (and also divides) literature and politics. Valéry is talking about the definitions of literature and politics but his statement applies to what goes on in those fields as well. He says, "Every answer to your questions depends on the ideas one gets [*des idées que l'on se fait*] of politics and literature" (1: 1148), where the phrase *se faire des idées*, which can mean everything from "form, produce, develop, improve, get or give ideas (for or to oneself)," to "wallow in illusions," aptly describes a production that takes place "prior to its further implication in epistemological determinations of truth and falsehood," as Kevin Newmark succinctly puts it in writing about what Lacoue-Labarthe means by fiction.[19]

How very far Heidegger is from understanding the work of art in aesthetic terms is evident from Lacoue-Labarthe's timely reminder of the way Heidegger uses *Dichtung* (poem). The poem, a language production co-originary with thought (its imprint, says Lacoue-Labarthe), is the highest form of production (*technè*) and, as such, is of critical importance since it is by *technè* that man situates himself in history, and thus in the political. By *poem* Lacoue-Labarthe understands that Heidegger does not mean "versified verbal construct" only. The extension of meaning can be seen, among other places, in Lacoue-Labarthe's hypothesis that the essence of the political "is sought by Heidegger in *technè*. And it is rather as art, and (principally as poetry) that *technè* itself, in the movement of retreat, comes to determination" ("Poétique," p. 187).[20] Wherever production, the installation of a world goes on, we are in front of poetizing.[21]

At the same time that Lacoue-Labarthe shows Heidegger extending *Dichtung* to fit more than verse, he also shows the latter to have restricted and condensed it greatly. Not all versified verbal constructs qualify as poem: "Thus the poem is not just any poem. It is truly poem only *where it speaks itself as poem*" (my emphasis, "Poétique," p. 194). Heidegger's simultaneous extension and restriction of the term so that it no longer coincides except in a few places with what, speaking aesthetically, we would call "poems," provides clear testimony for Lacoue-Labarthe that, besides speculating that the poem is a work not aesthetically determined, Heidegger is emplacing us differently in the language. A poem is not or is no longer a container, say, a cup or vase, but is rather defined in terms of production. A shift in the topography of the poem is apparent, and with it, a shift in the constructing and stability of place, now taken as installation (Lacoue-Labarthe's term) or, in Samuel Weber's strong translation in *Mass Mediauras*, emplacement.[22]

Heidegger's discussion with National Socialism in the texts following 1933 takes the form of a struggle over the place(s) of art in the polis and, also, over what is art. The work of art construed in terms of production and not aesthetics, and one like poetry concerned with installing man in history by installing him in language, is not an art that tries to define the political place along the model of a container whose borders delimit precisely the territory ruled, or a monument elevated in a stable, central place around which a community gathers. Poetry does not withdraw *out of* the world and *into* a tower. Instead, it withdraws from place itself, construed as formed and delimited space obeying a stable distinction between inside and outside, public and private. From its retreat it speaks its essence, which is "the Open: the play space of the struggle between world and earth, of *polémos*" ("Poétique," p. 196).

What is lost when the regime of art as formal entity is ended is the prerevolutionary emplacement made possible by the stable monument: the notion that place is static and homogeneous, totalized, contained, and bounded. For Weber, Heidegger's thought on *Technik* is bound up with his thinking on the breakup of the Aristotelian notion of place "defined in terms of immanence, stability and containment, as 'the innermost motionless boundary of what contains.'"[23] "In modern technics," he says, "this 'innermost boundary' is forced, driven out of its motionless state. It begins to move." One consequence "of an ordering that can no longer be taken for granted," as Weber puts it, is that place is not only differently mapped (no longer as inside/outside), but is in the process of continual remapping.[24] The modification Heidegger effects in what is called *poem*—restricted, concentrated, and condensed into the poem where it speaks itself as poem, and also dispersed everywhere—goes along with "placings" no longer secured by the stable model of a container or a visible monument, but instead heterogeneous, pocketed, enclaved, unsecured and shifting, making shift to secure where place is not a given. Because the places "thus set up are the result of emplacement," says Weber, "they can never simply be taken for granted. Places must continually be established, orders continually placed. As emplacement, the goings-on of modern technics thus display a markedly ambivalent character: they arrest, bring to a halt, by setting in place; but this placement itself gives way to other settings, to the incessant re-placing of orders through which new places are set up and upset."[25]

This breakup of the Aristotelian place has less to be anxiously controlled and traumatically repeated, than the energy of the disruption harnessed through thinking it. Says Lacoue-Labarthe: "The call to begin again the Greek beginning is thus the call to repeat the irruption of *technè*, of knowledge as essence of technique. This does not mean that it is a question of a call to dominate technique, but rather an attempt to find, together with its domination, a relation to the 'excess power' of such a domination" ("Poétique," p. 186). What is wanted is less a mere control of technics than a relation to the excess power released by dominating it. Lacoue-Labarthe thinks with Heidegger on this point, as well as on the critical redefinition of *mimèsis* in terms of production.[26]

When Heidegger privileges *Dichtung* over the other arts as giving a relation to this excess power, however, Lacoue-Labarthe thinks *against* Heidegger. Here the French philosopher suspects an incomplete undoing of formalism and a return of mimesis as imitation, in the form of a fiction of unity attributed to the people displaced from the stable Aristotelian place by *technè* but restabilized by their common identity as speakers of a language. For Heidegger, according to Lacoue-Labarthe, poetry provides a cohesive founding myth for the German-speaking people, replacing the shared and delimited *place* with the shared and delimited national *language* as the unifying element. Poetry (as distinct from the novel or the drama) has a critical role to play in the development of national identity, in a view of the political that Lacoue-Labarthe baptizes national aestheticism (*Heidegger*, p. 58). Heidegger's break with Platonic metaphysics is therefore not complete. The poem is not in retreat into the space of play only, for it also returns from its retreat to address a myth of a common origin to a community of speakers. It enables a community attributed the characteristics lent by traditional aesthetics to the polis—Lacoue-Labarthe cites in particular formal plasticity, the privilege on Western and especially Greek art, and above all the view of the polis as organic totality—all of which show up in myths of national identity and especially of the national type. Heidegger is thus "left *without his knowing it* [*à son insu*] prisoner of a mimetology that is in the end traditional, that is, Platonist: the one that relates *technè* to fiction" (*Heidegger*, p. 131). Lacoue-Labarthe sees the current task to be to think this unthought, in the hope of ridding the modern epoch of the mimetology that causes the needle to skip and again replay the long-playing record left by the Greeks. This drives Lacoue-Labarthe's interpretation of the Extermination as a caesura, the pause in which Heidegger failed to recognize the definitive collapse of the Platonic program of totalization. Auschwitz, says Lacoue-Labarthe, is "the refuse of the occidental idea of art" (*le déchet de l'idée occidentale de l'art*) (*Heidegger*, p. 72). This is not to lessen the event, but to accord it greater moment as the catastrophe of a program set in place several thousand years ago.

It is impossible to do full justice in so short a space to this admirable analysis, indispensable reading along with Jean-Luc Nancy's *Inoperative Community* for any consideration of literature and the political. Among the implications of this interpretation, based on Lacoue-Labarthe's long experience with the philosophical texts of German Romanticism, is a revised understanding of post-Rousseauian, pre–World War II modernity as the incomplete, convulsive, and repetitive attempt to liberate the political from mimetology. The French Revolution and the model for revolution that was its legacy—termed "revolution as permanent process" by Hannah Arendt—looks a fertile ground for an analysis based on such principles. It lets us look at the nineteenth century as the modern epoch during which the recurrence of this logic dominates, with the Revolution picked out as a decisive event installing it.

Take for instance one of the old chestnuts in the literature on the Revolution dividing Tocqueville and Michelet—whether 1789 was the outcome of the ancien régime's centralizing policies or the moment of invention and self-fashioning when a new actor and a new idea of place burst on the scene.[27] Both sides could be reinterpreted in the light of Lacoue-Labarthe's discussion as moves in the same mimetologic. Thus, Michelet's mythologizing view, his identification of the people as a new and inventive actor on the stage, is evidence of a dream of a founding myth reasserting itself in an upsurge of national aestheticism. Michelet may well have been wrong from the perspective of class about the importance of the people's contribution (the Revolution may be that of the bourgeoisie and not of the masses) and still have been on target in terms of the shift of the political place away from polis to demos and the invention of French national identity.

As for Tocqueville, his ironic vision of the monarchy's collapse in the wake of its "successful" pursuit of policies that centralized power and fragmented and isolated the Estates works very well as an analysis of the forces leading to the breakup of the unified, totalized place. In his account, the House of France was a lineage conceived as a proper place, a place organized as a house in terms of inside and outside, center and periphery. Taken in by this metaphor, the House of France tried to centralize everything, and was pushed flat as the pasteboard "House of Cards" that it was the moment that—all resistance against it overcome and the metaphor revealed to be one—it achieved its goal of centralization.[28] Truly, for Tocqueville, the monarchy fell from its own success at producing the city as a perfect work of art.

What is more, in keeping with Lacoue-Labarthe's cogent discussion of the return of mimesis as imitation, Tocqueville recognizes a fundamental continuity between the centralization policy of the ancien régime and that pursued in subsequent governments. In his discussion of the social glue needed to hold the Estates together, Tocqueville theorizes the role of society and culture as supplements on which the government depends. He sees that at the very moment that the feudal, land-based traditions that opposed and supported the monarchy in its quest for centralization are made meaningless and the monarchy collapses, new customs of thought arise that play the same role for the increasingly centralized governments of post-Revolutionary France. The fiction of unified place is not completely undone but returns to haunt the scene in the form of new customs based no longer on land, but rather on the national type. This national type is, again not coincidentally, modeled on "the instincts, the turn of mind, the tastes, and even the eccentricities characteristic of the literary man."[29] In this return of the work of art in the model of the French citizen as literary man, a version of Lacoue-Labarthe's return of mimesis as the myth of a community of speakers can be found.[30]

Some recent work on culture, especially on Revolutionary culture, could also be illuminated by this logic. Consider the central thesis of the work of the eminent historian Lynn Hunt, for whom a chief contribution of the Revolution to modern politics is political *culture*, where the "revolutionaries acted on Rousseau's belief that government could *form* a new people."[31] Revolutionary culture looks like another name for national aestheticism because, as Hunt describes it, it is both the product of and the means for producing the people as an unfinished project, a work-in-progress. The symbols and symbolic practices Hunt discusses represented the newly formed people to themselves as a renascent people; they also provided the people with a convenient project to work on, a means for perpetuating the Revolution itself in the discussion and elaboration of such practices. In Hunt's discussion, *culture* no longer means a set of autochthonous traditions, capable of obstructing as well as of stabilizing government. In the Revolutionary sense, culture involves a positing of something—a people—that wasn't there before. The symbols are not adopted as expressions of something, but are inventive and self-creating:

> Liberty trees, patriotic altars, Jacobin clubs, and electoral procedures were established in nearly identical fashion everywhere. This symbolic framework did not so much reflect already-present feelings of nationalism or the democratic strivings of the masses as it created them. The processions, the swearing of oaths, and the circulation of coins with the image of Liberty or Hercules elicited and consolidated the new Nation that revolutionary rhetoric posited in the first place.[32]

To make a revolution it is not enough to overhaul a government, tear down a building, or write new laws. One has to design, mint, and circulate symbols of the revolution, since the act of positing is the act over and over to be imitated. Revolutionary culture, as Hunt describes it, is revolutionary precisely in its actualizing the dream of producing a class whose very habits, traditions, and practices did not exist prior to the positing of the class. Lacoue-Labarthe positions this political culture for us very nicely, as part of the afterglow of Western metaphysics.

More immediately to the point for the essays that follow, Lacoue-Labarthe's analysis suggested a possible framework for rereading the poetic texts of the nineteenth century, so as to bring out areas of overlap or difference between the poem's topography and that of the polis. Certain thematic elements, certain functions poetry sees itself as fulfilling, can be viewed in terms of the struggle over how place is to be construed: as stable space constructed around a perceptible church or monument, or as the work-in-progress of a people. Mimetology lets us read the apparently most apolitical of poems as bearing on the political, since in the representation of representation, in poetry's questioning of itself as ultimately art object or mode of production, it positions us in terms of place and of production. The Ivory Tower is set up only to be instantly toppled, ironized, or mourned as the aesthetics supporting a model of the walled city. In terms of analyzing the poems of the period—poems in retreat from politics that concern themselves with the transformation in the base of the political—the possibilities are endless. For instance, the opening pages of Nerval's prose poem *Sylvie* show us a narrator who, by refusing to isolate himself in the "Ivory Tower of the poets" (which he terms a paradox of Platonic idealism), also refuses to remain within the boundaries of representation as grounded in the inside/outside polarity. Instead, he acts out a withdrawal from representation, and prefers the sublime, stormy, and sophistical discussions of a circle he locates at the edge of a theatrical, representational space: "Thus it was that, *quitting the theater* with the bitter sadness left by a vanished dream, I went willingly to sup in the society of a numerous company, where all melancholy gave way before the inexhaustible verve of a few spirits, sparkling, lively, stormy, sometimes sublime—spirits of the sort that are always to be found in periods of renewal or decadence" (my emphasis).[33] The politics of such a positioning would be the politics of a modernity arrested on the threshhold, having undone the myth of the city as work of art, but a forerunner of national aestheticism in its inability to do without myth entirely.

Within the more narrowly defined field of the reemergent nineteenth-century lyric, an art that exceeds the limits of the beautiful—in mode (the sublime, the grotesque), in figure (allegory, irony), or in genre (anti-lyrical tendencies of the lyric)—can be seen to betoken the breakdown in the notion of place discussed by Lacoue-Labarthe and Weber. In the various systems mobilized by a poem (its tropes, its syntax, its use of po-etic form) can be found evidence of a struggle between forces tending toward recontainment and retotalization and those tending toward over-condensation and dispersal. The poems of Chénier, Hugo, Baudelaire, and Mallarmé studied here all stage as one crisis the liberation of poetry from the confines of aesthetic determination and its construal as work-in-progress, as site of multiple possibilities. It is not impossible to make those struggles to resituate the poem in terms of what it says about itself and the act of poetic production at least parallel to, and thus significant of, a struggle going on in France in the nineteenth century, say to pro-duce a new myth of a democratic republic owing everything to a Greek, and nothing to a more recent feudal, past.

At one end of the eighteenth century, Chénier turns away from the classicism of the seventeenth century in irritation. His appraisal of trans-lation and even plagiarism as more inventively daring than imitation, and his positioning of a comet *aux crins étincelants* at the moving "cen-ter" of his poetic universe, are a few signals that the Aristotelian place is in revision, and that the poet is preoccupied with representation as a mode of production.[34] Where the poetic cup is not just a container of divine ambrosia, but can also serve as a weapon upsetting the status quo, it is possible to discover conflictual notions of poetic language, of the poet, and of the locus shaped by the poem.[35] An aesthetician, this *"ébéniste* [cabinetmaker] *de Marie-Antoinette"* (Baudelaire, *Oeuvres com-plètes*, 2: 239), works on the cup; but with the improvised weapon stands revealed a producer, a poetician, the "romantic" Baudelaire also calls him (2: 408). In the light of Lacoue-Labarthe's discussion, Chénier's famous line calling for an invention of antique verse—"Sur des pensers nou-veaux / Faisons des vers antiques" (On new thoughts / Let us make an-tique lines) (p. 127), can be interpreted as signaling both poesis as pro-duction, and the unthought return of aesthetic formalism, with "antique verse" as the key term recalling its allegiance to the Greek program. At the other end of the century, Mallarmé's well-known experiments with a poetics of *"le doute du Jeu suprême"* (the doubt of the supreme Game, in both senses of the genitive)[36] where representation is in question, and his lesser-known examination of a residual *beau* (beauty) haunting such unlikely places as the *tombeaux* (tombs) of poets or the *lambeaux* (fragments) of a sentence, are signs of a conflict within these poems, suggesting that the undoing of the space of representation is indeed not complete. The poem gets its energy, its "urge," and itself as work from this incompletion.

The problem, as it emerged from this second hypothesis, was to discover how each poet mythifies and puts a face on poetic production. Since the point was the discovery of a figure of mythic proportions, anthropomorphism, it seemed, would likely be the figure of choice. Hugo's poem *La Révolution*, in which the very monuments of the city are imagined as kings on the march, provides a gripping image of a crisis that consists in both the necessity and the impossibility of redefining a stable place. So too, the significant comment of a returning ghost in one of Mallarmé's poems, "tremblante de (s)'asseoir" (p. 69) indicates that she is trembling *to* find a place, desirous and perhaps fearful of seating herself, but also, with that marked ambivalence of which Weber speaks, trembling *from* having found a seat, quaking in anticipation of the loss of a seat recently found—all that in a language whose very thickness of meaning signifies that the poem is fulfilling its function of installing us in the language. This is a satisfying coincidence: on the one hand, the dramatic fall of the monarchy and the founding of a Republic, together with a new culture of the people as the living work-of-art-in-progress; on the other hand, the resurgence of a poetry no longer interested in imitation, but remapping itself instead as a building site, a Rimbaldian *chantier*.

Notice that, in this hypothesis, poetic language is ultimately synonymous with a temple where the priestly poet interprets what is finally a preeminently intelligible and intentional construct (where the gods draw near or depart ["Poétique," p. 197]), whatever its ambiguity, multivocity, or contradictory character. The sacerdotal function recurrently accorded the poet in the nineteenth-century lyric—even by Baudelaire's slipped halo—gives credence to the view that the nineteenth century might have so construed the function of the poet and of poetic language. It is presumably not only the sort of construction held sacred but even the sacerdotal function per se that is affected by the radical break that is the Extermination. Postwar poetry, as exemplified by Paul Celan for Lacoue-Labarthe, is a poetry of silence organized around the caesura, and if Celan still speaks of God (and of metaphysics), it is, the French philosopher asserts, not in terms of incarnation, but in the face of the dead, of the exterminated.[37] In brief, the narrative we have been examining is persuasive enough that all the essays in this book have to grapple with it in one way or another and are haunted by the questions and frame it provides. It is a strong story, even an indispensable story, positioning us as the survivors of the collapse of a program, in the midst of a need to think the possibilities for the political unleashed by that collapse.

Mais c'est trop beau. It's all too neat. It's too neat first because it is a narrative. Despite Lacoue-Labarthe's claim that his tale is built around a *caesura* rather than a *conversion,* despite all the precautions he takes not to anticipate a new politics, the story nonetheless positions its survivors as determinate beings possessing a more sophisticated knowledge of the modern predicament that is lacking to the more naive precursor, the abortive modern. It is true that in a poem a caesura is not a conversion moment, but when it qualifies the determinate historical event of the Extermination, it plays that role so far as the story to end all stories is concerned. One thing that a story does is provide the impression that all that suffering was not in vain. The past is done with, an error we have gone beyond, leaving us free to rethink the political in the light shed by heightened understanding. Now that Roman fever is over at last and the Greek ghosts laid to rest, we are free to open ourselves to "something else entirely" (*tout autre chose*) and to choose "perhaps, an art without precedent" ("Poétique," p. 200).

It's also too neat as an account of poetic language. Besides asking where the language is with respect to a community of speakers, besides giving language thick with intelligibility, installing us in a world, the poem has always already asked about the writing system, been preoccupied with legibility or illegibility of its message, installed in a scene dominated by repetition and the economies of the mark. Lacoue-Labarthe knows this, but also—in laying out a historical scheme where the poetry of the past is celebrated for a mythic function—forgets it. The caesura is not just a one-time pause or for silence in general; it is the term for the singular cut of rhythm marking every French poetic line. It signals more than the interruption of any meaning-centered interpretation by an interpretation attentive to form and recuperable as a distinctive trait of the poet's voice.

As singular as they are repetitive, caesuras mark where the voice breaks and the poem points to another way of reading, in terms of writing and of the memory of the letter.[38] Extrapolating from the caesura, poetry is not to be understood in terms of speech or speech acts; it is inscriptional, and as such concerned with how the play of the letter, the play of the text as machine, affects the outcome of that kind of play understood as Heideggerian, the *polémos*, the struggle between world and earth. To dispense with the poem's attention to the letter as it appears in the poem (and not simply as a concept, a synonym for disruption) is to dispense with what it has to say on the relations (linkage or gap) between its existence as art object or unifying myth and as technique (as mnemonic device, for instance). It is to dispense with what it has to say about its ability to survive as whatever sort of message it brings us about survivorship, silence, and so on. An effective device for remembering messages like alliteration, for instance, can also call the attention away from the primary message to extra messages about the literal dimension of the text. There is a third reserve to the poem, that is neither a withdrawal from the empirical world into an ideal space, nor the re-presentation of the tired language as refreshed, active, and capable of invention. This third reserve is that of a poetry full-up with monotonous gassing about the letter and the chanciness that affects it.

Similarly, poetry can worry about what we might call, for short, obliteration (*oblitterare*, "to efface or blot out a writing, letters"; related to *oublier*, "to forget"). By obliterating, one makes something illegible or effaces its memory. In French, one obliterates stamps, that is, one postmarks them so that they cannot be used again, for instance, to send the same envelope again. Robert's *Dictionnaire historique de la langue française* explains that obliterating is the practice of imprinting that "marks something to make it improper for any use." The poem does not only deliver the language as *fit* for use, with new gods near and old ones departing, install a people in it as in a temple, produce the language fresh-minted for use. It also instantly uses it up. No one can ever write or say again what the poem writes in its unique combination. In this it is close to Flaubert's ambition in his *Dictionnaire des idées reçues* of silencing the bourgeois. If one tries to say the poem, one doesn't speak; one dots one's speech with heterogeneous matter. Poetic language is not just language plus, language become fetishized commodity. It is also language minus, made unusable as speech in a certain order or combination. The poem may stamp the language for use but it also counter-stamps it as instant hieroglyph, in what Chénier calls "une écriture antique et non plus un langage" (an antique writing and no longer a language) (p. 405).[39]

Alliteration and obliteration point toward (*ad-* and *ob-* mean "to, toward") the letter and its supplementary orders. They give notice of gaps between the language as spoken topology and as written topography, between its understanding and its reading. If only in the name of a more complete view of the relation of poetic language to its politico-historical dimension, these gaps and the way the individual poems couple them to representation have to be considered. They may not appear invested with the dramatic character of an epoch-ending or -beginning event. Nonetheless, they may bear messages about the political because they mark places where the myth of a unified language carried by voice breaks down, where language is affected by heterogeneity or by fracture lines. One has only to look at Tocqueville's observation, quoted as the epigraph to this chapter, that the men of his generation habitually reproduce the literary style of the preceding generation even as they have forgotten how to read the books they ape. For at least one historian, the disjunction between interpretation and reading is rife with historico-political significance. It is what goes on in history, and he directs us to the texts to read it.

The Text and the City: The Case on Appeal

It may seem a bit far-fetched to suggest, as Tocqueville does, that the recurrent cycle of revolution in which his century was caught might have been halted had anyone known how to read the books from which they took their habits of thought. A more modest claim is possible. We will broach the third hypothesis from Plato's *Republic*, where at least one indication suggests that Socrates' confirmation of a sentence of banishment against poetry is ironic, and that the accounts of the city with poetry are not closed in terms of mimesis at all, whatever the sense one gives the word. In Book Ten, at the moment that Socrates confirms the sentence of banishment pronounced in Book Three, on the grounds that the poem is harmful to the polity of the soul as subordinate mode of production, he also declares what amounts to an unlimited right of appeal to the poem. He says:

But nevertheless let it be declared that, if the mimetic and dulcet poetry can show any reason for her existence in a well-governed state, we would gladly admit her, since we ourselves are very conscious of her spell. . . . Then may she not justly return from this exile after she has pleaded her defense, whether in lyric or other measure?[40]

Having declared poetry's right to appeal her sentence, Socrates goes on to state that the appeal can be made either by others who plead her cause in prose or by poetry herself:

And we would allow her advocates who are not poets but lovers of poetry to plead her cause in prose without meter, and show that she is not only delightful but beneficial to orderly government and all the life of man. And we shall listen benevolently, for it will be clear gain for us if it can be shown that she bestows not only pleasure but benefit.

How could we help being the gainers? said he.

But if not, my friend, even as men who have fallen in love, if they think that the love is not good for them, hard though it be, nevertheless refrain, so we, owing to the love of this kind of poetry inbred in us by our education in these fine polities of ours, will gladly have the best possible case made out for her goodness and truth, *but so long as she is unable to make good her defense we shall chant over to ourselves as we listen the reasons that we have given as a countercharm to her spell,* to preserve us from slipping back into the childish loves of the multitude, for we have come to see that we must not take such poetry seriously as a serious thing that lays hold on truth, but that *he who lends an ear to it must be on his guard* fearing for the polity in his soul and must believe what we have said about poetry. (my emphasis)[41]

Instead of limiting the appeal to advocates, literary theorists arguing in prose who might show poetry's benefits without displaying her dangerous charms, Socrates allows poetry herself the right to speak in her own defense. But this right is qualified by his recommendation that, so long as she has not fully replied to objections, she not be awarded the right to be heard.

Lest the charms and spells cast by mimetic and dulcet poetry upset harmony in the Republic and the polity of the soul, the judges are to avoid listening to it. As poetry presents her lyric defense, the judges are to recite over to themselves the reasons given in the *Republic* for poetry's banishment. Socrates' language is riddling, as riddling as he calls the poet Simonides' definition of justice at the beginning of the *Republic.* How can judges, in justice obliged to listen to poetry's defense, actually *hear* it (with their ears or understanding) if, in order to maintain good order and good judgment in their soul, they are obliged to chant over reasons to themselves (aloud or in their understanding) that would drown out the appeal? Socrates does not explain this riddle.

Nevertheless, we can suggest a response, suitable to the riddle because it is a riddling sort of answer. How but because it is an appeal one does not have to hear, because it arrives otherwise, as a writing? The siren's voice of poetry is not to be heard. Instead advocates speak for her, or she makes her defense by such means as do not require voice, as the mute Philomela's tapestry made known her story. The appeal is to be won or lost in a hearing that is neither literal (with the ears) nor figurative (with the understanding), but instead, something else—a reading.[42] Poetry doesn't appeal in the senses of charm (imitate) or actively call up (produce); it mimes its appeal.[43]

Socrates indicates a possible ground for a defense of poetry that would take into account a gap between the poem as mimetic, and thus as a modification of the logos ordered with respect to truth[44] and a poetry concerned instead with its dependence on techniques, a dimension of language that has not been ordered with respect to truth and is not reducible to meaning.

My third hypothesis evolved, in the wake of the collapse of the narrative associated with the second, from its debris and from reading the poetic texts. The hypothesis was that poetry emerges to mime withdrawing itself from the marketplace and legislative, foundational work to write the relation of its logos-dominated, mimetic dimension to its scriptural, miming dimension. That relation is not fixed but is subject to modification in the form of sudden or slow capitalizations and losses affecting the meaning system, which are tied to chances and misfortunes associated with the scriptural system. It opened several directions for work.

The Lots of Paris

Let me examine them further, and counter the relative dryness and abstractness of this formulation, in an example. The example is the city par excellence for nineteenth-century France, Paris, as it takes shape in some poetic texts, notably those of Baudelaire and Valéry. In the spate of recent books on nineteenth-century Paris inspired by Walter Benjamin, Christopher Prendergast's *Paris and the Nineteenth Century* is one of the most richly detailed. It relies on all sorts of materials—from poems and novels to pamphlets—to provide its panoramic view, and has grasped, in the problem of representation of identity, a central thread in those texts. As Prendergast states it, those who obsessively represented themselves and their identity in the city were faced with a mirror that was itself already a representation. He outlines his project in these terms:

> What, then, does the city represent, and how to represent the city, to see it as form and "identity" (in the double sense of giving identity to the city and finding identity, individual or collective, in the city)? These, in connection with Paris in the nineteenth century, are some of the questions of this book. But to pose them thus risks resurrecting Balzac's fantasy of omnipotence and control, assuming privileged access to what lies "behind" tautology and stereotype, to what, in the "Avant-propos" to the *Comédie humaine*, Balzac calls the "sens caché" of the modern world. The issue of the identity of the city, and of identities within it, constituted a veritable nineteenth-century obsession. . . . The endless reports and proliferating nomenclatures of the urban bureaucracies (from the police to sanitary inspectors), not to mention the cataloguing descriptions and ordering plots of the novelists, suggest a massive enterprise of mapping the city as a means, both practical and symbolic, of keeping tabs on "identities."[45]

Two of the functions that the obsessive representation of Paris can play are provided here, in a slightly idiosyncratic and interesting formulation that makes it clear that tautology and stereotype are the stake: to represent the city is to represent one's individual and the collective identity, either in the form of a plot of recognition ("finding identity") or in terms of a plot of self-production ("giving identity"). But, because the city is already a representation, when one finds or gives an identity, one turns out to be rediscovering or reproducing some earlier ideal—hence the sense of moving in a recognizable landscape filled with familiar images of oneself. Hence too the strain of obsession and paranoia running through the texts Prendergast discusses: to meet oneself again, one must have lost oneself first; one wonders, is the double encountered a true or false double; and so on. In Prendergast's account, tautology is the effect of too much representation; just as too much representation is the effect of the fear of having lost oneself, encountered a false double, and so on. In the texts on the city, we see a people obsessed with its individual and collective identity.[46]

It is of course possible that the fear of losing one's identity is a cover-up for the more terrifying worry that one never had an identity to lose in the first place. Prendergast's interpretation relies on the assumed stability and priority of an existing thing represented, be it ideal or actual, with the problem being simply to name, to catalogue, or to describe that thing adequately. A more paradoxical claim can be made about the predicament Prendergast describes: in the stereotype one does not recognize a type one has seen before; in the stereotype one finds a form one has never seen before but that one instantly recognizes as everywhere repeated because it is the iterable itself that comes into view. This claim is made by Baudelaire, who states the privilege of genius and the poet's task as "Créer un poncif" (Creating a stereotype) (1: 662). A *poncif* is a plate for reproducing designs for which there is no original. To understand what Baudelaire means by his dictum, we would have to consider a Paris that exceeds all representations of identity, personal or collective, which always presuppose the priority of what is (be it an empirical or ideal being) over reproduction. Besides all the representations of the modern city and its people provided by Baudelaire's *Tableaux parisiens*, besides Haussmannized Paris with its idealized regularities and the more unkempt city of the *flâneur* which leave Paris the inheritor of the *Republic*, Paris is something else for the poet. It is an instance of the open possibility that a city built to plan, its parts contributing to a story of self-recognition for a collectivity, might have chances for constructions owed to iterability and be shadowed by fates unforeseen by the Greeks.[47]

Paris can represent the chances of iterability for Baudelaire because it is a case of that sort. Paris, the proper name for an existing place on the map, the capital city of France, the seat of government and culture, the scene of uprising and revolution, the space of the beggar, the *flâneur*, the speculator, and the *arriviste*, also, quite by chance, spells something else. It spells the plural of the common noun *pari*, meaning bet (as in *le pari de Pascal*, Pascal's bet). In *Présence de Paris*, Valéry comments on this chance association in one of the epithets by which he describes the city: "PARIS, gaming table where every face of fortune, every lot of destiny, shines to every eye" (PARIS, table de jeu où tous les visages de la fortune, tous les lots du destin, brillent à tous les yeux) (2: 1012). The English word *lot* gets across quite well the coincidence that brings together a place organized in terms of legally determined property (a lot is a measured and surveyed parcel of land, with fixed and legally recognized boundaries) and a piece in a game of chance (a lot is the object used as counter in determining a question by chance, as also the stake won in casting lots). A poet concerned with language in all its aspects and identities as they are represented by and in the city could hardly escape having to reckon with an accident that joins the proper name *Paris* to its homonym. In a highly economical piece of language like a poem where every word counts multiple times, the sign *Paris* would mark a place where the poem as work of art points outside itself to its fates or chances as *written* text, to surplus chances attached to its technical side. Such accidents are ultimately owed to writing, to the iterability of the mark—as Derrida calls it. They have to do with the fact that poetic language does not disappear as it is uttered, that it has counted on repetition and on the return of the unmastered remainder. *Paris* is a *poncif,* an instant stereotype, a plate that can be run off more than once and for which there is no original, because it is a point of intersection where two ways of meaning fall together in a singular pattern. It is the lot of Paris that its very name, the proper name that names the place in its specificity, is affected by a productive repetition through the homonym.

This signpost PARIS that points in two different directions is not only a place of mishap and misreading, where some unfortunate soul can lose sight of the real city and the public good, to stray off into a fantastic city of her own devising. For the pun to matter, the accident has to arrive as a *significant* accident, staged as something more than just an accident, say, as a sign where modification in the meaning system and the representation of what is will have been taking place. It has to appear as the dramatic opening up of a gap between saying and meaning, speaking and writing, and so as an element in a unique pattern that allows us to think the meaning of that gap, without that pattern being derived from any prior idea or in imitation of some existing thing. Itself only a by-product of an effort at communication, the homonym threatens *and* recharges the meaning system. It provides a heteroclite element, shocking evidence of disarray, that negates signification but that can immediately be resemanticized (as meaning the death of meaning). Paris-as-bets renovates a dilapidated sense system. It collects elements hitherto uncollected or collected otherwise. That is quickly obvious in the *Fleurs du mal,* where the stray pun from the *Tableaux parisiens* transforms utterly one of the *Spleen* poems from the first section. In "Spleen I," the poet, as part of a convincing portrayal of his dejection, has borrowed characters from a Pushkin novel, "the handsome jack of hearts and the queen of spades" (1: 72). In context, the poet is bewailing his lack of a voice and inspiration (he says he has the "sad voice of a chilly ghost"). His ventriloquizing of the fictional characters of another, presumably more inventive, Romantic writer helps get the point across. But retroactively, by means of the reading of Paris as "gambles" and the introduction of a gaming plot, the line gets another meaning. Pushkin's characters were citizens of a uniquely Baudelairian Paris, cards *avant la lettre* in its game of chance. No plot of self-representation and self-recognition Pushkin could devise could have predicted the precise, legible manner in which his characters have been reinscribed as members of Baudelaire's phantasmatic city. This reversal, which is not the symmetrical one of a mere imitator become inventor (for Baudelaire is rather the reader than the inventor of this legible Paris), requires the consideration of such gaps in terms of poetic language and of the goings-on in the polis. What questions does it raise? I will discuss four areas of inquiry here.

Homonyms I: The Poet and His Double

It leads to another perspective on the authority of the text of *Fleurs du mal.* Some of its images of Paris are not routed through the sensuous imagination, relating to the poet's image of self, or to the aim of totalizing, finding, or restoring a perfect order in a community of speakers by means of the poem.[48] Some are derived through the work of the "literal" imagination, or memory, as it may as well be termed, associated with the resemanticized signifier *bets.* The poems collected as a homogeneous unit under the title of *Tableaux parisiens,* for instance, would quite likely be owed to more than one source. A text like "Le Crépuscule du soir" with its gaming tables appears produced by a very different route ("unhealthy demons" working at night wake the poet [1: 94]) than its companion piece from the same section, "Le Crépuscule du matin," where the imagination moves from the everyday, visible image of an awakening worker to an allegory: "somber Paris, rubbing its eyes, / Grasped its tools, old laborer" (1: 104).[49] In the *Tableaux,* Paris is built by workers according to plans that might have been drawn up by Plato. But it is also a phantasmatic city of dreams, a city owing sites to a demonic imagination linked to memory and the literal. The undecidability of the *Tableaux*'s source is significant. It turns the attention to a gap between Baudelaire's visible Paris, regulated by the orders of the day (perception, cognition, recognition, and representation) and his Paris-by-night, regulated by the orders of the inky night (dreams, disruption, crime, prostitution, and, also, chance). It suggests that Baudelaire's city verses are shadowed by an impish, perverse double. The scene of Paris is of Paris, plus one.

There are implications for the context in this analysis. Baudelaire's poet is at the tip of the iceberg. One of the denizens of Paris but hardly one of its most reliable citizens, he moves around the city on the alert for encounters where his identity will be called into question, and which will incite him to exercise his special poetic powers to stage his spectacular death as poet. His work is energized where his stable identity collapses, and he achieves his most vertiginous artistic feats only where he is courted by, or courts, death.[50] The poet is not cast out of the city but has already withdrawn from it; he has not withdrawn in order to help bring it into existence, but rather by virtue of service to rules of a game of deadly outcome in a "city of muck" (1: 195). As a sometime seeker of thrills, of encounters with a negativity that undoes him as subject, he is apt to fits of asociality that make him a suspect. What is more, he sacrifices everything to the thrill—not just himself, but also whomever he meets. He does this because—on these occasions, from the very limited perspective of the poet's concerns—others do not interest him as subjects encountering another subject. They attract his attention only insofar as they solicit him as an artist to stage the annihilation of the subject and the appearance of an alterity that affects the human without being determined by it.

In a poem like "Le Mauvais vitrier," for instance, the I stages a meeting with a glass-seller that cannot be understood only as meeting between rival purveyors of glass (transparent or roseate), nor yet a dialectical struggle between master and slave. It is staged rather as a devastating (and devastatingly funny) encounter between a bored first person subject looking for something on which to exercise his considerable powers ("feeling myself pushed to do something great, a scandalous action" [1: 286]), and a placeholder, a mute and uncomprehending worker, against whom the poet immediately conceives an overwhelming enmity. This encounter by no means takes place between two subjects, as a dialogue between two members of a community who share a language. The glass-seller never addresses the poet in human language. For his part, the poet addresses the glass-seller insistently, but his words, consistent with the overriding figure of hyperbole, overshoot the mark, as if he were aiming over the glass-seller's shoulder at someone else. For instance, the cry "hé hé" with which the poet summons the *vitrier* is not the answering cry of a client so much as an invitation issued, a challenge to a duel, or even, the vocal exercises of a poet tuning his instrument. Following Pierre Pachet's tack, we can construe the encounter as taking place between a subject and a first-comer, nobody in particular, who bears a meaning for the subject of which this passerby is completely unaware.[51] In the case of the poor *vitrier*, the detail that accounts for both the poet's hospitality and his rivalry is found in the epithet by which the passerby is first designated: "the first person whom I glimpsed in the street" (*la première personne que j'aperçus dans la rue*) (1: 286).[52] The first person passing by in the street is a first person of another order than the I, the discursive first person in the sentence. The poet is the first person as subject, by right of speech and consciousness, perception, passion, will, generosity, and so forth; the glass-seller is a first person in name only, mask or persona rather than subject. In the struggle that ensues, the poet's object is to hyperbolize the problem of the link that ties him as representative subject and poet to this replicant. His first action construes the connection as potentially that of likeness. He invites the glass-seller to ascend to his room, as he would invite a brother poet:[53] both are first persons, both cry out, both can reach the aerial abode of the poet only by dint of much labor, both are dealers in windows. But the discovery of a critical difference shows the likeness to be misleading: the one, the first person in name only, deals in the clear panes of a transparent language of naming, whereas the poet's windows are fitted with the colored panes of a rhetorically aware language.

This difference once found, the poet next stages the relation as that of disconnection by a series of contrasting actions: he rejects the seller's wares and his pretensions to rivalry, calling him "impudent"; in intentionally pushing him from the room, the poet causes the glass-seller to trip; looking down from the balcony he deliberately drops a flowerpot, as the unwitting man emerges below after a tortuous descent, and scores a direct hit. In every case, the contrast is between the poet with his masterful production of illusion and the glass-seller, errant and uncomprehending, who bears his literal panes. But once again, the differences, which might lead us to conclude that Baudelaire is reiterating the superiority of the poet in his tower over the man from the crowd, turn out to be misleading. The windowpanes and the flowerpot that shatters them (in Barbara Johnson's perceptive reading, a figure for the *Fleurs du mal* and their aesthetics) *together* produce the high point of the poem, the "burst of noise of a crystal palace shattered by lightning." The figure teaches that the poet's rhetoric and the glass-seller's transparent language are related as the parts of a *same* structure that is both transparent and artificial, a crystalline palace whose enveloping structure is suspected only at the moment that its parts are mobilized, collide, and de-structure it.

Neither likeness nor difference regulates the relations of poet and glass-seller. Rather the scene shows that the assumption that opposition rules their relations is of the order of an ideological assumption, which naturalizes as a relation between subjects what is in point of fact a relation between a subject and the structures, including linguistic ones, in which it dwells. There are implications for the representative subject and poet, who throws away everything—rationality, morality, aesthetics, and personal salvation—for poetics, for a sound that derives from a disseminatory tendency associated with the letter (the shattered *palais* can be translated as *palate*). There are also political implications. One point would be that naturalizing the relation does not shelter one completely from the violence wreaked on man by structures (for which plenty of evidence is forthcoming both in the vicious cruelty of the poet and the apathetic suffering of the laboring glass-seller), but merely ignores its source. On the other side, the destruction of the ambulatory fortune of the glass-seller suggests the price of this knowledge is high. The "Mauvais vitrier" undoes the poet's aesthetics and the dream of a transparent language that it helps buttress, and provides the stakes for political man of pursuing that undoing in the public sphere.

Homonyms II: The City and Its Double

What might look like a one-time accident is an open possibility in the poetic text. Paris, undecidably name and word, is what Andrzej Warminski calls, in the context of a related discussion of undecidability in Hölderlin, a "place-holder for a gap."[54] The gapping that this case of undecidability locates and makes intelligible is a gapping that neither the pun nor the knowledge it makes available can fill. The vocable stands for it as just one in a list of placeholders. The gap cannot be closed; the language that tries to close it off by naming it (and that's Paris, *both* a planned city where people work, meet, and recognize one another, and a placeholder for the chance constructs associated with the letter) also always opens it again (another chance Paris lurks around or within the written sign *Paris*, even Paris whose field of meaning has been extended to cover both its aspects).[55] That other chance could be delivered by another pun or a larger syntactic structure. For instance, besides the crepuscular poems representing Paris as a place with views by night and day, another near homonym, *peri* (around), could be proposed as the source yielding a poem about a suburb of Paris "Je n'ai pas oublié, *voisine de la ville*" (I have not forgotten, *neighbor to the town*) (1: 99). Critics have tended to read this poem as an excursus on Baudelaire's part into a nostalgic, autobiographical style out of keeping with the rest of the work, but the pun suggests a way to make it consistent with the collection's celebrated secret architecture. Similarly, in Baudelaire's poem called "Rêve parisien," at least one image is explained by the peristyle, those colonnades surrounding the inner courtyard that fold the outside into the inside of the house: "Non d'arbres, mais de colonnades / Les étangs dormants s'entouraient" (Not by trees but by colonnades / Were the sleeping pools surrounded) (1: 102). It is as though the proper, familiar space of the poem as representation of a city scene were opening to include cysts or pockets of negativity, digressions or parentheses, owed to a different inspiration. In its role as placeholder for a gap between two language functions, the pun bridges a gap that as bridge it can reopen. Paris is (Paris plus one) plus one.

Once again, the undecidability of source has consequences for the context. A first consequence is that some "places" in the city are taken as privileged places to explore the way that the city's growth and destiny may be affected by accidents of its name. We tend to assume that a city grows in terms of an economy of need, with sectors of luxury latching onto and parasitizing those of need only where needs are being filled; or, conversely, that the accumulation and conspicuous spending of tremendous wealth stimulate growth. In these assumptions, language economy, the production and using up of metaphors or the writing of poems, is a minuscule part of that small part that is the luxury sector. But Paris might owe something, its luck as city, to the surge of energy delivered by the discovery of a new placeholder; or its misfortunes, the sudden disrepair into which a whole sector falls, to the collapse of a metaphorical system. Are we so sure that the concentration of capital and population in Paris led to the production of gambling dens, which spawned further growth, and only then to the metaphor of the city as an "immense gaming house"? Might the surplus production enabled by the free-floating signifier not have played a role in turning Paris into the immensely con-

centrated center it became in the nineteenth century?[56] One may conjecture that the growth of the city is the result of the coincidence of two incompatible principles (one, a rational plan, a representation of oneself in
the city, the other, chances, associations owed to a metonymical law).
The interest of the conjecture lies partly in the obligation it puts us under
to consider the regular operation of heterogeneous principles in the formation and life of cities. It makes room for the consideration that among
the reserves to be tapped in the city are those provided by its language. It
allows us to consider the surplus speculation authorized when the signifier appears as potentially standing free of the context, and then, having
been made to signify that freedom, is taken to permit the realization of
returns from this subsidiary economy.

A second sort of narrative for the building of the city puts in an appearance. This narrative does not rely on the desire to represent one's
identity, but rather on the problem of what to do with the debris of the
ideal images that have already been undone, with surplus or by-products
from the work of self-representation. Baudelaire's "Le Cygne" provides a
particularly arresting version of it, in the poetic proposition that Paris is
not the latest inheritor of the logos-centered Greek city, but might instead inherit from the letter-oriented Trojan losers of the battle and the
ruined Troy.[57] The poetic argument is buttressed by the false etymology
linking the name of the French city to the wife-stealing Paris who caused
the Trojan war. Behind the many plausible likenesses the poet finds between his situation of mourning the "old Paris" destroyed by Hauss-
mann and Andromache's situation of mourning Hector and the grandeur of Troy, stands this disruptive gesture that superimposes the two
cityscapes by way of the likeness of the name. It is the destiny of Paris to
bear the name of no city founder, but a name that resembles that of the
lucky and unlucky cause of a walled city's destruction. To inherit from
Paris is not to inherit as a child born into a lineage is handed the property of parents. Hecuba and Priam abandoned Paris on a hillside where—
for good and for evil—fortune became his parent. All this exposed son
has to hand on is his lack of a continuous relation to tradition and to
property, and a reliance on luck.

Such an allegory reveals the mechanism that allows the placeholder for
a gap to be converted from a placeholder into a place. The sign *Paris* just
stands in for the disjunction between meaning and saying, for the always
open possibility that the most arbitrarily chosen of names can also func-

tion as motivated sign. But it is immediately taken as a significant coincidence, meaningful of all such occurrences. This conversion of the homonym into a supplemental source of meaning is a means for energizing and enriching the city. It allows Paris to be increased by gambling dens, by night views, by peristyles, and by suburbs, by populations unaccounted for in an ideal republic. The accident that at first appears an obstacle to the ideal of the orderly city can be turned instantly to use, pressed into service for the work-in-progress of constructing the city. Instead of appearing as menacing, the disjunction is translated into meaning, the placeholder determined as a place and the freed signifier made the source of enrichment. However, the startling, energizing disruptiveness of the pun is immediately used up by the conversion and the area opened, like some Southern Californian housing development, as already out-of-date. The productions resulting from this conversion are a key to this instant banalization. What is exploited—the means as standing free of meaning—carries in every case the same, monotonous message about the means. Moreover, the operation of translation is one-way here: Paris is enlarged by zones that have come into being through a nonreversible operation, based on a heterogeneous principle.

Homonyms III: Memory and Its Double

"Le Cygne" makes available another line of thought concerning the effects on memory of translating the letter into intelligibility. Here, the distinction between text and context becomes moot. Where memory is concerned, in a city's public monuments and archives or its palimpsestic use of the site, it is always a matter of text. As for the poem, again in terms of memory, it points outside itself as reminder to a language community of a nonliving side to its language. In remembering Paris's textuality, one has inevitably to translate it into the logic of place (of inside and outside, of specular oppositions). One has to forget that the freedom of the signifier can only be a *conjecture* for which only verbal evidence can be forthcoming. One has to treat it as free in fact, and thus as susceptible to appropriation, determination, economization. In doing so, one forgets about the disruptiveness of the disjunction, the threatening mechanicity of linguistic play. Forgetting about it does not mean that the potential for violence carried by the letter has gone away. It has simply been covered up in the location where it first emerged and might reemerge elsewhere abruptly and without explanation. The attempted dissimulation and abrupt return of the mark are the twin aspects under which Paris is set in its historical dimension by Baudelaire in "Le Cygne," as a brief commentary of the following passage will establish.

> Andromaque, je pense à vous! Ce petit fleuve,
> Pauvre et triste miroir où jadis resplendit
> L'immense majesté de vos douleurs de veuve,
> Ce Simoïs menteur qui par vos pleurs grandit,
>
> A fécondé soudain ma mémoire fertile,
> Comme je traversais le nouveau Carrousel.
> Le vieux Paris n'est plus (la forme d'une ville
> Change plus vite, hélas! que le coeur d'un mortel);
>
> Andromache, I think of you!—this poor stream,
> This melancholy mirror where once shone forth
> The enormous majesty of your sorrowful widowhood,
> This lying Simoïs made great with your tears,
>
> Suddenly quickens my fertile memory,
> As I cross the new Place of the Carrousel.
> Old Paris is no longer (a city's form
> Changes more quickly, alas, than a mortal's heart);
>
> *(1: 85)*

In "Le Cygne," Baudelaire picks a puzzling but instructive link to clinch the ironic filiation of the French city with ruined Troy. He considers as the decisive detail fecundating memory, the river, "This lying Simoïs made great with your tears." The detail draws attention to the widow's tears, tears that in literally feeding the river also impart it a figurative grandeur. It is tempting to read the figure of the river as one of triumphant recuperation, in which Andromache's weeping is supposed to show her faithfulness to the memory of Troy and Hector. The poet's remembering of those faithful tears—in a sort of invocation of the spirit presiding over the remembered city—would then constitute a further, poetic compensation for the destruction of Troy and the loss of Hector's line by the translation of a Virgilian topos into an epic in the modern style. The epithet attributed the river complicates things, however. The poet calls the river a liar here, so Andromache's tears feed and give grandeur to a lie.

What exactly does the poet mean by saying her tears swell a *lie*? It is possible to understand the river's lie in two very different ways, with the reading of the modern city's relation to its past turning on how we read the line. The river may be a lying Simoïs because it is a river in Epirus that does not fit in the landscape reminiscent of Troy where Andromache sites the tomb. It lies in not being the Simoïs, a river in the Trojan plain, and as such, it is the chief obstacle to revivifying memory. Her tears, as much as those of an inconsolable widow, are those of an artist weeping at the failure of art to assimilate the river into her tomb for Troy. In weeping, she feeds the river that gives the lie to the illusion she is trying to perfect, with Andromache exiled from a past plenitude she can neither forget nor recapture. The allegory points to her tearful recognition of a gap between a present, fallen state where one can only construct a tomb to the city irretrievably lost and a past, mythic moment when Troy was Troy.

The passage allows another reading, however. Andromache has situated her cenotaph so as to take advantage of a fluvial feature of the Epirote landscape that has reminded her of Troy. Her siting of the tomb landscape on the banks of the river in Epirus is a decisive act. Whether she sought out the river with a view to building the cenotaph, or was inspired by it to a reconstruction, the river is a reminder of Troy. The river in Epirus is not a river of Epirus. It is the gash by which the wasteland around Epirus has been re-marked by Andromache as a site apt for the construction of the tomb. The river maps the site as reminiscent of Troy and is therefore not a natural river. If the river lies in such a case, it is because, instead of appearing what it is, a reminder, gash, or mark, it appears as a natural stream, watering an Epirote landscape. It lies by bearing a name other than the Simoïs. If Andromache weeps, it is because her reconstruction is so successful that it has partially erased the loss for which the river was to serve as reminder. Her tears enlarge the lying river, because they too dissimulate. They are supposed to show her memory of Hector, Troy, and the Trojan heritage. Instead they show her forgetting them by reinstalling the nature-artifice distinction, the very model collapsed and lost with Troy, through a reminder that appears disguised as a river. Like the mysterious clefts and fissures in *The Narrative of Arthur Gordon Pym*, seen from above, by angels, the river would show up as a mark or letter, but to the fallen (and Andromache, for Baudelaire, is indeed fallen) it seems natural.

At stake in these two readings of the river's lie are nonconvergent notions of the relation of history to myth. In one explanation, Andro-

mache lives in a historical present that is characterized by loss, alienation, substitution, and artifice, and that she measures as fallen with respect to the mythic past of heroic suffering. The explanation shows her
registering the gap between the two times by her tears. In the other explanation, Andromache's tears wash something out. They erase the mark
of her violent imposition of the Trojan landscape onto the Epirote wasteland. Myth is not in the past; fiction comes alive in the present dissimulation of the gash that marks the site as textualized. In this explanation,
myth hides the violence of history as it occurs. Myth is not what distinguishes an age that comes before the historical time, nor yet the means
by which history takes place. It is rather the means by which we dissimulate the mark; actual history is of the mark.

But, and this is the larger meaning pointed to by the first explanation
of the emblem, at any point the reemergence of a scriptural side to the
picture can occur to let the fiction be cast off as past. "Le Cygne" provides an example of this. Our reading so far has depended on the assumption that the poem is a translation, in the tradition of the epic
(however failed), of a Virgilian theme onto the modern scene. As a meditation on memory and forgetting, history and myth, it provides an instance in the "Simoïs menteur" of a placeholder encapsulating its chief
dilemma, and expressing what history and myth are for the nineteenth-
century French as they reach back to find their own beginnings. But
nothing prohibits originating the poem, including even its most conse-
crated images, rebus-like, from another source and according to another
logic. Baudelaire's choice of Virgil's Andromache at the river may have
been itself determined by the sort of mechanical associations it talks
about that have nothing to do with the resonant meaning of Virgil's image, and everything to do with the literal, inscriptional side of the cita-
tion. Baudelaire may have espied in Virgil a chance to translate the *tu-
mulus . . . inanis*, the cenotaph in Epirus, into a Seine-otaph in Paris.
The poem would then originate in the translation of the empty tomb
that is the sign, rather than in an attempt to revive a content.[58]

Of course, this would be a very artificial procedure for engendering
the text, and we cannot assure ourselves that a poem of the stature of "Le
Cygne" was written in that way. It seems impossible that a poem that
theorizes about memory associations available because of the sign's lack
of groundedness could have been constructed by such associations. But
we cannot utterly reject the hypothesis either, since if the poem's theory

holds any water at all, it has to be applicable even to itself, as a poem about such constructions. The mere positing of the hypothesis of such an artifice as conditioning the birth of the poem is enough to make it impossible to see the poem as a modern epic. The myth it seems to perpetrate—of a Paris that inherits like Virgil's Rome from a ruined Troy—falls away here as the poem stages its rupture with the very tradition of the epic in which it has placed itself.

In this predicament, remembering the source of the city in the Seine or the cemetery has two shapes, both oriented toward the future. It is apparent from the emblem that the choice consists not in acceding to truth, but in trading one sort of lie against another, one sort of memory against another, and one sort of future against another. The emblem presents a choice: in one reading, there is a future of nostalgic mourning for a mythic past, accompanied by a present of slow degradation (as Andromache falls from the hero Hector, to Achilles' less than heroic son Pyrrhus, to Pyrrhus's slave Helenus), as imaged in the lying river elongated by salty, sterile tears (*grandit*). In the other reading, as predicted by the lying river made great with tears (*grandit*), the future is one where the dissimulation of violence through naturalization shelters the city by hiding its faulty cornerstone, at the same time that the dissimulation points to the inevitability of a recurrence. A set of chances that affect the forgetting and remembering of the letter, and a rhythm or speed associated with them, are at stake. In nineteenth-century Paris, for the poet, the memory of the letter is the question of the future.

Homonyms IV: Public Remains

A legible Paris shadows the intelligible city and endows it with openings or chances on which the poet or city builder alertly speculates. But the drag or inertia of the system has also to be considered. To add a new placeholder to hold the gap in lieu of the one absorbed and appropriated, capitalized on, built, used up, is not to add anything new, but rather to add the same thing again. When the same thing is added again, the whole system, now concerned with repetition, is transformed. But this transformation doesn't take place without leaving refuse, a debris that doesn't go away. This can be seen especially in Baudelaire's accounts of new groups of humans in the city. One striking example of this new sort of being is Baudelaire's "sinister old man who reproduced himself" in "Les Sept vieillards" where one placeholder, his very stance as the upright man of Ovid compromised by the prosthetic device of the cane, takes the place of the first, in a monotonous succession (1: 88). Each is an instant stereotype, incapable of change or education, sprung to life fully formed, born decrepit like its predecessor. The *vieillard* can only be replaced by another, equally vigorous in its alienation and equally incapable of internal change. The placeholder for the gap shows up in the emergence of groups of people ("Reader, I am sorry to say, a very numerous class indeed," claims De Quincey) associated with the life of the letter and its costs.[59] This calculation with the letters and techniques of writing increases the size of the city, enriches it with secret pockets, folds in adjacent territories where speculations of various sorts can occur. It leads to openings for memory. But from another side it is a speculation concerning whole zones where are collected the refuse of this process of producing a city. For the rapid changes in the shape of the city, especially those changes that sever it from its own past, accumulate populations who have effected the very changes that have rendered them obsolete. The city of "Les Petites vieilles," for instance, is haunted by "weak phantoms" and cluttered with the "Debris of humanity ripe for eternity . . . Ruins! my family!"—the old women of the title who listen at concerts recalling to public memory the heroic, military past, but who are themselves left unremembered or noticed only by mocking children (1: 91). Trashed populations, heterogeneous groups whose function has been reduced to returning with the memory of the repressed letter, fill Baudelaire's city: gamblers, out-of-work clowns, prostitutes, addicts, drunks, on which parts of the city's complex economy, and especially its future memory of its repressed past, depend. Here the critical gesture of a poem like "Le Cygne" is its refusal of transcendence as a means for getting "beyond" (or rid) of refuse. Unlike narratives, which have to feign to believe the narrator's claims to having gone beyond error, the poem takes everything the poet-as-garbage-collector finds and dumps it in our lap—trash gilded along with lilies. It recollects all the chances refused in the appropriation of the city, and returns them in a last-chance speculation concerning the readability of the system and the crowd, forgotten in its heterogeneity.

~

I have suggested four areas where Baudelaire's poetry conjectures that chances owed to the letter may intervene to stimulate and disrupt the economy of the city. In the first two of these areas, a closed system is in operation, under the aegis of a ruling metaphor. The stakes are the poet's individual authority as master of the *chantier*, and, within the system, the unity of the poetic voice, the stability of the poetic order legislated or the aesthetic form produced. Once it is understood that the city space is construed along the model of the work of art (with the banishing of the poet a ploy to guard that secret), the testimony from the text's nonaestheticizing, linguistic side has a relevance. It bears news of the operation of a different model that the city variously suspects and censors, or welcomes and tries to appropriate. Be it in terms of the undoing of a ruling metaphor, the interruption of a formal harmony, the threatening of vocal unity from within by an ironic self-division, or the breaching of a boundary trying to close the inside off from the outside, the force derived from the poem's speculation on its mandate as literal, written text is critical of formal orders and ideologisms. Its disruptive force, when it emerges to topple an ideology revealed as constraining, is reenergizing; it bears with it a breath of air and renewed freedom as the old convention is lifted, and the new one has not yet made its weight felt. The disruption appears absorbable in each determinate location where it strikes. But, from a more general perspective, the letter's effects are too disseminated and incalculable in their timing to be appropriated. It is not surprising if the letter's force should sometimes be felt as dangerous so that the attempt will be made either to set bounds on its freedom or to reduce it to an innocuous game. The point is not only to slow things down so as to absorb, register, and take profits from the latest reenergizing. It is also to re-occult the automaticity, which suggests that the life of cities is more like that of a textual system than like that of an organism. In short, the question of order—order construed as formal arrangement arrived at along a rational principle and also, in the plural, as the disruptive orders issued by the letter—can be discussed in terms of the reserve of the poem, its holding itself apart in, as holding the secret of, the city.

In the second two areas discussed, the problem considered is not the closed, presumably autonomous system set up, partially breached, and then potentially recouped by way of a larger metaphor. Instead, the poems turn out to be concerned with open-ended systems—history, memory, allegory, the textual debris collecting in the archive. Here, the aestheticizing gesture, as per Lacoue-Labarthe, would position the poet in a fallen present of elegiac lament, removed from the grandeur that was Greece or Rome, and seeking to restore its promise. Against this memory as mournful nostalgia or triumphant rebirth, the chances associated with the poem's literal side bring out a more disjointed and uneasy relation to the past, in which the memory of the sign (as conditioning nostalgia and as subject to sets of accidents and a recollection of its own) plays an important part. In this history, the monuments left by the past do not just attest to a past over and done with. A present more riddled by a past more riddling is made available once one considers the testimony of the remainder as such. To recollect the debris left in the project of organizing the city space is to consider, for instance, the present as fractured by an unsuspected fault line of the past, haunted even as it shakes off the past in monumentalizing and transcendentalizing gestures, by castoffs. The reemergence of a textual remainder suggests that the city is the De Quinceyan palimpsest or Poesque sunken city, where sudden, sweeping erasures and submersions can occur, or half–wiped out letters resurface, or a reinscription with broad implications take place. In such a city, the monuments erected in public squares to honor the dead in representational works are of course up for grabs. They can be removed one by one from their pedestals, melted down and others raised in an economical gesture of public refashioning of the sort analyzed by Christopher Prendergast or Lynn Hunt.

Moreover, even Hunt's model of history as a succession of monuments is in question here, for what comes into prominence is not the monuments but their supporting pedestals, the columns with their shafts and capitals, or the frontons of public buildings, left as litter of the melted-down symbols. According to an economy of symbols, one generation's symbols can be replaced by others without remainder: to replace a figure by another one is still to engage in an ongoing process of substitution, and the loss of particular monuments leaves intact the process. But the leftover pedestal is not a symbolic work of art, a representation based on an inside/outside correspondence. It is not merely a useful object, nor is it entirely taken up in the symbolic mode of the statue. Indeed, if we take its name as a clue, it participates in both logics: it is a case of a name indistinguishable from a work of art, a figure, since it is given by a wild metaphor, a catachresis, a term borrowed for which there is no other word. What is to be done with the block of stone that supported the statue? Just like its name for which there is no other term, the pedestal is not subject to substitution in the same sense. If we destroy the pedestal we destroy what supports and reminds of the costs of the process of substitution. Just so, in wiping out a name we obliterate it from memory, relegating it to oblivion without hope of return. The footing left lying around without any monument to support places the viewer in front of a decision: whether to destroy the pedestal as *disjecta membra* that reminds too visibly of the violent act of overthrowing and yet that is unique and irreplaceable in saving some part of the archive from ruin; or to save it and thus burden the city with the care of preserving the reminder, be it by putting it to work as a building block for a present construction, or by placing it in a museum, or in some other way. The events that concern the poet are not contents, something that happens in the real world that is then saved in a sign; they consist rather in these decisions to preserve or to relegate to forgetfulness a set of signs that are undecidably name and figure. When Baudelaire speaks in "Le Cygne" of "Ces tas de capitaux ébauchés et de fûts" (these heaps of sketchy capitals and shafts) (1: 86) the word for shaft, *fût*, is the homonym of the past subjunctive of the verb *to be*, *qu'il fût*. The text points to a heap of "would or might have beens," of events not yet actualized, whose actualization requires the preservation of the shaft. With the column and the archive come into view a memory and a forgetting reliant on a set of inscriptions and affected by the accidents that can befall them.

The essays of this volume are divided into groups corresponding to a division between the address of poetry to place and position, and its address to temporal, historical issues. The first group of essays is thus concerned with the setting up and undoing of metaphorical systems, whereas the second group is characterized by a turn away from totalizing figures, to the mark and toward literary modes expressive of temporal difference like allegory and irony.

The first two chapters consider texts, one at the dawn of the century (Chénier's "La Jeune captive" from 1794) and one at its close (Mallarmé's "L'Action restreinte" from 1895), both of which issue, as it happens, from the very particular spot of a retreat anything but pastoral, coded instead in terms of entombment and reemergence from the tomb. Chénier's poem was written during his incarceration in the St. Lazare prison; Mallarmé's piece is situated in the poet's study in the rue de Moscou, in the *quartier de l'Europe* that grew up around the St. Lazare train station. In both cases, the poet writes under the long shadow thrown by the *genius loci* Lazarus and is concerned with an old order losing its grip, and a new order in formation. Both chapters examine the role of the lyric in helping question or erect idols through the naturalizing of linguistic structures.

The three chapters of the second part are concerned chiefly with history and memory, and approach the lyric in terms of the failure of the epic on account of its narrative. ("An epic poem is a poem that can be told [*raconter*]. If one *tells* it, one has a bilingual text." [Valéry, 1: 1456]) In the poetry of Chénier, a poet usually credited with a nostalgic classical revivalism, a logic is found that identifies Egyptian hieroglyphic writing (undeciphered in Chénier's day) as a forebear of an atavistic French. The fragmentary epic *Hermès* is mined for evidence that in bringing out this legacy as *antique écriture*, the poem is concerned with the chances and misfortunes shadowing it. The second essay, on Hugo, considers the memory of the specific event of the French Revolution as it haunts the century in odd memorials—pedestals left vacant by the melted down statues of kings, empty public squares and streets silently awaiting popular manifestations, the scaffold with its guillotine. The march of history is then figured, also paradoxically, as a repetition (the kingly statues roam the city in search of a new placement and a more totalizing mastering metaphor). Against this future, the future of the Revolution as repetition, Hugo suggests futures given by the written text. In the final chapter the focus is on the censoring of one of Baudelaire's poems from *Les Fleurs du mal*. Here, the question is not the content censored so much as the model of memory and history implicit in the government's repressive act, set off against the model proposed by the poem. The critical claim is that the work transgresses against the ideal of the poem as autonomous entity providing a view of the language as an intact body, and against the ideal of nostalgic, revivifying memory. Instead, the poem meditates on a fractured memory and a dated language that threaten to divide a people from its past.

The observant reader will notice how important a role the relatively obscure poet André Chénier plays in this book. This may seem an unwarranted elevation in status, elevation all the more suspect for occurring in a book that purports to study the *nineteenth-century* French lyric. It is true that scholars are not very certain of the dates of composition of most of Chénier's poems, but we are safe in asserting that all of Chénier's composing was at an end after July 25, 1794, the date of his decapitation. Chénier is clearly an eighteenth-century writer. But the date and circumstances of the publication of his poems present a different picture. Prior to his death, André Chénier had published only a few political articles and two poems on political subjects; when the eighteenth century spoke of Chénier, it meant his brother, Marie-Joseph, Jacobin and dramatist. André Chénier's work is very much a nineteenth-century production. Its appearance was owed to Henri de Latouche, who labored to make a collection of finished poems out of a fragmentary work at the urging of Chateaubriand, and brought Chénier's work to the public in the 1819 edition read by Hugo, Baudelaire, and Gautier. As for the characterizations of the poet and his life, like those found in Giordano's *Andrea Chénier*—singer of a love for women even more than for freedom, caught up in political events outside his ken—they are legends largely invented by the nineteenth century. Sainte-Beuve summarizes the situation: "André ressuscité / Parut" (Resuscitated André / Appeared [or even, since *paraître* is what books do, "Came out, Was published"]).[60]

This curious situation, of a writer on political subjects whose reputation and very work as a poet were invented from his *Nachlass*, is part of what makes Chénier a central figure for this study. He never sang at all, except posthumously. Moreover, while the works published during his lifetime show him literally up to his neck in politics, his emergence in the nineteenth century as the lyric poet of the *Bucolics*, *Elegies*, and narrative poems involved the disregard or outright forgetting, if not of his partisan leanings, then of the more nuanced positions taken in his political writings (for instance, his polemics against partisan politics). Chénier never sang lyrically, except through a neglect or partial repression of his political writing. When he did emerge as a poet, it was in the lurid light of the scaffold; Chénier's "voice" gained pathetic force and reach as an effect of this positioning. Just so "sang" the head and lyre of the decapitated Orpheus, received by the river Hebrus. The nineteenth-century production of the seductive legend seems to have gone on, in the case of Chénier, rather more helped than hindered by the lack of an authoritative text. There is a less seductive side to the posthumous appearance, however. For one thing, Chénier's *Nachlass* proved over and over subject to the accidents of the letter. That was true in terms of the manuscripts, whose survival and rediscovery proved chancier than that of many. It is also true of the texts themselves, which were left as fragments, puzzlingly polished and yet unfinished.[61]

Needless to say, Chénier comments in the work on his destiny as posthumous poet, and thus on the siren quality of his legend. This led to a more important reason for foregrounding so apparently marginal a figure. It is my contention that the critical legacy of Chénier's poetry for the nineteenth century, a legacy largely neglected by the critics, is neither his fin de siècle neoclassicism, nor yet his Romantic lyric voice. Rather, he claims to have discovered a French related to and, as it were, worked over by, the Egyptian hieroglyph. This cryptic heritage is claimed by Baudelaire and Mallarmé (and in America by Poe), among others. It is worth noting a strain that counters the vision of the poem as aesthetic object or as verbal act at the moment that the lyric reemerges. Besides the model that makes nineteenth-century France the effect of policies pursued in an earlier régime, or that sees it has having broken with the recent past in its return to classical republicanism, a third model, where the city space is dominated by the obelisk, is proposed in Chénier.

The Writer's Tower

The *terminus ad quem* of this study is probably not Mallarmé but Valéry, whose well-known silence (twenty years without a poem) is a vivid enough suggestion of a further modification in the status of the Ivory Tower having occurred toward the end of the nineteenth century to dispossess the lyric poet of voice and centrality. In lieu of a systematic study of Valéry's poetics and politics (or as he called them, *quasi*-politics),[62] I would like to offer a brief commentary on a passage from the short essay I began by citing, where Valéry registers that a new medium has dispossessed poetry of its position and job as purveyor of culture. At the same time Valéry says something about the responsibility and arena left for the poet, whom he designates a writer. This is what he says:

> The effects of ideas in the political universe, the simplifications they must undergo, the unexpected and opposing consequences that they produce show that often *the one who thinks to act does not act* (or acts against her own designs) and that the one who did not dream of acting engenders, without wishing it, profound modifications. It happens to the Ivory Tower to emit powerful waves, unknown to itself. Nothing is more interesting than watching ideas, extracted from the intellect where they were conceived, isolated from their complex conditions of birth, from the delicate analyses, the hundreds of attempts and relations that have preceded them, become *political agents, signals, arms, stimulants*—and these products of reflection be employed purely for their motivational value. . . . How many examples in the last 150 years! . . . Fichte, Hegel, Marx, Gobineau, Nietzsche—even Darwin . . . used, spouted in fixed and crude formulas.

Another word [*Encore un mot*]. It seems that France today feels no sort of "mission." Our general attitude is expectant. Nothing wiser, no doubt, in an epoch where the universal confusion makes one think that everything is possible at every moment, where stability in everything seems the out-of-date property of a world before the war. Nothing wiser, but perhaps also nothing more dangerous than so reasonable a state. I do not think it without peril for our youth. Who will find a new ideal object for youth to desire with all its force? Without participating in public life, without care to parties, without losing anything of oneself, a *writer* might consecrate to that the height and solitude of her Tower. (Valéry's emphasis, 1: 1149–50)

One of the most interesting features of the passage allowing us to conclude that Valéry is registering an epochal modification in the status of the Ivory Tower is the metaphor that collapses under the single term of *Ivory Tower* both the Tower of Literature whose influence is waning, and its inheritor, the Radio Tower. The Radio Tower is a technological advance made possible in part by the recognition that words have, besides a meaning function, a poetic function. As an acoustic entity a word has a phenomenal existence and can enter into patterns and be reproduced without regard for meaning or context. One has to be able to construe the signifier as separable from the meaning function, and thus a language free of context, to be able to imagine a radio. Like poetry, which for Mallarmé arises to remunerate the "defect" in languages that makes *nuit* sound clearer than the night it means (or than the word for day, *jour*), it relies on the gap between language as tool and as object of the senses. From what Valéry says, then, we can deduce that the Radio Tower is one of the unwitting "waves" of the retreat where the nineteenth-century lyric poet experiments with language as sensuous form. The Radio Tower as diffuser of culture and information inherits its dominant spot in the city from literature, with the city's borders extended by it to include all those reached by its electromagnetic waves. The collapse of the Tower of Literature has been taking place slowly (over the 150 years that separate 1933 Europe from the Revolution) and also all at once, with unprecedented speed, in the subsumption of the Tower of Literature by a Radio Tower that has itself been abstracted from its "complex conditions of birth."

The takeover of the poet's tower by the media tower is not the occasion for any wailing and beating of breast by Valéry, and that despite the Nazism deftly and soberly evoked, despite the clear message that the radio is efficient at broadcasting crude formulas, despite the overarching point that the signifier, far from standing free, has already been reabsorbed as a message about the dominance and power of the medium. Nor is it the occasion for a celebration of the broader notion of community associated with the new medium.[63] The dubious cult of the aesthetic is no more practiced by Valéry than the dubious cult centered around a technology and the lowbrow pleasures of hit lit. It should be noted, however, that the Radio Tower takes over more than just the ability to make waves beyond the context; it also takes over an ignorance. What is occupying Valéry is the life of a peculiar illusion perpetuated by the Ivory Tower and what it stands for, its claim that fiction can stand free from any determination. The very existence of the Radio Tower—side effect of positing the freedom to the signifier—demonstrates that claim to be problematic. Valéry is neither a partisan of Radio Culture, nor a reactionary recommending that poets take back the tower. He describes and analyzes a recent modification.

One of the more interesting features of the metaphor likening the two towers is that it relies on no visual or audible similarity for its transfer of terms. By no stretch of the imagination does the Ivory Tower of poetry, itself a chimera, look like the Radio Tower, any more than the waves the former emits (the lines of the poem, according to the traditional topos, are waves) sound like the electromagnetic waves beamed out by the latter. The transfer is allowed by an overlap in vocabularies which the poet does not produce so much as note. A certain part of the poet's usual job description—the part that consists in making up for the arbitrariness of the sign by mining the freedom of the signifier, in making the message derive from the medium, in imagining metaphors—has been taken over by the Radio Announcer. As shown in Valéry's own operations, the poet's part is reduced to registering the outlines of an area where a new sort of likeness, a likeness between vocabularies, is exploited, and to delimiting an area where a blurring or loss of difference occasions a search for remainders in need of an account. Valéry puts his finger on one such remainder in the difference between the poetic and radio wave—the second of which is an analogy based on a resemblance between sound's movement and the visible movement of water, and the first of which is more usually a figuration of the written page as the troughs and billows of a sea. The recollection of difference would call us away from the seductive spell of the signifier as sonorous inanity capable of meaning itself through the image, toward the consideration of the material conditions of writing that have not been taken over by the Radio Tower.

So Valéry does more than register and explain a collapse. He also suggests a task and obligation for the writer (and reader) whom he summons to her table by a *mot d'ordre* of his own devising: *Encore un mot.* Another word, yet again a word, and also, a word that is still a word, not used only as stimulant, political agent, or motivating signal. The point is not to emit a word, to project it to others as one does a liquid, a voice, a signal transmitted by electromagnetic waves—for pleasure, for profit, to exhort listeners to action, or to freeze them listening to the voice of radio technology as to the voice of a master. The task Valéry has in mind as remaining for the writer is that of finding a "mission" in the midst of a hyperrationalized space regulated and naturalized by the sound waves of the radio. The spell he seeks to break by another word is the spell cast by a speaking edifice, a tower from which an artificially produced voice emanates, as if naturally, like the waves of the sea. The writer is to search out a new object to desire, and we get a glimpse of what that object might be like in the tower of the writer.

The writer's tower can be differentiated from the Ivory Tower of poetry or radio. In the latter case, we have to do with a construct, an edifice with an inside space of retreat dominating those who can hear the words it diffuses. In the former case, the tower is measurable, says Valéry, by the yardsticks of its own altitude and solitude (and not by those of its inhabitant). The writer's tower consists rather of an irreplaceable heap; it has neither outside nor inside. It could be, for instance, a heap of volumes, like Valéry's own *Oeuvres,* appearing in a new edition in the early thirties. Valéry appeals to the writer to think the material conditions of the birth and collapse of ideas in works that acknowledge a participation in the logic of the remainder (*encore un mot*), and not just that of domination and seductive totalization. He appeals against a blind submission to the fatality that says that fictions posited as standing free of the complex conditions of their birth should then be left to carry out mindlessly the orders programmed in that positing. He appeals for recollection of distinctions operative in the complex network in which the hypothesis came into being. He diagnoses as the ill of his time an ignorance: the expectant attitude sets a choice before one when in point of fact, the undecidable question has already been decided once a conjectural freedom is taken as real and effective. To take on the burden of the determinations to which indeterminacy is subject, to render an account of them and to render oneself accountable for them (instead of just accountable to them) is the task of a writer alert to the material conditions for the birth and collapse of idealisms. The Valéry of 1933, at any rate, puts his money on another word as a chance to remember responsibly those conditions.

PART ONE

On Shifting Ground: Poetry's Orders

Already the autumn of ideas is at hand
And I must use shovel and rakes
To gather up again the inundated soil
Where the water has dug holes big as tombs.

And who can say if the new flowers I dream
Will find in this ground washed like a strand
The mystical food that will give them vigor?

—Baudelaire, "The Enemy"

§ 1 (Dis)Arming Minerva: Of Performatives and Prosthetics in Chénier's "La Jeune captive"

> In the final instance, all literary texts have as their object—and this seems to be their real "philosophy"—the non-adhesion of language to language, the gap that constantly divides what we say from what we say about it and what we think about it. . . . Provided that it is rigorous, literary rhetoric relates to the ideology of an era only insofar as it brings it into conflict with itself, divorces it from itself, brings out its internal conflicts, and therefore makes a critique of it.
>
> —Macherey, *The Object of Literature*

In tracing out the patterns made by Chénier's figuration of the political, we inevitably come across gender. A poet giving voice and face to an abstract or absent entity has also to endow the persona with a gender, and thus to inscribe the poem and its problem within the arena of sexual politics. In some of Chénier's lyric poems contemporaneous with the Revolution, gendered personae show up in particularly arresting shape, bearing double, ambiguous, or crossed gender markings. Most often these strange shapes emerge at points of crisis in the last odes, where Chénier, exploiting the form's potential for swift mood changes, clashing images, and a mixture of public and private themes, is concerned with characterizing freedom and revolutionary action, as also with formulating poetry's task with respect to it. These figures are interesting in political terms, since where they occur ideology is at stake, and also in poetical terms, since they put into play tensions between language as representation and as inventive or disruptive of representation.

One surprising feature of these figures is that they are not invariably evaluated negatively, as might be expected in a poet whose dramatic end leads one to suppose he must have had counterrevolutionary tendencies. Instead, they can be colored differently even in the same poem, with the poet apparently more concerned with the metamorphoses undergone by the figure than with defining or observing gender norms. A poem from what one critic sees as Chénier's period of moderate antiroyalism, the

ode *Le Jeu de paume* dedicated to the painter David, provides two allegorical figures for Poetry and Liberty that change gender over the course
of the poem. First seen as a divine Hebe bearing a cup of ambrosia to a
kingly David (p. 167), Poetry Triumphant is then figured as a virile, ma-
jestic Cybele, of august and proud grace, with great step and towering
forehead encircled by light, who lends her *"fraternal* aid" to freedom in
stanza 2 (p. 167).[1] As for freedom, first called "male liberty" (*la liberté
mâle*) (p. 167), it undergoes multiple transformations, appearing triply
marked in stanzas 2 and 3. As an emanation of the "young and divine
Poetry" addressed by the poet, it is a desired woman in flight: "C'est de
tes lèvres séduisantes, / Qu'invisible elle (la liberté) vole" ('Tis from your
seductive lips, / That invisible it [freedom] flies) (p. 168). In its actions,
it is a wily Odysseus escaped from a feminized fortress:

> et par d'heureux détours
> Trompe les noirs verrous, les fortes citadelles,
> Et les mobiles ponts qui défendent les tours,
> Et les nocturnes sentinelles.
>
> and by happy detours
> Outwits the dark bolts, the strong citadels,
> And the drawbridges that defend the towers,
> And the nocturnal sentinels.　　　　*(p. 168)*

In its reign, it is like an unborn child of indeterminate sex, a seed germi-
nating in the hearts of the wise: "Son règne au loin semé par tes doux en-
tretiens / Germe dans l'ombre" (Its reign sown abroad by your sweet
conversation / Germinates in the shade) (p. 168). By stanza 11, reani-
mated Freedom has taken on the virile attributes of Poetry Triumphant:
"de ces grands tombeaux, la belle Liberté, / Altière, étincelante, armée, /
Sort" (from these great tombs, beautiful Liberty, / Haughty, throwing
off sparks, armed / Issues forth) (p. 172), only to end as a pious daughter: "la sainte Liberté, fille du sol français" (holy Liberty, daughter of
French soil) (p. 177). The poet's central concern is the solemn verbal act
of the Tennis Court Oaths, which, besides transforming the playspace of
a gymnasium into a temple and cradle of the law, has the effect of bringing a people into existence.[2] The metamorphosis in the gender of the
two figures is a vehicle for the celebration of the verbal act.

By contrast, in the violently anti-Jacobin "Ode" celebrating Marat's as-
sassin, Charlotte Corday, praise is heaped on an even more dramatically

virilized feminine figure. A solemn, classical comparison of the heroine in the tumbrel on the day of her execution to a beautiful, brilliant bride riding in her hymeneal chariot is followed by an apostrophe to Corday as the woman who acted as the sole man in a crowd of eunuchs: "Seule tu fus un homme, et vengeas les humains. / Et nous, eunuques vils" (Alone you were a man, and avenged humanity. / And we, vile eunuchs) (p. 180).[3] Similar figures of problematic gender thus arise both in the poem celebrating the Tennis Court Oaths as the act of freedom giving itself the law and in a poem celebrating the assassination of Marat as of a monster. The political positioning cannot be identified as anti-Jacobin or antiroyalist, left or right, on the basis of how the figures are gendered. If we want to read what the poems have to say about the political—about freedom and law—it will not help to think in terms of partisan politics.

In *Le Jeu de paume* the central problem is the verbal act of the Oaths and its representation. In the "Ode à Charlotte Corday," the doubly sexed figure also appears where the poem's language is passing from description to apostrophe, from a language of tropes grounded in a witnessed event (Corday's tumbrel ride) to a language that foregrounds naming as power. That is the kind of revenge the poet wants to wreak on those historians and poets immortalizing Marat: he calls Corday's deed by the name of vengeance, its motive by the name of virtue, its reward by the name of glory, its doer by the name of man. The poet says how deed and doer are to be remembered, how honor and virtue are to be redefined, and what is henceforth to be called *man*. By such figures Chénier seems to posit and try to bridge a gap between one regime of signs (tropes can substitute for proper names in a world knowable through appearances, one where men look like men and women like women and we can rely on experience) and another (where inventive verbal action is necessary and names have still to be given in order to recognize or classify a new sort of experience), as between one rule of law and the other. Because the verbal act has to be set down in the grammar of the gendered language that is French, the poet has also to take into account both the resources that grammar provides and the violences that it may do to those figures of mythic proportions. This has to be shown, and its implications and permutations developed, in the reading of a poem.

Before one undertakes such a reading, some cautionary statements are in order, so as to allow the specificity of the lyric genre to emerge as it pertains to gender issues. With the performative, Chénier's interest in language clearly coincides with the events occupying the political stage in his time: the swearing of the Tennis Court Oaths, the adoption of the Declaration of the Rights of Man by the National Assembly, the writing and ratifying of a series of constitutions, and so forth. In narrating the acts of swearing, naming, declaring, praising, or blaming that have occurred, but also in imitating them by swearing, naming, declaring, praising, or blaming in turn, the poet is doing what an austere and republican sort of poet (in Plato's terms) might do—limiting his poem to the representation and imitation of heroic, virtuous acts (of speaking). A poem may reflect questions that have arisen in the context. For instance, during the Revolution a redefinition of public and private space and of human rights and responsibilities was undertaken. Intense hermeneutic pressure was brought to bear on concepts ordinarily taken for granted and it became a matter of debate how to distinguish in legal terms a friend from an enemy, a human from an animal, or a man from a woman. It would be not surprising to find traces in Chénier's poetry of this debate in the problematic gender of its figures.

But in ascribing gender to a speaker, a group addressed, or a presiding influence—in sexualizing the speech situation—the poet consults a logic internal to the poem that may diverge from historical events and even from such a presumed aim of the successful performative as the aim of stabilizing identity—witness Corday imagined both as a virginal bride and as dragon-slayer in the space of two stanzas.[4] The problematic gender may simply be the thematic form given an indeterminacy in *language*—say the problematic difference between performative and constative, or between inventive verbal action and its conventional repetition. Chénier's determination of the gender of poetry might then be a place where he is taking a stance on poetry's legalities and freedoms with respect to linguistic indeterminacy. Such gendering would have implications for the context and the Revolutionary process of redefinition, but no quick translation of the terms of one into the other would be possible.

Gender in the Lyric: Caveat Lector

The first, rather obvious precautionary statement thus concerns the status of gender themes in the lyric. In the case of a representational genre like the novel, it is possible to start from the premise that the gendering of characters in the fictional world is part of the framework at the author's disposal for setting up potential conflicts and alliances among characters conceived as representative human types. Gender is one means the author has for opening the window onto the family romance, the emotional life of a character riven by desires and repressions. It allows relations, conflictual or harmonious, between the passionate life of individuals and the conventions and demands of public life to be represented. Since numerous social conventions are devoted to the smooth management of desire, and since the social structure itself relies on repression and sublimation, the gendering of characters in the novel marks off zones where conflicts are likely to emerge and reconciliations to be made. The world of the novel, filtered as it is by the author's mediating consciousness, can then be approached dialectically, and it becomes quite possible to ask about the author's stance with respect to gender constructs.[5]

It is not at all evident in the case of the lyric that we can approach the theme armed with the same presuppositions. A poem takes its point of departure in a query as to the obstacles in the way of its arrival. It knows itself imperiled in its capacity to represent experience. This is true for a poet like Mallarmé who represents the world as it absents itself in language. It is also the case with Chénier, whose translations and imitations of the poems of the *Greek Anthology*, for instance, are at a far remove from the *peinture de moeurs* we find in his contemporary, Laclos. A poem does not separate itself entirely from representation, but approaches it from a different bias, as a problematic possibility. As a result, gender as it appears in a poem can be an unanchored structure, what the French might call a *bâtiment* (*bâtiment* is a word for grounded structures like buildings, but also for floating ones like ships), one whose attachment to the referential world of empirical relations between the sexes and to gender structures is not a priori given.

Barbara Johnson starts from this point about difference in poems in a useful essay where she criticizes "the ideal of a woman's poetry of experience" as "uncomfortably close to Baudelaire's . . . construction of Marceline Desbordes-Valmore—and indeed of the woman poet as such—as a *sujet supposé sincère.*"[6] For Johnson, to reduce Desbordes-Valmore's poetry to an expression of woman's experience is to deprive it of what makes it poetry at all. Instead, Johnson considers Desbordes-Valmore's poetics in terms of a complex process of gender construction and identification that acknowledges the potential freedom of the poet from biological determinism, in a position to question the polar oppositions of logocentrism. By uncovering a difference affecting the poetic voice with doubling, Johnson is able to show the role readers play in determining the status of that difference. In the case she analyzes of Desbordes-Valmore's poem "Son image," difference gets read as sexual difference and the poet's language as the sincere, literal language of a confessing feminine subject. In the case of Baudelaire, by contrast, the same difference is read as ironic self-difference; his hysterical self-splitting is thought of as an enacting of a "right *to play* femininity" (p. 178) for some serious hermeneutic purpose (such as an inquiry into the nature of desire). It is a short step to suggesting that a change in the way we read difference can empower. Johnson makes the step explicit at the end of the essay when she calls for a "different kind of reading," by which it is to be assumed she means more than simply granting Desbordes-Valmore the right, symmetrical to the one enjoyed by Baudelaire, of playing at masculinity. Presumably, what one gets by according seriousness to Desbordes-Valmore's ironies is an inquiry into the rationale behind reading self- and sexual difference in poems, which means an inquiry into poetic language as concerned with linguistic force and action. How does the poem strike us, that its doubling can strike us differently?

A second precaution to take in reading gender in the lyric concerns the attribution of gender to the lyrical voice. Johnson's point is that one reads difference differently according to whether the poetic voice is heard speaking *as* male or female.[7] But, in a poem like Chénier's *Epître à Lebrun*, where the poetic persona claims to speak with an "altered voice," it is in the midst of a larger boast that the very voice of the origin, "the Greek chorus," has been mixed by the poet's daring insertion of French songs into it.[8] The term *altered* does more than raise the specter of impersonation and ventriloquizing, of brutal operations that threaten the integrity of the body, either mutilating it—by damage inflicted to the speech apparatus (de-tonguing in the case of Philomela), by castration—or, more radically still, by beheading. It suggests that voice is not a given but has to be made—for instance, by the introduction of a mechanical sound box or prosthetic device that produces the illusion of a speaking voice. Such was the case with Ovid's dismembered Orpheus, worth recalling in the context of Chénier, whose emergence was as a posthumous, decapitated poet: "Wonderful to relate, as they floated down in midstream, the lyre uttered a plaintive melody and the lifeless tongue made a piteous murmur, while the river banks lamented in reply."[9] Artifice intervenes first to produce the supposedly "natural" voice, and then in the subsequent undoing of the illusion that the poem is voiced language. It is the greater part of the poet's craft, not to mimic voices, but to *mime* voice.[10] The attribution of gender to the singer—usually the same as that of the poem's signatory—is part of a strategy for covering over the threat posed to voice. It enables the poem to appear in the last analysis as the unified song of the poet, be that poet expressing the nature of his individual desire, or, in the case of a woman poet, of her gender.[11] Gendering the poet's voice—and it seems almost impossible not to attribute gender to the persona—lets us forget that there is a gap between the poem's force as song, and its actual existence as text, thereby ridding us of the need to consider what Peggy Kamuf has called "signature effects."[12]

A glance at *Epître sur ses ouvrages* shows the relevance of this discussion for Chénier's poetry. The poet does not claim an existence as song for the poems: "Combien de chants de faits?—Pas un, je vous assure" (How many songs made?—Not a one, I assure you) (p. 158).[13] Instead, the poems are called textiles woven from heterogeneous materials. The poet *points* out the heterogeneity, *shows* the seams stitching foreign colors to the stuff of the text: "Mon doigt sur mon manteau lui dévoile à l'instant / La couture invisible et qui va serpentant, / Pour joindre à mon étoffe une pourpre étrangère" (My finger on my cloak immediately unveils to him / The invisible seam that goes snaking throughout, / To join to my fabric a foreign purple) (p. 159). In Chénier, the poet's language is one of mute gesturing; unveiling is not a gesture of revealing a truth behind appearances, but instead, of pointing out seams and stitches in the veil.

Chénier's lyric poems ask, What does it mean to arrive as mute texts (antilyrics) to which the liveliness and unity of a speaking voice is attributed? The rhetorical figure that allows foreknowledge of this destiny is prosopopoeia, the figure whereby an absent or dead entity is given voice and face, or in Chénier's usual term, gets a forehead (*front*) with which to face the day.[14] With prosopopoeia, poems are concerned with the conditions under which, and the effects produced when, one grants human voice to what does not have one.[15] Through the analysis of a poem, I'd like to develop further the possibility that the attribution of gender to the poetic persona is a strategy for defending the integrity of the person, as invested in the poet's *own* voice.

But first, a final caveat, this one about the gendering of the figure of

Poetry itself. Indeterminacy also affects the distinction between poetic and nonpoetic language or within two kinds of poetic language. It would thus affect our very ability to make the sort of statements we have just been making about poetic language (as distinct from the novel, or as marked internally by a difference between lyric and antilyric tendencies). One tenacious notion about poetic language is that it is a transgressive language with respect to normal discourse conceived as a message-bearing, translatable language that respects a prescribed grammar and obeys given semantic constraints in the production of intelligible utterances. We assume that, like M. Jourdain, we ordinarily speak prose; poetry is thought as a deviant, imaginative use in which a normal utterance has been embroidered upon to make an *objet de luxe*. The *Princeton Encyclopedia of Poetry and Poetics*, for instance, explains in the article "poetic license" that it is the freedom in practice "to *depart* in subject matter, grammar or diction from what would be ordinary prose discourse" (my emphasis).[16] The presumption is that one could get at the meaning of the poem by recognizing "o'er" as a poetic term for "over," or by putting the words back into their "natural" order, but that the poet—preferring beauty to meaning, everywhere marking a preference for form—has the license within the narrow confines of the poem to pay attention to rhyme or rhythm, in short, to the poetic function of language, rather more than to its hermeneutic function. Where, exceptionally, language is allowed this license, it is because it is construed as the natural idiom of an I ordinarily constrained by civility, but here, in this limited place of lyric expression, given freedom to voice itself. In such an interpretation, the identification of the Muse as feminine helps tame the poetic function of language by endowing it with a sensuous, natural body on which the poet can labor. Linguistic difference is figured as perceptible to the senses. Gender ideology would work in tandem with the ideology that makes poetic language an inspired deviance with respect to the logos.

However, in generalizing what has just been said about the undoing of lyrical voice, we are led to put things another way. Poems do not so much depart from prose as operate according to another law entirely. The theory of the poem about its language is that there is no other way to say it here than by using *o'er* and the inverted structure. That means first of all that in the inversion or elided letter, a chance to manifest the poem's language as a unique and untranslatable configuration has been seized. What sounds transgressive or ungrammatical from the angle of the speedy delivery of a message has been worked by the poet who hears in it a chance for a poem until it exhibits itself as ineluctable or commanded. The precarious autonomy of the poem is that of an entity operating in strict obedience to its unique law (like a Derridian hedgehog or a Pongian oyster). Its survival is decided by its success at converting the supposed breaching of a rule into the occasion for the manifestation—good for one time only—of poetic law. It follows that the singular legitimacy of a poetic utterance could never be a given but is what the poem strives to give.

In such a hypothesis, ordinary prose discourse is not *opposed* to poetic language. It is a matter of more or less. Prose is more forgetful of its obedience to untranslatability, of its surreptitious observance of such laws as those of rhythm, of an ever-threatening fictionality. Poetry would propose itself as a guardian, but not the sole possessor, of this memory of rhythm in the language.[17] It would call attention to the traits of harmony, rhythm, balance, number, order that are exhibited by ordinary prose, but that, in the hurry to reduce language to the logos, have been set aside, repressed, or confined to a limited sphere. Where this memory of rhythm is concerned, the "natural" order of a sentence, *over* in the place of *o'er*, would be imprecise language.[18] That does not mean, however, that *o'er* and the inverted order of a sentence would be the idiom of an individual lyrical subject. The singularity of the text is that it is the *only* way of putting it that observes poetic law. In "La Poésie de Mallarmé est-il obscure?" Maurice Blanchot states this succinctly:

> The first characteristic of poetic signification is that it is linked without possible change, to the language that manifests it. Whereas in language that is not poetic we know we have understood the idea into whose presence the discourse brings us when we can express it in different forms, making ourselves masters of it to the point of freeing it from any determinate language, on the contrary, in order to be understood, poetry demands a total acquiescence to the unique form it proposes.[19]

All these gnomic formulations point toward a situation with implications for any discussion of gender. On the one side, following out the same thesis concerning poetic language as problematically removed from reference, we end with the thorough evacuation of the thematics of the poem as they concern gender. If we always have to bear in mind the determining importance of rhythm, for instance, the decision to make the Muse feminine in French poetry could well owe less to theme or tradition than to the relative frequency in French of syllables rhyming with *elle*, to the odd accident that many of these rhyming terms are central to any statement of such poetic topoi as memory and beauty (for instance, *celle, belle, appelle, rappelle*), to the fact that French is a gendered language and *poésie* a feminine noun.[20] Where words step out obedient to measure and rhythm, chosen in response to "the immortal needs for monotony, symmetry and surprise,"[21] gender may be a matter of rhyme or cadence.[22]

On the other side, however, at the precise moment that our discussion of poetic indeterminacy tempts us to conclude that it makes no sense to speak about gender in poetry at all, except perhaps as a place where a formal or grammatical problem is being translated into a theme, a second approach to the problem can be seen to emerge. The poem, we have asserted, seems to provide a unique sort of self-legitimating act. The law it follows does not predate it, but is always given by way of it, through the "seizing of the occasion" (a carpe diem of sorts) for its manifestation.[23] As such, it is a law bound to a case. Nor is a poem's law ever anything but unique and irreducibly singular. In this, it is different from codes governing rational subjects where the ideal is of universality and whose logic is that the law precedes the case, the subject becomes a subject by respecting the law, and so on. Such codes as those of the legal system, partly by way of a logic that sees the idea of property and of a proper language as embodied in the possessors of penile appendages, have a well-known tendency to favor the gender as the model of the supposedly "reasonable man" being legislated.[24]

Poetic law, among its other specificities, recurrently bears the gender marker of the feminine.[25] What is the rationale for calling poetic law in the feminine? It cannot be because poetry is "like a woman"—innocent, wily, capricious, sensuous, sentimental, mysterious, beautiful, natural, or any of the other ways of constructing her around a lack—because all of that assumes that woman *has* certain properties, be it only the property of lacking property of her own, and that the observant poet thus personifies poetry on the basis of a perceived resemblance between woman and poetry, which "share" this property of a determinate lack, of "being" the appendages or others of man and the logos. But that is precisely what we deny in saying the poem tends toward untranslatability and gives itself a precarious legitimacy from its observation of that law. The lack of a proper term is not a deficiency to be supplied by just finding or fabricating one by way of a metaphor that can, in the last analysis, be shown to be a metaphor, an exchange of terms based on the observation of a resemblance. The poem points to an ungroundedness to language that makes the status of its metaphors an open question.

Blanchot makes this point when he says that, while "the first reflex faced with some poetic lines that discursive reason would like to elucidate is to give them another form," the poem resists transforming paraphrase, and thus, further metaphorization: "But its resistance allows no metamorphosis. Here we have to understand without feint or detour, and by exchanging the poem only against the poem."[26] The poem's figures cannot be further exchanged. Blanchot remarks that it is to misunderstand poetry to look there for abstract ideas in the name of which we can make new exchanges and against which we can measure cases. Instead, poetry exhausts figures, bringing them to the point where they become obsolete and unusable:

> La signification poétique ne relève pas de cette généralité pour laquelle plusieurs moyens d'expression sont possibles et qui peut s'appliquer à un certain nombre de cas. Elle ne sert qu'une fois et elle rend indisponible le système d'images, de figures, de consonances qui lui est indissolublement associé. Elle appartient à la catégorie de l'Unique. Elle est non seulement ce qui dépend essentiellement du langage, mais ce qui rappelle le langage à son essence et l'empêche de se confondre avec ses buts.

> Poetic signification does not arise from this generality for which several means of expression are possible and which can be applied to a number of cases. It is good for one time only, and it makes unavailable the system of images, figures and consonances indissolubly associated to it. It belongs to the category of the Unique. It is not only what depends essentially on language, but what recalls language to its essence and keeps it from being confused with its goals.[27]

Chénier's famous statement—"Sur des pensers nouveaux faisons des vers antiques" (On new thoughts let us make antique verse) (p. 127)—is close to this Blanchotian view of poetic language as confronting us with the orientation of language toward untranslatability and Babelic ruin.

If Blanchot is right and poetry each time has to exhibit its belonging to the category of the unique, then how is it that poetry seems always to get personified by one gender, in the feminine? Blanchot's commentary, just to take a handy example, personifies poetic signification in the feminine: "Elle . . . sert . . . elle rend . . . Elle appartient . . . Elle est . . . ce qui dé-

pend . . . et rappelle." (It is good for . . . it makes . . . it belongs . . . it
is . . . what depends . . . and reminds.) What's so unique about this personification that happens each time anew? In a gendered language like
French, it could be simply that grammar demands such a determination:
la signification poétique is a feminine noun, so the pronoun *elle* has to replace it. But that doesn't solve the question, since it is simple enough to
find nouns of masculine gender, or to rearrange one's sentence to avoid
the personification. Indeed, in the sentence immediately preceding the
passage quoted, Blanchot has used such a noun, *le sens*. In Blanchot's text
at least, the writer has obeyed grammar in accepting the gender of the
noun *and* has chosen to allegorize the intervention of grammar's command in the feminine. Each time, a persona in the feminine gender
would arrive and be chosen to stand for the intervention of a dimension
to language that exceeds its hermeneutic function. But it isn't by a gener-
alizable rule. However often it recurs, it would be at the point of collapse
of the metaphorical system and its replacement by another logic (here, a
grammar capable of positing an anthropomorphic figure). Poetic language is language worked until it cannot be exchanged any more, and it
is that horizon of untranslatability that is seized and held in the feminine, as a singular form destined never to be repeated or reformulated.[28]

Notice that it is not woman or women but the feminine gender that is
invoked. Whereas the attribution of gender to voice seems to occur
along the lines of an opposition between subject and object, and is likely
to prove a defensive maneuver in the face of a threat to one's narcissism,
the allegorization of poetry in the feminine seems to occur along a different axis, to personify a certain freedom of language in its poetic function, as well as an inexorable demand to determine that freedom in singular form. It is as though two logics (or a logic and a poetics) for
gendering were interfering with one another in the production of the
overall pattern—characterized by points of suture and by gapping—of
the poem. In the overlap or the disjunction between these two orders,
shifts and disruptions to the meaning paradigm would be in evidence,
and these would be the concern of anyone reading the gender system.

From these precautionary statements, it is foreseeable that gender in
the lyric will play two very different roles that are bound up with those
of the lyric itself. It will have a defensive, essentially conservative function of unifying in a single figure, misconstruing an inhuman situation
as human, reinscribing poetic language within the logical oppositions

of logocentrism, making it translatable, reducing it in the last analysis
to a language conforming to idealism: in a word, of disarming language
by making it seem natural and full of expressive possibility. But, it can
also mark out an arena where the program of logocentrism falters and is
disregarded by poetic law, where unread possibilities and unique configurations are given, and where we find ourselves attending to "the non-
adhesion of language to language" as providing the chance for (and
menace of) a shift.

Among Chénier's poems devoted to the overlapping areas of and conflicts between the jurisdictions of law and poetic law, and characterized
by gendered figures, one of the most fully developed is "La Jeune captive," the famous ode written in St. Lazare shortly before the poet's execution, and smuggled out of prison, according to one legend, in a bun-
dle of dirty laundry. While, at first glance, the gender structures appear
predictable, the poem contains some surprises that make it worthy of
lengthy consideration.

The Fearful Beauty of "La Jeune captive"

La Jeune captive

"L'épi naissant mûrit de la faux respecté;
Sans crainte du pressoir, le pampre tout l'été
    Boit les doux présents de l'aurore;
Et moi, comme lui belle, et jeune comme lui,
Quoi que l'heure présente ait de trouble et d'ennui,
    Je ne veux point mourir encore.

Qu'un stoïque aux yeux secs vole embrasser la mort:
Moi je pleure et j'espère. Au noir souffle du nord
    Je plie et relève ma tête.
S'il est des jours amers, il en est de si doux!
Hélas! quel miel jamais n'a laissé de dégoûts?
    Quelle mer n'a point de tempête?

L'illusion féconde habite dans mon sein.
D'une prison sur moi les murs pèsent en vain,
    J'ai les ailes de l'espérance.
Echappée aux réseaux de l'oiseleur cruel,
Plus vive, plus heureuse, aux campagnes du ciel
    Philomène chante et s'élance.

Est-ce à moi de mourir? Tranquille je m'endors
Et tranquille je veille; et ma veille aux remords
   Ni mon sommeil ne sont en proie.
Ma bienvenue au jour me rit dans tous les yeux;
Sur des fronts abattus, mon aspect dans ces lieux
   Ranime presque de la joie.

Mon beau voyage encore est si loin de sa fin!
Je pars, et des ormeaux qui bordent le chemin
   J'ai passé les premiers à peine,
Au banquet de la vie à peine commencé,
Un instant seulement mes lèvres ont pressé
   La coupe en mes mains encor pleine.

Je ne suis qu'au printemps, je veux voir la moisson,
Et comme le soleil, de saison en saison,
   Je veux achever mon année.
Brillante sur ma tige et l'honneur du jardin,
Je n'ai vu luire encor que les feux du matin;
   Je veux achever ma journée.

O mort! tu peux attendre; éloigne, éloigne-toi;
Va consoler les coeurs que la honte, l'effroi,
   Le pâle désespoir dévore.
Pour moi Palès encore a des asiles verts,
Les Amours des baisers, les Muses des concerts,
   Je ne veux point mourir encore."

Ainsi, triste et captif, ma lyre toutefois
S'éveillait, écoutant ses plaintes, cette voix,
   Ces voeux d'une jeune captive;
Et secouant le faix de mes jours languissants,
Aux douces lois des vers je pliai les accents
   De sa bouche aimable et naïve.

Ces chants, de ma prison témoins harmonieux,
Feront à quelque amant des loisirs studieux
   Chercher quelle fut cette belle.
La grâce décorait son front et ses discours,
Et comme elle craindront de voir finir leurs jours
   Ceux qui les passeront près d'elle.

The Young Captive

"The new-born ear of wheat ripens respected by the scythe;
Without fear of the winepress, the vineyard the whole summer
    Drinks the sweet presents of dawn;
And I, like that one beautiful, and young like that one,
Whatever the troubles and cares of the present hour,
    I do not want to die yet.

Let a stoic with dry eyes fly to embrace death:
Me, I cry and I hope. At the north's black breath
    I bend and again lift my head.
If there are bitter days, there are some so sweet!
Alas! what honey never left some disgust?
    What sea has no storm?

Fecund illusion inhabits my breast.
On me the walls of a prison weigh in vain,
    I have the wings of hope.
Escaped from the nets of the cruel bird catcher,
More lively, more happy, toward the countryside of the sky
    Philomena sings and soars up.

Is it mine to die? Tranquil I go to sleep
And tranquil I wake; and my waking to remorse
    Nor my sleeping are not prey.
My welcome to the day laughs at me in all eyes;
On dejected foreheads, my aspect in these places
    Reanimates near joy.

My beautiful voyage is yet so far from its end!
I depart, and of the young elms that line the road
    I have scarcely passed the first,
At the banquet of life scarcely begun,
Only an instant have my lips pressed
    The cup in my hands yet full.

I have only reached spring, I want to see the harvest,
And like the sun, from season to season,
    I want to finish my year.
Brilliant on my stem and the honor of the garden,
I have only seen shine yet the fires of morning;
    I do not want to die yet.

Oh death! you can wait; take your distance, take your distance;
Go console hearts that shame, fear,
     Pale despair devour
For me Pales yet has green asylums
The Loves kisses, the Muses concerts
     I do not want to die yet."

So, sad and captive, my lyre nonetheless
Awoke, hearing these complaints, this voice,
     These wishes of a young captive;
And shaking off the burden of my languishing days,
To the sweet laws of verse I bent the accents
     Of her lovable and naive mouth.

These songs, of my prison harmonious witnesses,
Will make some lover of leisures studious
     Seek what was this beauty.
Grace decorated her forehead and her speech,
And like her will fear to see end their days
     Those who will pass them near her.   *(pp. 185–86)*

The ode is characterized by an abrupt change in speakers that has proved
one of its cruxes. The first seven strophes consist in an eloquent plea by
the captive of the title that she be allowed to live out her natural span.
The gender of the speaker has to be established internally by the adjective *belle*, confirmed in the framing song by the nominalized adjectives
captive and *belle*, since the title by which it is popularly known in all
likelihood was not owed to Chénier.[29] The last two stanzas are those of
another singer, this time a male (as marked by the adjective *captif*), who
claims to have "bent" her accents to the "sweet laws of verse."

   The shift has been felt as disconcerting and has divided interpreters. It
has seemed a matter of moment to work out why Chénier should have
put the eloquent plea for life and liberty in the mouth of a woman captive, whereas the male speaker should meditate instead on such apparently tangential matters as poetic form and the poem's posterity. Two of
the poem's chief commentators, Francis Scarfe and Leo Spitzer, are in
marked disagreement over the poem's change in voice and divided on
Chénier's aesthetics and place in literary history as a result. For both critics the issue is a conflict between the natural objects of perception (the
given, sensuous world of stalk, vine, sweet honey, and bird) and the theoretical structures of reason (the world of doctrines, laws, and confining

institutional structures exemplified in the "troubles and cares of the present hour," stoic virtue, the nets of the bird catcher, and so on). The two voices of woman and man, like the two voices of Shepherd and Goatherd in Chénier's dialogued poem "La Liberté," are taken as providing differing views on the same issue, with their final reconciliation in a single harmonious song taken as the problem of the poem. Since this is one of Chénier's last poems, written "at the foot of the scaffold" (p. 193), the stakes are high. On its success at reconciling the two perspectives rides Chénier's ultimate success as a poet. Both Scarfe and Spitzer find the reconciliation to fail, and see the poet as choosing one of the singers over the other as the dominant figure. It is worth bringing out the way each critic tries to resolve the conflict, so as to provide a backdrop against which a third model attentive to the points of overlap and disjunction between the two logics can be made to emerge. In the last stanza, the poetic persona predicts that the poem will receive divergent readings, so we are justified in considering that the reconciliation of its two speakers may not have been envisaged.

Throughout his detailed intellectual biography of Chénier, Scarfe reads his subject through the lens of an emerging Romanticism, insisting on Chénier's passion, sentimentality, and lack of a true ethical dimension. It is therefore not surprising that under his pen "La Jeune captive" should be turned into something of a Romantic elegy, one of several poems in which the imprisoned poet is taking leave of poetry. As Scarfe reads it, the poem may have been inspired by a real-life woman—either Aimée de Coigny or Mme de Saint-Aignan—but she is so transfigured as to have lost any but the most tenuous of connections to her model, coming to stand for the lyrical impulse by her "spontaneous song," "exuberance of protest," and celebration of "pastoral pleasures."[30] In the second part of the poem, the poet abandons indirection to sing undisguised, from the perspective of open melancholy and superior knowledge, providing a commentary that Scarfe sees as adding the dimension of a reflection on the pleasures of society that are missing from the woman captive's song. Scarfe finds the Lucretia-like victim's eloquent lyrical plea to the Tarquin-like "tigers judges our masters" (Chénier, p. 193) to have been framed and distanced from the first by the poet. Writes Scarfe:

> . . . the poet's own view of life is *obliquely expressed through the song of the "captive"*. . . . The expression "l'illusion féconde" is a key to the *Bucoliques*,

elegies and odes, which all have that very *personal mixture or "alternance" of enthusiasm and melancholy that marked his character.* Throughout, the lyrical flight is held in check by the superior knowledge that nothing is perfect, but, against that, stands the conviction that life is something to be lived to the end, be it good or bad. *It is the voice of a mature man, then, and the "captive" is only a beautiful vehicle for nostalgia. The last two stanzas are a brake to sentiment and enthusiasm: the poet comes into the open, but had been there, keeping the balance, all the time.* All that is left, really, is the pleasure of art. (my emphasis, p. 334)

Scarfe proposes a resolution for the mixture of tone in Chénier's work, exemplified by the shift of speakers in this ode: first the poet speaks obliquely, through the mask of a fearful woman, expressing himself in the high-pitched tones of a lyrical enthusiast, and then he drops the mask to speak directly, in the grave and melancholic tone "of a mature man." Retrospectively, however, that male voice turns out to have been there "keeping the balance, all the time." The alternation of speakers is thus explained as a dramatic means to express the maturation process of a single voice: the voice of the boy poet with its dulcet tones, "smooth and persuasive," deepens with maturity to become the grave tones of the self-conscious male poet. Unsurprisingly, Scarfe finds Chénier to have "a conventional and irritatingly superior attitude toward the other sex" (p. 30), and an immature one at that.

Certainly, the theory that under the skin a woman is an adolescent boy who hasn't fully developed his voice would testify "to an immature idea of women" (p. 30). But is it Chénier's in this poem? Scarfe's theory is that any incongruence between the songs of *captive* and *captif* can be accounted for in terms of a shift within a single, ultimately unified, voice. But the break in the poem, marked by the end of the quotation and the white space between stanzas, is a gap between two sorts of language: a recited song with a refrain, and a brief comment on the poet's activity with respect to the recited song that looks forward past his death to wax prophetic about future readings of a text made of two disparate parts. At the very least we have to consider why the poet insists that her song is not "my" song. The break between the first and the second parts of the poem is too great to be resolved by absorbing the repeated song into the frame as a moment in the poet's development. Instead the poet puts his finger on the seams the *Epître* talked about, pointing up a discrepancy between its parts.[31]

At the other end of the literary historical spectrum and with an inter-pretation of the gender scenario superficially quite different from Scarfe's, Leo Spitzer demonstrates in patient detail that the poem is a classical ode, with the captive woman's song owing everything to the harsh, moral lu-cidity of a Racinian heroine.[32] Of Spitzer it has been justly said that he "invites us to think that nothing in a form is accidental,"[33] and much of his essay on Chénier confirms the excellence of this method. On the basis of a single detail—that Phèdre did not say "Que ces ornements me sem-blent vains" (How vain these ornaments seem to me) but rather "Que ces vains ornements me pèsent" (How these vain ornaments weigh on me)— Spitzer is able to establish Racine's character as an intransigent moral judge of her own passion, show proof of the "muting" effect he finds characteristic of classicism, and demonstrate the filiation of Chénier's Epicurean captive with Phèdre. In what sounds to Spitzer like Chénier's equivalent classical line—"l'illusion féconde habite dans mon sein"—the captive asserts her knowledge of her delusion, all the while stating the force and persistence of her heart's Pascalian reasons that reason doesn't know. None of the enthusiasm Scarfe detects characterizes this speaker for Spitzer. Her claim to our attention is that of a rational, ethical being asking only that her passions be given such hearing as is their legitimate due. Spitzer insists on the moral strength and "intellectual clarity of the young woman" (p. 100). Her will to life has nothing "agitated or at all hysterical about it" (p. 99) and her protest—framed with exceptional so-briety and an artistry that conceals itself—takes on the force of a "natural occurrence" (p. 99). When she speaks, it is as though nature itself were saying: I know all that, but listen to me anyway (*je sais bien mais quand même*).

Spitzer cannot be accused of covering up the discontinuity between the two parts of the poem. On the contrary, he reads the captive poet's song as all but disconnected from that of the captive woman, and as in-ternally inconsistent to boot. For instance, he agrees with most critics that "a certain break" separates stanza 8 and the first lines of 9 from the last distich, with its ornate compliment to the beauty (p. 103). Spitzer heaps scorn on the poet who intrudes in the last stanzas. *He*, it seems, is a bungler, a late-eighteenth-century gallant who spoils his poem with a rococo compliment to a high tragic figure he has authored but utterly failed to understand. In the best possible construction, the style in the last stanzas degenerates into mannered "play in the face of death" of the sort characterizing the blind and decadent aristocrats of the last days of the ancien régime (p. 102). Spitzer amasses evidence of the poet's impotence: Chénier's poet doesn't just disrupt the mood by intruding, but he does it pedantically, by telling us unnecessarily what we already know, namely, that he is the author of her verse, in lines that are not even grammatically correct[34] and whose temporal perspective is moreover unclear.[35] Spitzer is so displeased with this impotent poet that he uncharacteristically acts against his own dictum that the critic be the apologist for what is on the page, going so far as to substitute a few verses of his manufacture for the inadequate eighth stanza.[36] He wreaks violence on the last distich in a translation that makes the poem more mannered than it is[37] and closes his attack with a summary dismissal of the last two stanzas as unworthy of serious consideration (p. 104). Spitzer has set up a strong, artful, *herrlichen* ("splendid" but, literally, "lordly, masterful") female figure who spreads moral strength and joy, in contrast to the moral and aesthetic weakling of the forgettable last lines against whom the critic has turned his considerable polemical verve.[38]

From the structuring of the captive's discourse as a disavowal (*je sais bien mais quand même*), from the petrifying effect she has had on the poet, from her use as an apotropaic device by the critic on a rampage (flailing away at the poet and slicing away at his poem), from the deleterious effect the poem has on the critic's own theory of respectful close reading, we can identify the figure Spitzer appears to have glimpsed and with whom he is attempting to side. It is that of Medusa.[39]

It would hardly be a surprise to find a Medusa in a poem written under the shadow of the guillotine, and whose situation could well elicit the "litany of nervous questions" that Neil Hertz has conclusively demonstrated as underlying nineteenth-century representations of revolution as a Medusa's head:

> questions that give expression to epistemological anxiety (can I trust my eyes?), to narcissism (can I hold myself together?), to sexual anxiety (can I hold on to my penis?), to—beyond that—social and economic fears about property and status (can I hold onto anything, including representations of myself?) or—put more grandly by one of this century's grand hysterics— Can the center hold? or is mere anarchy to be loosed upon the world?[40]

Such questions might quite plausibly run through the mind of anyone incarcerated in St. Lazare in 1794 and could be found as a subtext in the poem. Chénier was not a stranger to the Medusa theme, as we know from "L'Invention," where the birth of a poem is compared to that of Minerva, who

> formed in an instant,
> Sprang armed from Jupiter's forehead,
> Shaking the blade and the warrior's helmet
> And the horrible Gorgon of murderous aspect.
>
> *(p. 131)*[41]

But if we search "La Jeune captive" for traditional Medusa symbology (hair, snakes, stones, mirrors, shields, swords) it is not forthcoming. Indeed, with the possible exception of the last distich, the overall mood is stated to be that of tranquillity rather than terror. There is a puzzle then: the poem does not provide us with explicit Medusa symbols, but the gestures of a critic distinguished by a keen sense of stylistic nuance suggest he has picked up on something in the poem productive of the anxiety usually associated with the figure. How are we to explain this puzzle, which is a puzzle of importance because, if we can discover how the poem can be interpreted as a scene of desire and castration anxiety, we might also discover how it resists such translation?

A penetrating comment from Hertz can point us in the right direction. Discussing the contradictory and complex symbol of Medusa as it is analyzed by Freud and Laplanche, Hertz writes:

> Following one strand of associations, for example, the snakes curling around Medusa's face are penises; following another they are the pubic hair surrounding the castrated (and—to the terrified boy—castrating) sex of the mother. The symbol wouldn't function *as* a symbol . . . if such condensation and concentration weren't operative; further, in addition to the effects of "consolation" Freud attributes to specific elements in the mix (as when Medusa's grim powers of petrification are translated, reassuringly, into the stiffening of an erection, or her snakes into replaceable parts), Laplanche insists on the primary apotropaic power of symbolic concentration itself. The symbol of the Medusa's head is reassuring not only because its elements can be read in those ways, but *because it is a symbol.* (my emphasis)[42]

Whereas Freud argues that anxiety and its compensation are concentrated on specific elements in the Medusa myth, for Laplanche anxiety and consolation accompany symbolization itself. A language cut off from reference, symbols bear the terrifying scars of deprivation; but they also console by a compensatory realignment of an intelligible concept with a corresponding perception, in the case of castration anxiety, "a theory (of how women got that way) with a perception (of what their bodies look like)."[43] Symbols provide fixed, complex, condensed structures in which a cognition is given sensuous form. They can thus accomplish what Spitzer calls the "overturning of the negative into the positive," because they can turn the scary "want" or "nothingness" itself into a visible thing, and thus make it available as meaning. Hertz goes on to conjecture that the symbolization of revolutionary violence by the Medusa fantasy is largely a defensive maneuver. It has as its aim the preservation of "one's own more natural ways of looking at things" like property, even at the moment that the revolution is suggesting that property might instead be imposed by "'unnatural' systems which interpret the historical world with willed and artificial coherence."[44]

Taking a hint from Hertz then, we may ask whether Spitzer has glimpsed an unsettling overindeterminacy to the poem's chief symbols that he is trying to limit by recourse to the Medusa fantasy and by the detachment of the *captive's* song from its frame. We can then go on to ask, following Hertz, whether a more patient, and ultimately more historical, account is available in the poem of its incongruent parts that even so astute a reader as Spitzer is overlooking by reducing the poem to one of Medusal aspect. The best way to get at what Spitzer is seeing, and what he is trying to ward off, is by examining the symbolic system as it is set up around the young captive, since that is where the threat is concentrated.

Reading Gaps: "Qui sont ces belles, si ce sont des mortelles?"

The opening stanzas establish the utter destitution of the singer, stripped of any tie to the historical world: name, condition, property, personal history.[45] The very crime for which she has been incarcerated is unknown, as are the specific "troubles and cares of the present hour," the name of the jail that holds her, the dates and length of her sentence. Deprived of a proper language, she does not even have the imagination and eloquence granted through nature to help her; for she is immured in a prison, far removed from natural landscapes.[46] Her eloquence has its source in memory, and her memory is that of a being reduced, like Wilde's "wistful eye looking upon that tent of blue / Which prisoners call the sky" to finding her natural landscapes among similar "campagnes du ciel."[47] This suggests the genre of the poem is ultimately that of inscription, not of lyric. The *captive* is the spirit of the place. Her songs are doubly those of prison: considered as lyric they voice the desires of countless nameless prisoners, testify *from* the prison *for* them; but as prison songs, they testify to their prison, to its walls, as the writing on its walls. That is what the poet says: "ces chants, *de* ma prison témoins harmonieux" (these songs, harmonious witnesses from/of my prison). The prisoner sings to escape her prison; but also, the prison sings through the prisoner's song.

Read as an inscription, the early stanzas serve chiefly to persuade us that the singer is enough unlike the inanimate stalk and vine for her likeness to them to require establishment. Should Wordsworth's Lucy Gray sing that she feels like "the rocks, and stones and trees" with which death has intermingled her we would probably not worry about the minor miracle of feeling stones, so intent would we be on the major miracle of her reanimation. What Chénier has done is get us to accept the major illusion, and to focus instead on the minor one of the comparison. We need to bear this in mind, that the I, the deictic, persuades that the singer is unlike the mute things of which she speaks. Among other things, it focuses the first part of the poem on the act of speaking, on the poem's ability to persuade that it is a discourse appealing a judgment and calling for a review of a death sentence.[48] We will return to this prosopopoeia, in the context of the opening comparison where the persuasion is first made to operate.

One of the most enigmatic lines in the poem is the deceptively simple line in the first stanza where the *captive* claims herself the beauty of the poem. In this line, the speaker articulates an analogy between her situation and that of other natural entities, an analogy on which she is presumably grounding her appeal. Upon inspection, the analogy not only does not ground her appeal, but it opens onto an abyss threatening to engulf the poetic figure. She says: "Et moi, comme lui belle, et jeune comme lui" (And I, like that one beautiful, and young like that one).

The first difficulty surfaces around the third person pronouns: there are two antecedents—*le pampre* or *l'épi*—both masculine nouns, either of which could be plausibly relayed by the two pronouns, *lui* and *lui*. The line may complete a chiasmus of sorts, restatable as "comme celui-ci [the latter, the vine] belle, et jeune comme celui-là [the former, the ear of corn or wheat]." But nothing forbids reading the order instead as that of an *enumeration*, with the grain mentioned first as the beautiful thing, and the vine second as the young thing. The line is grammatical, but it does not let us decide which of the two natural entities has which of the properties the speaker is purporting to borrow. Pronoun substitution, far from serving the function of "syntactic representation" that Benveniste accords it, and allowing the more efficient transfer of meaning, fails to make the necessary difference.[49] The tool slips, and instead of a relaying substitution, we just get a pronoun repeated. This tiny lapse is significant, as a structure that ceases to differentiate. It is a detail that in Blanchot's terms is not a detail at all, since it stands allegorically for similar breakdowns affecting communication.

What does it matter which property belongs to which entity, one could retort. *Epi, pampre*—both are young, both are beautiful, both are natural entities having the qualities common to Nature's children. A cornucopian Mother Nature cannot much care about ownership: she dispenses the same to all equally by natural right.

An ellipsis strikes the sentence that destitutes the concept of Nature itself of the determination necessary to confirm this reading. Goes missing the verb that might tell us whether the speaker is comparing properties of autonomous entities to reveal their essence ("je suis comme lui belle, jeune comme lui") or rather modes of appearance ("je *parais* comme lui belle, jeune comme lui"). Anxiety attends this open question as to whether Nature is a being in the process of unfolding or a procession of simulacra, especially given the proximity of the twin metonyms for death, scythe and winepress. The stakes of the passage are quite large if one considers that the captive is trying to base an appeal against death on natural right. This prisoner, fearful victim *of* the Terror, can make a plausibly fearful figure *for* it.

This is established by considering what it would mean to stay death in each interpretation. If *appearances* are compared, the speaker would seem young in the same manner as the vine seems young—to the judging eye of the winemaker. The vine can be spared death because death cannot happen to it any more than age; its youth, maturity, or death can only seem such by the pathetic fallacy, to a human observer, busily applying human terms and fitting human ends to it. The poet would be recognizing that when we allege nature as a basis for our decisions we are actually alleging ideology, that is, a fiction whose status as fiction has been lost. Vines are pruned to bear the biggest harvest, chopped up when they cease to bear fruit, not when they have lived out the span "nature" accords them. *Nature* would be the term for a symbolic system, part of the prison immuring her against which she is in revolt, had the speaker said "I seem like vine and grain." In this case, the captive's analogy would be a preliminary concession made in a larger argument seeking to establish her crucial *difference* from the natural entities she otherwise resembles. She, unlike them, is a being who can undergo death. In this spirit, the last line of the stanza would stand out as strikingly dissonant with the rest. There she speaks as an I possessing the features of a *human subject*: her knowledge of her mortality, her desire to defer death, her freedom as moral being in need of legal protection: "I don't want to die yet."

On the other hand, the speaker might be saying she partakes of Nature's essence, her secret of perpetual youth. Nature can live forever by turning all forms into the occasion for her rejuvenating action of metamorphosis. The execution of grapes can be stayed on this account. Considered from the perspective of the unfolding being of Nature, the appearing of natural entities is a transformation of matter. But so too is their "disappearance" a metamorphosis that provides a further occasion for nature's spontaneous self-renewal. Natural entities do not die; even corrupting carrion can be thought as being in mutation (witness Baudelaire's "Une Charogne"). In Sade's *Justine*, the libertine Clément argues for murder on just such grounds:

> Through tastes given by nature, I will have served the ends of a nature that, working her creation only by means of destruction, never gives me the idea of the latter except when she is in need of the former. That is to say, from a portion of oblong matter I will have made three or four thousand round or square ones. Oh, Thérèse, are these crimes? Can we so name what serves nature? Does man have the power to commit crime? And when, preferring his own happiness to that of anyone else, he overturns or destroys everything he finds in his way, has he done anything but serve nature whose first and surest inspirations order him to make himself happy, no matter at whose expense?[50]

Clément's Nature is indifferent to the extinction of the individual and of the species: she maintains herself by the creation and destruction of forms. Similarly, the scythe and winepress can be construed as abetting natural process in Chénier's poem. As the voice of Nature and of Nature's intention to maintain itself as process by innumerable transformations, the captive would not sing of the fall of a past ideology so much as celebrate the installation of a new one by speaking for mute Nature, giving one form to its transformative possibilities. Inseparable from Nature in life and in death, her identity entirely submerged in it, she would sing as its mouthpiece. Because she speaks for Nature[51] her death would have to be deferred until her song is done.

The elision of the verb means that we do not know whether Nature is elided as an old ideology slipping away, or as a new one in process, made necessary by the recognition that more than one form is possible. Given a nature so indeterminate, it is predictable that the captive's appeal against death should easily flip over into an appeal for more destruction. That is evident in the rather chilling ambiguities of the sixth stanza, with its insistent repetitions: "Je veux voir la moisson.... je veux achever mon année.... je veux achever ma journée." Each phrase can be read as a *request to defer death* so as to allow for a completion (I want [to live] to see the harvest.... I want to finish *out* my year.... I want to finish *out* my day), or as a *demand for a hasty death* and the satisfaction of closure (I want [to get] to see a harvest.... I want to finish *off* my year.... I want to finish *off* my day).[52]

Spitzer's glimpse of a Medusa figure in this captive is comprehensible now that she has emerged as considering the impossibility of grounding an appeal for putting off death, never mind a system of law, in natural right. The speaker presents a symbolic system on the brink of collapse (or in formation), no longer (or not yet) able to negotiate the passage between visible and intelligible, form and content, outside and inside, promised by the comparing term *comme*. The analogy is too incomplete to tell us what she means: Defer my death because I am human, with the consciousness and autonomy natural beings lack? Or, rather, defer my death because I speak for natural right, as the spirit of a self-renewing and incomplete Revolution?[53]

If the singer cannot borrow properties from a nature so indeterminate, does nature then borrow its stability from the singer?

Gender Agreement: O Belle (Son Nom; Pas le Véritable?)

Remember what Hertz said about the apotropaic power of the symbol, which consists in finding a visual equivalent for the theory elaborated, so as to make things reassuringly legible.[54] It is significant that the examples Hertz cites all appeal to vision—be it the iconography of the

Revolution (paintings, drawings, statues) or, in the case of written texts, descriptive passages of what Hugo so aptly calls "things *seen*" (*Choses vues*). No such visual symbol is available in the prison setting of "La Jeune captive." Dawn, for instance, is not seen but recalled, and recalled in its dew-bearing rather than its light-giving aspect ("boit les doux présents de l'aurore").[55] Indeed, one of the most important effects of the song is to set its singer up as a sort of substitute sun "in these places" from which the light of nature has gone out.[56] This relative sunlessness is characteristic of Chénier's poetic universe even prior to the poems of the Revolutionary period. The celebration of the sightless poet Homer whose "divine words" help set up the city space in "L'Aveugle" is only one example of this consistent organization of Chénier's poetry around the performative dimension of language in lieu of its descriptive possibilities, and it is what makes Chénier a closer contemporary of Baudelaire's prose poems than of Hugo. Given the absence of light in "La Jeune captive," the singer cannot display a visible lack, as in the Hugo passage cited by Hertz where a woman lifts her skirts to show her genitals.

How then does the singer supply the missing perception (of a lack), and so allow the stabilization of a symbolic system where organized, regular exchanges might be possible? The answer is, by the I's assertion of gender through the qualifier: "Moi . . . *belle.*" But what is the value of this assertion? It is a speech act, but not quite a conventional one. It does not follow the grammatical rules of adjective agreement any more than it indicates the natural sex of the speaker. It cannot obey those rules because, as is evident from the fact that there is no prior noun with which the adjective might be agreeing, neither an outside referent nor the internal system of grammar can explain the case.[57]

When la Zambinella steps onto the stage in Balzac's *Sarrasine* the naive hero does not know that women's roles in Italy are sung by castrati, and he falls in love with a role, a prima donna who is no *donna* at all. The critical information was theoretically available; a short and timely course in Italian culture would have helped Sarrasine avoid this fatal mistake (although, once the passion had been conceived, it seems to have had to follow its course, like any verbal hypothesis).[58] In the case of Chénier's captive, where no prior noun is available and no referent is provided, we have only *moi*'s word to go by. By *belle, moi* actively assents to something; *moi* agrees to agree with, outside of any law or context from which the agreement would follow as legal.

This act of claiming agreement is in several senses without precedent. It doesn't take place in an already given context, where *belle* might refer to some real-life female prisoner. Nor is there an antecedent noun with which *belle* agrees; any visible shape to the mouth from which the song issues has to come from the poem. *Belle* turns temporal succession around, starting out with an act of agreeing ahead of anything with which to agree. It lays claim to agreement, assents in advance of any convention for conventions to come. The poem talks about this turn in stanza 9's framing discussion of the future referents that seekers will find for "belle." In the absence of a previous noun, "belle" accepts to qualify any number of subsequent nouns: from concrete ones like "Aimée de Coigny" or "la victime," to abstract ones like "La Révolution," "La Terreur," "La Guillotine,"[59] "La Liberté," or "L'Histoire," to name just a few of those apposite when considering the political implications of the poem.

We can call this performative an inaugural performative. It is inaugural because it does without the covering of a prior name or law. It is a performative because it does more than state a predicate. It covers itself in advance by the law, agrees ahead of time to respect a convention without the convention having been given with which it will have been in agreement. The performative works as a performative because the old symbolic system is bankrupt. It is language freed from, yet assenting to, reference, freed from, yet assenting to, signification.

Why *belle* and not *beau*? One reason was suggested near the beginning of this chapter. French grammar dictates that the masculine gender dominates the feminine form where two nouns are grouped by a single adjective or article. In this poem, the feminine form appears at the moment that the system based on the noun and the transfer of names is no longer operative. Instead, what appears in the feminine adjective is a case of the always open possibility of positing whatever grammar lets us say. The claims of French grammar reach us through this feminine form. This is an observance occurring with enough regularity to be worth noting, that the feminine form dominates where texts stage the interference of grammar in a specific case, as what befalls from inhuman language. Why does Balzac say "*la prima donna* . . . elle" in *Sarrasine*? Because grammar makes him say "elle"? Or rather because, having chosen to remark that grammar can stand free from what we mean to say, and make us say something we don't mean, he seizes upon "la *prima donna* . . . elle" as a one-time chance to make the point? Chénier's choice of *belle* to mean the free election of and subjection to grammar is wilder, because the adjective has no antecedent noun. But the function is similar. It signals the entrance of a linguistic order, an order to obey that comes from language and not from some person. The inaugural performative gendering *moi* as *belle* occupies us with a promising, agreeing side to language that operates—for better or for worse—independently of human promises or agreements.[60] The feminine gender has nothing to do with an outside referent and everything to do with the singularity of a case where a fiction is posited as bound only to grammatical law.

However, we haven't accounted for an aestheticization, evident in the thematics of beauty as well as in internal rhymes like "quelle fut cette belle," which draws attention to the signifier's formal effects, and seems to bar access to the inaugural aspect of the performative, to make it appear as incomplete or other than a free positing obedient only to inhuman grammar. *Belle* is one of those adjectives in French that allows you to *hear* the agreement of forms. The modifier *belle* is not simply a feminine form of the adjective; it also has a sound associated exclusively with the feminine form of the adjective (in contradistinction to *jeune* or *tranquille* which are invariable adjectives, or—reaching outside the poem—to adjectives like *inconnu/e* or *aboli/e* where the difference is not audible). Like the nominalized adjective *captive* audibly distinct from *captif, belle* cannot be confused with *beau*. The word capitalizes on poetry's ability to bring the language to our ears through rhyme, rhythms, and so forth as formally beautiful. It brings language before us not as an inhuman system, but rather as a natural body that can be experienced in a perception. Through a rhyme effect, *belle*, which sounds enough like *elle* to persuade of *elle*'s immanence, drags along from the outworn system a last possibility of symbolization by providing the perceptual equivalent of the freedom of the signifier. The gendering of *belle* sounds as a bell, alerting us to a last-ditch attempt to restore meaning in a natural language where words mean what they say.

The move is restorative of the old ideology, not just reflective of it.[61] Here a linguistic indication of language's ability to operate independently of reference is phenomenalized (taken as a freedom of which we have some experience). In the *Essai* Chénier comments on the pleasure a reader may take in the signifier, "a vain noise . . . number, cadence, rhythm which please his ear" (p. 687). That pleasure, he goes on to say, has inspired many a bad poem in which the poet, without considering logic, piles up "words that seem to him by their sound to represent the thing he wants to depict" (p. 687). The echo word *belle* suggests that what one paints in sound to compensate for the loss of everything else is language as a thing perceptible to the ear.[62] Where there is an anxious Narcissus about, which would certainly be the case where specular exchanges based on vision were in question, it is not surprising to find an Echo. The performative act of assent, carried as it is by the signifier *belle* that sounds its gender so convincingly, carries the past system over, makes it appear as if it were still in process, promising a renewal both of meaning and of its undoing. The symbol is apotropaic because, despite the threat of a renewed loss of meaning, the ultimate correspondence between the meaning and the vehicle seems assured: language signifies itself as a body by the signifier. The Medusa fantasy has a connection to the fatal song of the invisible Sirens, where an aesthetics based on the perception of the signifier is available.

Adjectives grammatically gendered in the feminine carry an extra burden for Chénier, the burden of the difference made by the signifier. We can think of this as an extra burden, or else as a signal of a slackness or freedom, a place where the signifier sounds the bell of freedom from the signified, and which can be picked up and resignified in some way. There is a chapter to be written—perhaps as a sequel to Alice Kaplan's autobiographical discussion of the powerful seductions exerted by the French language on its students—about the agreement of the feminine adjective as diverting one from the content of the utterance to pleasing reveries about the situation in which the utterance occurs and about what adjective agreement might imply. For instance, it allows fantasies about native speakers who learn to make this agreeable agreement at their mother's knee (what is a native speaker? is anyone ever a native speaker of a language?), reveries about a language naturally beautiful and harmonious, dreams as well about the eventual correspondence of grammatical rules with natural gender (the docile agreeableness of women like the sounded agreement of the adjective, the dominance of the male, just like the dominance of the male adjective). What is this seduction exerted by the so-called feminine form that lets us hear the same word differently, as a signifier whose meaning is affected by sound, and to construe that difference in ideological terms? With the feminine grammatical gender, language appears on the scene as ungrounded fiction, as sheer appearance. But that is also where the last-ditch symbolization takes place and drags with it the no-longer-grounded system. It is as if the radicalness of the break inhibited the performative's clear reception, and it were getting instantly parried by a blow from a reassuringly intelligible, descriptive language. We have to modify our original hypothesis somewhat, and say that so far the reading of the poem does not show that the attribution of gender is *sometimes* defensive and *sometimes* disruptive, but rather that it is *at once* and *indistinguishably* defensive and disruptive.

The anxiety focused on an incomplete performative has a clear analogue in Chénier's political writings: the fear is that the future would hold a series of speech acts made by "shameless clowns who invade the empire in the name of liberty, who dare to decorate with the name of *the people's wish* their insolent caprices and tyrannical fantasies" (p. 295). In making an appeal to the contract model one might merely substitute, for the bankrupt system where the king stood for God's rational plan for the world, a reckless tyranny of the imagination, and a succession of further performatives, each equally empty, each vying for supremacy as the best expression of the vox populi.[63] This is the interregnum described by Chénier at the beginning of *Avis au peuple français sur ses véritables ennemis* as a time when "nothing can be looked at as finished [*fini*]" (p. 201), since neither is the past regime over (*fini*) nor the new order brought forward, accomplished (*fini*). Hannah Arendt analyses in similar terms the French Revolution hamstrung by its "attempt to derive both law and power from the selfsame source."[64] For Arendt, the inability to separate the two functions of disruption and law led to a relentless cycle of production of decrees, each of which could be done away with because none could ever be granted stabilizing authority so long as the unverifiable virtue of its speaker was its problematic basis.[65] *Belle* inaugurates such an anxious period. The captive inhabits a prison: the more the speaker breaks with convention, strikes an unprecedented agreement in advance, the more it sounds as though she were simply carrying over the same old forms, getting stuck undoing what at every moment gets restored. The strongest poetic statement of this repetition occurs in the seventh stanza where the speaker pleads again that she doesn't want to die *yet*. Because the refrain is repeated, literally an encore, the line sounds like it could be saying something else: I don't want to die *again*. Baudelaire's comment—"André Chénier, with his flabby antiquity in the style of Louis XVI, was not a vigorous enough symptom of renovation"—might be fairly applied to the captive's act of self-gendering that cannot seem to stop restoring the past here.[66]

In Which Manner Beautiful? The Prosthesis

It remains to be seen, however, whether Baudelaire's comment applies to Chénier's poem. We've been trying to understand what is *meant* by the deficient analogy (the failure of some conventional routes for transmitting meaning, the inadequacy of natural right to ground the appeal) and, given its failure, what the speaker *does* to counteract the failure and establish a ground for the appeal (agree to agree, claim gender in advance, but in terms that seem partially to restore the old regime of signs as still to be put in question). But so far, we haven't asked *how* the line is poetic, that is, how it transmits its meaning and act, and in so doing, aids or take a distance from the suffering captive. This question of *how* links the figure in its incompleteness and promise to the poet of the framing song, and especially to the poetic act of finishing the song by bending accent to law. It let us raise the question of Chénier's poetic method with respect to ideology, and to the lyric as ideological genre.

With the question of manner the poet considers the poem as something other than a versified message or rhymed verbal act. The poetic statement of this move is found in the eighth stanza, where the poet claims to have accomplished two related actions. The first is expressed as "secouant le faix de mes jours languissants" (shaking off the burden of my languishing days). *Languissant* means languishing, of course, but if we take the poet at his word and shake off the burden of meaning from it, it still *sounds* like something, languaging (*langu-issant*), which is one of the things poets do. It alerts us to the poem's concern with its mode and the effects of the signifier even in that part that seems to be only commentary and not very poetic. In the commentary Chénier is considering the outcome of the first part, the signifier's share in prolonging an interregnum. He is dramatizing a frenetic attempt to shake off the torpor associated with it. We know this attempt is frantic and dramatized as such because the poet does not say he shakes off the burden without also saying he just shakes it around: *secouant*, besides shaking off, can mean shaking, shaking around, shaking up.[67] The scene is one where the poet is enacting the impossibility of getting rid of the echo effect. The artificial heightening of the situation, the deliberate introduction of the signifier's effects into the metalanguage, shows the poet to have conceived his poem in response to that carryover. He looks for a view of language to oppose to the dream of "imitative harmony" and of natural language, for the means to allow the break that has already occurred to pass as such into history, to be remembered or forgotten, to occur as irreversible. The second action, that of bending the accents of a mouth to the laws of verse, shows the poet against this background of heightened echoing, subordinating voice and accent to something else. The action of the poet tells us what this might be: a bend, a fold, such as would produce an envelope or letter (*pli*), and so the text, the piece of paper on which Chénier's poem made its way out of prison.

If, armed with this question of *how*, we turn back to the first part of the song, we discover that it has been concerned with manner all along. It is there, after all, that the captive has drawn our attention to a bend (*je plie . . . ma tête*) and to a cut, a caesura made coherent (*la coupe en mes mains encor pleine*). As for the line from the first stanza that we have been discussing, it actually helps to read *comme* in its etymological sense: *quomodo*, in such a way or manner. *Moi* asserts itself *belle* in the manner of *lui*. The manner of talking about manner makes the line stand out as poetic in Blanchot's sense, that is, as unique and irreplaceable. By means of an inversion, Chénier juxtaposes the masculine pronoun *lui* to the feminine adjective *belle*. This is one of those "barbarous couplings" Hugo didn't know whether to admire or deplore in Chénier,[68] a "happy violence" of the sort that Chénier recommends the poet occasionally use (p. 687). It is correct, according to the rules of adjective agreement, since when two nouns of differing gender are being compared, the qualifier agrees with the first term of the comparison. In French, one says "elle est belle comme un épi ou un pampre," or simply, "Je suis belle comme lui."[69] But, at least to the grammarian Grevisse in *Le Bon usage*, discussing a related case of plural adjectives agreeing with nouns of differing gender, the immediate juxtaposition of nouns of one gender and adjectives agreeing with another is to be avoided as "having something shocking about it."[70] It is a matter of harmony, and affects only forms of *audibly* different gender. Grevisse wants us to say "une tête et un buste humains," rather than "un buste et une tête humains" because the juxtaposition of a feminine noun to the masculine plural, audibly different from the feminine form, hurts the delicate ear. Chénier's inversion with its juxtaposition highlights what sounds like a disagreement between the gendered pronoun and adjective. That disagreement, moreover, occurs in spite of the strict legality (in grammatical and logical terms) of the utterance. The poetic order adopted is not calculated to smooth over the discrepancy between grammatical correctness and good taste, but rather to bring it out.[71]

What are the stakes of the discrepancy? Grevisse does not state exactly what is so shocking that good taste has to be invoked to cover it up. But he lets us divine it in his definition of the distinction between natural gender (a matter of semantics) and grammatical gender (where the agreement of parts of speech is the issue). He says about natural gender that "in its semantic function, the gender of the noun is, *in principle*, an indication of the sex of beings" (my emphasis).[72] He goes on to number cases where the principle does not hold (many animate beings, all inanimate or abstract beings), but suggests that those cases still respect the principle, since they involve figurative extensions from it. As for grammatical gender, it is "defined by the agreement established between the *noun* and other words in the sentence (article, adjective, pronoun, participle)."[73] The grammar of the sentence is organized around the noun, and that noun has, in principle, a gender that is an indication of the sex of beings, and thus is anchored in the referent. Behind Grevisse's rule lies respect for a belief in an ultimate or originary convergence of grammar and semantics, in gendered nouns as articulating the smooth passage between the syntactical and the meaning function. That belief is wounded when the ear hears the juxtaposition of nouns and adjectives of differing genders. There is no passage between grammatical gender and natural gender, but, Grevisse seems to be saying, the French speaker ought to speak as if there might be such a passage. Grevisse calls for the distancing of masculine and feminine forms in the name of "harmony,"[74] precisely the same harmony promising the ultimate compatibility of grammatical and natural gender, the ultimate reassuring correspondence of form with meaning, of contiguity or grammar with figure we found associated with the adjective *belle*. At stake is the *appearance* of that system to the ear, its arbitrariness notwithstanding, as an integral body, internally cohesive. That is the belief Chénier leaves behind in electing to assemble the unlike as both qualified by *belle*. The unity and integrity of language's body is breached from within. The noun qualified is missing, and as such cannot provide the function of articulating grammar and semantics as a correspondence. The feminine ending of the adjective out of sync with the proximate masculine pronoun brings out language as mutilated, or rather, not comparable to a body at all. It is this breaching of the body of language that lets the performative reach us with the force of a binding performative.

Through the inversion producing the disjunctive juxtaposition, the poem folds into itself as a shock, the recognition that its language is not a voiced song charming the ear but rather a text, an inscription. Similar couplings occur with irruptive regularity in Chénier's poems. Chénier searches them out as places where the language appears affected by a "barbarous rust" (p. 132), in the etymological as well as extended senses of barbarous: they are foreign to the familiar notion of language as integral. The manner adopted recalls the language to itself in its supreme artificiality. By "folding" (the inversion is one fold much practiced by Chénier), the poet divides language as *belle* and bellicose body from language as something else. That is what he says in the important poem on poetics, *L'Invention*: "L'inventeur c'est celui qui / montre . . . à la nature mère / Ce qu'elle n'a point fait (The inventor is the one who / Shows . . . to mother nature / What she has not made) (p. 124).[75]

This shock is salutary in terms of the poetic situation. It is tantamount to an advertised break with the paralyzing formalism organized around the sounded signifier, a breaking off in midstream of the succession of performatives suggested by *belle*. It completes the singer's unfinished appeal by delivering it not as said, but as always already bent to some other rule, folded, recited—iterable and iterated (in the terms of Derrida). The speech act is not one in a series of equally ungrounded and equally authorized speech acts, each of which tries to persuade—in the absence of the provable virtue of its speaker—that it carries an experience of freedom. Instead, it is delivered as written, and as written, invested with an authority that does not come from the senses, is not human and intelligible, but legible.[76] The grounding performative does not get delivered as an act of a self-determined, autonomous being, but as grounded, showing a prosthetic leg, "avec sa jambe de statue" (with its statue's leg), as Baudelaire puts it (1:72).

In *Hermès*, so long as the lawgiver merely states decrees he claims to have been inspired by the gods, Chénier describes him as a demagogue, moved by his own desire for glory, reliant on the blindness and superstition of the people. When Moses descends Mt. Sinai with "the voice of God himself written on stone" (p. 398), however, he emerges as exemplary lawgiver by a "a great and holy lie" (p. 398). With the written text, no further transformation is possible in the decree, just as with the juxtaposition, Chénier's formula stands forth as unique and untranslatable. The juxtaposition has shocked the language free from its supposed oneness and made it available as broken matter ready for realignment, and thus, as subject to displacements of the sort that *Moi . . . belle* convenes for. It makes it available as inhuman, but that also means free from any idealism that has been attached to it, including even the idealism that attaches to the tyrannical freedom of the signifier. It gives it to us in its material aspect. That written law should entail a theology (the reporting of God's word) is less important to Chénier than that it be written down, because in his understanding writing allows the performative to stand out as remembered and binding, but also as what lets us forget that it is just an ungrounded performative, one imposed order among many possible ones. By writing, in the immobilization of the performative as the "voice of a nymph" in stone, the specter of a politics obedient to aesthetic principles of transformation is laid to rest.[77] Here again, Chénier proves in agreement with Arendt. For Arendt, the American solution to the revolutionary dilemma was to separate power and the law, placing the source of power in the people and the source of law in the supernatural. Jefferson's assumption of the sacrality of the law made the founding performatives of the American Revolution stick, whereas those of the French Revolution were nonstick performatives.[78]

The prosthetized comparison does not just leave behind any past aesthetics or ideology. It completes the inauguration of a new ideology by proposing a new aesthetics. A third model centered on manner is added to the two definitions previously advanced of beauty (an essence, *la beauté* shared by *lui beau* and *moi belle*, each according to its kind; an appearance agreed to by an act of convention, with nature tailored to fit). The juxtaposition proposes, in answer to the question, How is *moi belle*? the response, In the same manner that *lui* is *belle. Moi belle comme lui belle.* In what manner can *lui* be said *belle*? Not naturally (neither the phallic stalk nor the leafy vine branch are persuasive representations of a feminine). Not grammatically. But *lui* can be called *belle* if the devalued *lui* is considered in itself, as a word that can enter into patterns even when it ceases to relay meaning: as the homonym of a word for light, *luit* ("je n'ai vu luire encore que les feux du matin"), or the near homonym of the recently decapitated scion of the Sun King Louis (whose headless neck shakes in *secouant* and *écoutant*), as connected by alliteration or assonance to various themes (*plier, illusion, lyre*), as part of the arresting juxtaposition. In short, to make sense of *lui belle* we have to take *lui* as a piece of language entering into a pattern that can only be exchanged with or against itself, referable like *moi* to a third thing. The third genre in which both *moi* and *lui* have an equal share is neither masculine, the genre of the general and of humankind, nor feminine, the genre of gender and the difference attached to it, of sexual difference. It is an unkind genre where the poem breaks absolutely with translatable language and with sensible nature (visible forms, audible signifiers) to organize itself as a unique and untranslatable combination whose legibility is the question.

But the third genre is no sooner posited as not human, than it seems to get treated as if it were a category to which humans can be found to belong. That is apparent partly from the inversion tending to suggest *lui belle* is the model for *moi belle* (reading *comme* as analogy) and even more from the fact that by the end of the song a number of figures testify to the category of prosthetically extended or mutilated "beauties." One is Philomela, the tongueless victim persistently confused with her sister Procne, the nightingale.[79] Another is the *captive* interpreted as unhysterical woman à la Spitzer or as Scarfe's man in drag. Another is the *captif*, interpreted as Scarfe's nostalgic melancholic of soft tones or as Spitzer's hysterical impotent. Another is the deity Pales, the Roman guardian of the flocks, a deity sometimes reported as male, sometimes as female, and sometimes as having a combination of the characteristics of both.[80] The decking out of the St. Lazare prison as a pastoral retreat (*asiles verts*) is suggestive of this movement where the language is no sooner made to stand free as sheer system from language-as-body by way of a radical artifice, than it gets taken as a natural category, and examples found to testify to it.[81] So for that matter is Lazarus himself, whose resuscitation is too often judged a return to a natural life, instead of to the zombie existence that a cadaver wrapped in cerements and stinking of the tomb could hope for. The framing song, which freezes the adjective "belle" into an anthropomorphic noun, completes the process. At the precise moment it becomes possible to consider the effect of the text-as-machine on figure, illusion kicks in with a vengeance, and the artificial production is fostered as natural. Again in Chénier's terms, "l'inventeur est celui qui . . . montre et *fait adopter* à la nature mère / Ce qu'elle n'a point fait, *mais ce qu'elle a pu faire*" (the inventor is he who shows and *makes be adopted* by mother nature / What she has not made, *but what she might have made*) (p. 124).

When Nature is made to mother an artificial creation something is fin-

ished. An old ideology of nature is past and fallen into oblivion; a new
ideology has taken its place. The poet has not tried to stand outside of
this process. At first glance, he seems in the last section to have submitted
to it, to have chosen to conform himself to the new model of nature. The
weak rehearsal of the earlier formulation, the less successful juxtaposition
of clashing genders provided in the framing song testifies to this: "Ainsi,
triste et captif, ma lyre." Such juxtaposition has become a technique, a
sort of reproducible verbal twitch. This is the line Spitzer found weak
and ungrammatical. The poet appears enslaved to the lyre, a sad captive
forced to repeat a pattern meaninglessly. Spitzer's theory of an enfeebled
poet (neither electing order nor receiving it, but become a blind technician carrying out orders) is not unjustified. The stanza states this by ani-
mating the lyre (awake, its ear alert), in contrast to the poet's torpor.

But there might be a way to read the phrase as grammatically correct,
and a call to consider the order installed by the performative. Suppose
that "triste et captif" is not descriptive language, since it modifies neither the feminine grammatical subject of the sentence, *ma lyre,* nor the
too distant personal subject of the second clause, *je.* Take it instead as an
abbreviated apostrophe, a provocative vocative, a call put out to readers,
a phrase metonymically brushed by the adjoining *lyre,* to read (*lire*) the
poem: "(hé toi! lecteur) triste et captif" ([hey you!] sad and captive
[reader]). With the qualifiers, the poem would reach out to snag itself
readers, anticipating Baudelaire's "hypocrite lecteur,—mon semblable,
—mon frère!" (hypocrite reader,—my double,—my brother!) (1: 6), or
in the style of Chénier's abrupt ending address in "Iamb VIII," "Ce sera
toi demain, insensé imbécile" (It will be your turn tomorrow, senseless
imbecile) (p. 193). The poem, "ma lyre," interpellates a titular subject,
anyone overtaken by "triste et captif" who stops to enlist: Here I am,
ready and willing to serve.

But what does this Althusserian interpellation, this moment where the
machine puts out a call for readers to reproduce its tensions, have to do
with the gender situation?[82] We have gone to some lengths to show that
the poem proposes, in the place of the old idealism seeing grammatical
gender as ultimately harmonious with natural gender, a new and more
fluid set of configurations for attaching property to nouns. These new
configurations, so far as gender is concerned, allow androgynous, double-
sexed, prosthetically-extended, and mutilated figures as natural. But the
fact that these wandering adjectives that hail every subject democratically

and without differentiation as to sex do so in the masculine grammatical gender, the gender used for generalizing and whenever difference is being lost, suggests that the naturalization of the new configurations comes at a price.

A new naturalization, a new ideology forces the stretching of the body politic to fit its Procrustean bed. A readjustment and reaccommodation has to occur in the public arena. The poem shows that readjustment occurring in the last stanza, where the poem's readers are divided into two groups, in contrast to the first part of the song, where the captive's aspect gathers her fellow prisoners into a single community. One group has few, one, or even no members, "Ces chants . . . Feront à *quelque amant des loisirs studieux* / Chercher quelle fut cette belle." The other is an undifferentiated mass: "La grâce décorait son front et ses discours / Et comme elle craindront de voir finir leurs jours, / *Ceux qui les passeront près d'elle*." (Grace decorated her forehead and her speech, / And like her will fear to see end their days, / *Those who will pass them near her*.) The division occurs in terms of passion, but not intersubjective passion. Instead it is a passionate relation to time and to knowledge. A small group loves the leisure activity of study, and seeks knowledge of a beauty confined to the past. The larger group, spending their days in ignorance of their proximity to this beauty, live in fear of a future death. But the division into new groups is not the only effect. The mysterious bed of Procrustes was always too long *and* too short for those who lay in it. A shrinkage has also taken place. That shows up in the lines describing the smaller group, in the masculine adjective *studieux*, which yokes in a tight embrace the plural masculine noun, *loisirs*, and the singular masculine noun, *amant*: one studies the other, but we lose sight of which. Does the lover, studious of leisure, seek knowledge of beauty? Or is it rather studious leisure, through its lover, that seeks knowledge? The autonomy and self-motivated activity of the aesthete, lover, knower, dandy is in question here, where—like a pipe that smokes its author—leisure makes use of the aesthete to know itself. Marked is the loss of a difference between a leisured being, some lover or another, and a citizen under orders to an abstraction, having legal permission (*loisir*'s etymological meaning is "to be permitted") to engage in leisure activities so as to represent leisure time, with a consequent rationalizing and oversight of an enlarged area of the hitherto private space of leisure.[83]

As for the larger group massed around the beauty, another loss of difference is being effected through the use of the governing masculine adjective. Here, we cannot tell whether the members of the group are like the beauty because they fear their individual deaths, or rather, because they fear her death, that is the end of the reign the figure inaugurates. The possessive masculine adjective *leurs* in "voir finir leurs jours" is responsible for the confusion. It can anticipate the subject, *ceux*, the group's members, or refer back to beauty's attributes, "son front et ses discours." The difference between the system and the group that keeps it going is swallowed by the masculine pronoun. Fear and ignorance are harnessed to maintain the idol. The point of the figure would be to explain the necessity of maintaining the life of the sign system on which the lives of individuals depend. The poem could be set next to Baudelaire's *La Chambre double*, as a comparable study in "days" spent keeping an apparatus "alive."

In Chénier's work, a bed enlarged in terms of desire and the gender structure goes along with a bed shrunk in terms of the day compartmentalized into hours of leisure for love, art, and knowledge, and hours for keeping the new ideology alive. Ordinary days are spent going about one's business, receiving orders from the machine that hails us as "sad and captive," carrying out those orders as a technician. All are equal, equally addressed under the generic label, because all are enslaved.

～

We have read the poem as if its gendered figures were enigmatic and powerful because they could not be explained by recourse to a given ideology outside the poem. Instead, they had to be considered as figures thrown up in the gaps between figure and grammar to bridge as best they can the abyss between them. In the shift between the two parts of the song (the first a song of an incomplete break with the old ideology, and the second a song where a new ideology is operative), gender was the place where the lack of fixed connection between semantics and syntax, figure and grammar became apparent and the shift became conceivable. It was also where the last-ditch attempt to restore the old regime of signs was registered. In the light of this discussion, we have already had to modify once the initial hypothesis that gendering is sometimes a defensive and sometimes a disruptive gesture. In "La Jeune captive," considering the first seven stanzas alone, the attribution of a sexed body to language was an apotropaic maneuver, at once a recognition and a partial veiling of the consequences of the freedom of the signifier. The gendering of voice proved a ploy to postpone registering the breakdown in the old regime of signs, to maintain the Medusal interregnum of terrifying violence and consoling symbolization, and—ultimately—to leave intact the correspondence between grammatical and natural gender as the horizon the poem respects.

We now have to add a corollary to this statement, looking at things from the perspective of the break with speech and voice registered by the quotation marks and the poet's concern with manner. Here, gender helped in the naturalization (through anthropomorphism) of the prosthetized figure. It made the performative, its force lost, appear as a description of a natural being, and aided in restabilization of the new ideology. On the other hand, the difference carried by the feminine gender in "la lyre" was potentially enough to disrupt the vision of poet as lawmaker with which the poem ends. There is all the difference in the world between a poet who induces an interpreter, successfully or not, to accept a convention he has imposed on his own authority, and a poem that renounces authority and—singing by rubbing a lyre up against the decapitated head of an Orphic poet—awakens a reader with a call to notice what the lyric has to say about ideology formation. That difference is addressed to readers who, knowing that one never can see one's death ("voir finir leurs jours"), leave their eyes to read how it will arrive, say, in the choice between carrying out a program and studying its contours, including its cracks and its scattered or disregarded members—always a first step in any critique. Gender, as it suggested in the final stanza with its collection of *elle* words and its final insistence on a governing metonymy, or in the penultimate stanza by the awakening of the listening lyre, can prove a lever in critique. In "La Jeune captive," the trouble with gender is that where it looks most disruptive it is actually part of a defense against violence by apotropaic symbolization. But where it is at its most natural, "aimable et naive," it is the tip of an iceberg, part of a structure through which the dehumanizing relations characterizing the overall ideological structure can be glimpsed and critiqued. At least, that's one way to read the gap between the two parts of the poem.

§ 2 Mallarmé's "Bound Action": The Orders of the Garter

First Constraints / First Economies: The Poet

Mallarmé wrote as if constrained to make his work accountable to the strictest, most rigorous requirements of verbal economy that could be devised. Not only is there nothing in excess, but what little there is has found its place as a result of numerous calculations. Few major writers have left so scant a production (at the end of his career Mallarmé projected a complete edition of his poetry that was to contain 49 poems); fewer still have left so little neglected. It is not uncommon for even the most meaningless of marks—say the circumflex marking the disappearance of the letter "s"—to take on critical importance in a Mallarmé poem. To take only one instance, recalled by Yves-Alain Favre, Mallarmé appears to have spent some seven years in amiable discussion with his editor over the typography of the projected complete edition of his works.[1] Mallarmé has operated on the gratuitous language of poetry with the precision of a mathematician, taking one of the most restricted poetic vocabularies around and subjecting it to multiple calculations, with the result that the poem's potential to mean gets increased to a nearly intolerable degree.

In the analysis of a Harold Bloom, such economizing can be put down to Mallarmé's situation as a belated poet, in another version of the dilemma described by Valéry as facing Baudelaire, who arrives on a poetic scene dominated by Hugo.[2] As Valéry saw it, the enormous productivity of Hugo, the richness of his vocabulary and rhetoric, the encompassing sweep of his vision, created a situation of dearth for poets of the latter half of the nineteenth century.[3] Mallarmé ruefully noted something similar in "Crise de vers": "Hugo, in his mysterious task, brought all of prose, philosophy, eloquence, history down to verse, and because he was in person verse itself he confiscated, so far as anyone who thinks, speaks or narrates is concerned, almost the right to express oneself" (pp. 360–61). Hugo left his successors little but gleanings, and a Baudelaire or Mallarmé would have to exercise considerable ingenuity to increase even to a sufficiency, never mind to a treasure, the meager poetic stock remaining. What could be left over when the liberal arts had all been reduced to verse and verse had been personified in Hugo? Presumably only whatever could not be reduced to lyric expression in the idiom. Since Hugo had so far taken over literature as to have stolen "almost the right to express oneself," the anxious belated poet would presumably be exploring the literary scene for nonexpressive language. The poets of the new generation would have the task of writing nonlyrical poetry, working out of the crisis precipitated by Hugo's massive appropriation of all discourse to the lyric, which he first totalized by personifying it, and then took with him when he disappeared.

But to consider Mallarmé's work solely as a capitalization dictated by the straitened poetic circumstances of the fin de siècle poet is to ignore another set of accounts to which the poet refers the work. We can term this accountability politico-ethical, in the first place because, despite the absence in Mallarmé's work of the topoi of morality or of a Kantian discourse on freedom and the law, an ethical attitude is manifested in such decisions as the following: the active renunciation of the charms of self-expression; the uncompromising rejection of a poetry centered on the poet in person; and the consistent turning of the work until it addresses (the secret of) its address to others—be it in the occasional verses written in albums or sent as New Year's greetings, or in such major works as the *Tombeaux* poems or the *Eventails*. Very early Mallarmé assumes as a freely accepted obligation what we might think of as a mere effect of the accident of his belatedness. He is not deprived of the seductions of the lyric, he renounces them; he is not forced to give up personal poetry, he "surrenders," as he put it, "the initiative to words" (p. 366). At 24, he was already envisaging that his work would require twenty years of the strictest discipline, that he would have to cloister himself inside himself, and to give up all but the most limited publication. Setting aside literary glory as "worn-out foolishness" and announcing his death as a matter of fact, he looked forward to a work structured around the "Secret that each man has in himself," to be offered to the "reading of friends," in both senses of the genitive.[4] The verbal economizing we have been discussing has thus to be considered not just as an effect imposed by need on the belated poet, but in terms of this second set of accounts we are provisionally calling ethical. There it is rather a chosen practice, and as such reaches the poet from some source outside the poet's desires and anxieties. The poet acts as if doubly obligated: he is necessitous and driven by circumstance to desperate economizing; he has elected, perhaps out of an apparently boundless gratitude for some benefit conferred, to perform the most exacting and vertiginous of writerly feats.

I am recalling what is already old hat partly because the second obligation has tended to get at least partially misinterpreted or overlooked, causing a consequent skewing of perspective on Mallarmé's practice of speculative play, as on the dream accompanying it.[5] When the question of why the poet *elects* economy gets lost from sight, it is easy to get dazzled or frustrated by the over- and underdetermination of meaning associated with the signifier. The disruptive free play of the signifier can be quickly tamed to a technique productive of meaning, one that, while leading to knowledge of the instrument language as it affects its message-bearing function, provides a certain pleasure and return on the narcissistic investment of the interpreter. It is not an accident that Mallarmé's philological treatise *Les Mots anglais* should (albeit with considerable caution) evoke Science and the absolute meaning of the alphabet's letters—at the moment that an alliterative tendency in the dictionary of the language is being considered.[6] Mallarmé reminds us in "Le Mystère dans les lettres" that meaning in texts is presented "out of consideration for those from whom (the text) borrows, after all, for another object, the language," its chief function being that "one gains by turning aside the idler, charmed because nothing concerns him in it, at first sight" (p. 382). To the extent that the play of the signifier proves a rich source of meaning and stability in the poems, it is just a diversionary ploy by an author considerate of even such readers as tend to loiter in the poem's precincts. The passage suggests the poem has something urgent to say that is of concern to the speakers of the language, but whether the play of the signifier gives or blocks access to it is a question. The play of the signifier might be less a way to keep idlers out than a way to draw them in, for a closer look at what does concern them, as the got-up clown of "Le Pitre châtié" might have circulated among crowds at a fair to attract onlookers to the main spectacle further within.

The first reason for pointing to the poet's ethical attitude, here manifest in Mallarmé's insistence that an outstanding debt is owed to those from whom the language has been borrowed, is that it allows debate to focus on the verbal economy as a means of repayment (or deferral) of a recognized debt to the other. It points us away from the view, recently stated in Paul Bénichou's *Selon Mallarmé*, that Mallarmé's poems are obscure, ingenious, and beautiful to the extent that they are distinct from "clear elocution" by virtue of "verse and its laws, but also of the seeking out of expressions that are rare and . . . withdrawn from immediate intelligibility."[7] It suggests that the poet's duty, ethically speaking, is to render the language of the other, or even to render the language as other.[8] It makes the poem into something more or other than an aesthetic object closed in on itself, self-reflexive and beautifully vain.

Second Constraints / Second Economies: The Poem

But something else is brought into view by considering the ethical accountability of Mallarmé's work. We are brought to ask what command *poems* answer, what question excuses or impels their being written. The double economy we have been discussing so far in terms of the poet has to be considered in terms of the famous impersonality of the Mallarmean work. The passage from "Crise de vers" where Mallarmé is considering the task facing the post-Hugolian writer is helpful here. In it Mallarmé proves more concerned with a crisis threatening *literature* than with a problem facing any particular poet or generation. Since with Hugo all discourse became poetry, and since Hugo himself became poetry in person, when he died, poetry ended with him. After Hugo, poetry is finished, and with it "all of prose, philosophy, eloquence, history" (p. 360). The post-Hugolian writer has then to address a reader whose habits have been disrupted by Hugo's death, in a poetry whose very possibility is imperiled. This poetry has to answer to (and for) the disappearance of poetry. Nor is this a one-time crisis. Interruption, Mallarmé goes on to say, is the rule obeyed and testified to by French poetry throughout its history: "French poetry . . . bears witness to itself as intermittence: it shines a lapse; exhausts it and awaits" (p. 361). If poetry bears witness to its own repeated lapse, then it is obeying a paradoxical command: it breaks silence to account for its lapsing into silence.

A reader familiar with the writings of Maurice Blanchot will recognize that we have fallen on a preoccupation central to Blanchot's reading of Mallarmé, namely the preoccupation with the impossibility of literature, or as Blanchot put it in 1959 in *Le Livre à venir*, with a literature that "only founds itself in contesting itself radically and in interrogating itself 'even to its origin'."[9] In a short letter to Claire Nouvet published in *Literature and the Ethical Question* (special issue of *Yale French Studies*, 1991), Blanchot brings together this problematic of a literature in crisis and the ethics of writing. He answers his correspondent's request for a text on the topic with a question about what kind of act it is to put literature in relation with the question of ethics. This is what he says:

> And I remember a text on literature where it is said that it has a clear destiny to tend toward disappearance. Why then still speak of literature? And if one puts it into relation with the question of ethics, *is it to remind us that the demand to write (its ethics) would be nothing other than the infinite movement by which it appeals in vain [for] its disappearance [until its disappearance]* [est-ce pour nous rappeler que l'exigence d'écrire (son éthique) ne serait rien d'autre que le mouvement infini par lequel elle en appelle en vain à la disparition]. (my emphasis)[10]

There is at least a Derridean double bind in this Blanchotian demand to write: writing appeals *for* literature's disappearance, arguing for an end to literature, and writing appeals literature's disappearance, arguing against its end, or for its return. Furthermore, as Blanchot states it, this double imperative commands the scene *until disappearance*: for the time being, until further notice, literature will occupy us as the infinite movement of appealing, and appealing for, its disappearance.

From Blanchot's formulation, it can be deduced that the "conscience" of literature can only be clear when it turns out to have been asking about the demise and survival of literature. To pursue any other question in writing is to give one's writing something to have a guilty conscience about, because the command of literature is unambiguous: to appeal in vain (for) its disappearance (until its disappearance).

If we accept that Blanchot has, with a little help from Mallarmé, put his finger on what modern literature is about, then two things become obvious. First, literature's concern is terrifically narrowed and focused:

its ethical imperative is never to obey any other call or to respond to any other question than that "appealing in vain (for) its disappearance." But second, literature's sights are widened to such an extent that distinctions tend to get blurred. Where, for instance, could we draw the line and say that such and such a text is not literature, that is, ultimately or fundamentally concerned with literature's problematic disappearance and survival? To write ethically would be to write until the echoes of the call for / appeal to literature's disappearance make themselves heard. For instance, a critic trying to demonstrate Mallarmé's sources in popular culture, or at the other end of the spectrum, seeking to show that his work positions itself as high culture, and so proves suspiciously collaborationist with elitism, will be writing—with more or less nuance and cogency—about the (im)possibility of determining the point where the deviation that is literature emerges from or disappears into more popular forms of expression.[11] The poem takes the vanishing points—where literature withdraws into itself and its very narrow concern with its survival, and where it opens up to take on any theme as a version of its problematic—and gives them to us in a combination that is good for one time only.[12]

One consequence is that we have to consider every organizational pattern a Mallarmé poem shows as dictated by the double bind and thus as necessary. The story goes that when Berthe Morisot asking Mallarmé why he did not write so as to be understood by his cook he answered "What? but for my cook I would write in no other way" (*Comment? mais pour ma cuisinière, je n'écrirais pas autrement*).[13] The comment is not to be taken only as a refusal by an aesthete to cater to his cook and explain his meaning in clear language. It has to be taken seriously, as an expression of astonishment by a poet with a clear conscience. Having written exactly what had to be written, having produced an absolutely unique and singular combination that does just what literature is supposed to do—appeal (for) literature's disappearance—he can only say that to write otherwise would be to ask that his poems obey other rules than those that command their writing. At worst, it would be to ask for a muffling or attenuation of the poem's uncompromising ethical stance. At best, it would be to request the writing of another poem, one that by its unique combination would otherwise and again fulfill literature's strange ethical imperative. *Comment?* How could one *write* otherwise, even to oblige one's cook, Mallarmé asks.

A further complication is introduced if we consider that the poet might be astonished by something else that Morisot's question takes for granted, namely that his poetic language is an elite language for those in the know, a language not aimed at the cook.[14] In the introduction to *Les Mots anglais* Mallarmé makes a remarkable statement about the relation of poetry to ordinary speech. Citing some verse from *Piers Plowman* to get across his point that English is a language of the graft, Mallarmé justifies his recourse to poetry in preference to narrative or to documents. He says: "The radical sensibility of language, its decencies or its tendencies [*ses pudeurs ou ses tendances*] manifest themselves in poetry, always taken in this Study as the most exact type of speech proper to an epoch [*le type le plus exacte du parler propre à une époque*]!" (p. 913). If we apply this pronouncement to its maker and see his poems as the most exact type of speech of the period, then Mallarmé would not write differently for the cook for a very different reason: his poems give back to the cook the exact type of the cook's speech as the poem has overheard and manifested it. Nobody may speak exactly like a Mallarmé poem but that is because his poems are exactly the impersonal language of the period. In kitchen or salon, it is spoken confusedly and by individuals more concerned with expressing their personal desires or needs than with manifesting respect, in the manner of the time, for the radical sensibilities of the language. The cook, whose language is given back to her in its type, is no less apt to understand than any other speaker. A poet who undertook to represent exactly the speech of the period would no doubt be astonished when required to put things less exactly, lying about the state of language as he hears it from the cook. At the simplest level of household economy, in the case of a cook who obliges one everyday with honest, unadulterated food, to say things otherwise than as the poem demands them would be not to repay one's debt.

Now it certainly gives one pause to think of a Mallarmean poem as the type of fin de siècle speech, or to consider that he may have found his cook as prepared to read his poems as were lords or literary critics. We know that Mallarmé took some pleasure from the ability of postmen to read the rhymed quatrains he sometimes wrote as addresses for his letters, an ability demonstrated by the fact that not one letter so addressed went astray. But more curious still, *Les Mots anglais* has provided us with another source for the poem, also impersonal, that does not come from within literature narrowly understood.[15] Instead, the poem is construed as having arisen in generous response to a muddled plea by the speakers of a language for the most exact type of their speech. The poet is not needy so much as the epoch is needy, and it is to meet that need that the poem generously reaches such lengths of over- and underdetermination. The poem always appears in Hölderlin's "time of need."[16]

We now have two apparently distinct, impersonal calls to which the poem, in its singularity, responds: On the one hand, there is an ethical command coming from within the confines of literature, that the poem address nothing other than the question of literature, its impossibility, its disappearance. On the other hand, the poem responds to confused pleas, to echoes reaching it from the epoch, that ask it for the most exact type of speech, that want to know where the epoch is with respect to the language. To look to one without considering the other is to miss the double origination of the extraordinary verbal entity that is the poem, and to misconstrue the double and impersonal necessity (both neediness and law) that governs its every point.

How does a Mallarmean text respond to this double demand? How does it relate the two demands in its response? A prose text from the meditative *Quant au livre* called "L'Action restreinte" provides a convenient example. In it the poet is not only exercising verbal economy, he is also asking about the role of poetic language both in helping clear up a murky phrase about the need for action, and as itself possibly answering the request for action. The text opens with a brief anecdote, providing the pretext for the rumination that follows, and establishing the text as a distant descendant of Rousseau's *Fourth Promenade*. The passage reads as follows:

> Plusieurs fois vint un Camarade, le même, cet autre, me confier le besoin d'agir: que visait-il—comme la démarche à mon endroit annonça de sa part, aussi, à lui jeune, l'occupation de créer, qui paraît suprême et réussir avec des mots; j'insiste, qu'entendait-il expressément?

> (Several times there came a Fellow, the same, this other, to confide in me the need to act: what was he aiming at—as the approach with respect to me announced on his side also, in this young man, the occupation of creating, which appears supreme and succeeding with words; I insist, what exactly did he understand by it?) (p. 369)

The visitor's confidences raise questions for the poet. He wants to know what the fellow might have been *aiming at* by acting as he has acted in confiding in him, the poet (*que visait-il*); he also wonders what exactly was being *heard/understood* by the visitor when he pronounced the little phrase "the need to act" (*qu'entendait-il expressément*).

The singular repeated confidence of the visitor can be construed in two quite different ways. On the one hand, the situation represented is as follows: A visitor, the poet's line to the epoch, comes to the poet to drop a word in his ear. This speaker native to the time keeps returning until the poet finally hears the word as given, and—understanding it as a message from the period—sees it as needing poetic work and commentary. He is concerned with discovering exactly what reverberations the phrase has for the speaker, who seems to know as little what "the need to act" means *expressément* (that is, exactly *and* expression-wise) as Poe's raven understood what he meant by "Nevermore." The poet undertakes to write the text of "L'Action restreinte" to clarify what is understood by this garbled message that doesn't know if it is a slogan (we've got to *do* something), a warning or rule (we cannot not act), a commentary (action is a response to need; action is needy), or a reproach (you poets ought to stop fooling around with language, and act). He receives the word as it is given, as a given, and works it over so as to return to the fellow from whom he got it what is given by the phrase. The text here is a sort of Ronellian machine for picking up rumors, a phone receiving data to be unscrambled and given back in an exact formulation.[17] People keep on saying "the need to act" so often it must mean something and the poet has to sort out what is actually given of and to the epoch by the given. The piece does this sorting, with Mallarmé meditating in each section on possible meanings for action and its neediness, sorting out what is no longer meant by "le besoin d'agir" from what is more exactly meant by the speaker of the period. The poet is standing as a historian of the phrase as it reverberates with and for the time and not as an active participant. He listens with his epochphone to what will have been understood, expression-wise, by "the need to act."

On the other hand, the same anecdote is getting construed along very different lines by the I. His visitor does not come from the outside, but is rather a roommate, a *camarade* (etymology—*camera*, room) who presumably inhabits the same literary mansion, since, as the I explains, he is already showing signs of a literary vocation (*annonça de sa part, aussi, à lui jeune, l'occupation de créer*). The approach (*la démarche*) to the poet by way of a *verbal* action announces this literary bent in the other fellow. Here the concern is with the performative dimension, with a repeated *confiding* in the poet. The latter wonders what is aimed at by this act of confiding; what it means that the confidence should be addressed to *him*, a poet, as concerning him nearly; he wonders what the action of this representative of the next generation announces about the future of the "occupation of creating," as also what it says about his own (already past) generation; he considers the question of verbal action in terms of the supremacy of art, and in terms of success. These are just a few of the questions that are getting read out of this confiding and confident word—a poem in the making, a shared sign that links the two whose occupation is creating in an act of entrustment. The I reads this confidence as a kind of sign from the future of what will have been being done with words. He is thus concerning himself with the literary question of "whither literature?"

In short, the same pretext can be taken—according to whether the accent is on the *act* of confiding or on the *message* about action confided— as responding to a call from literature to reflect on its future, or as a plea from the epoch for clarification about what its language is giving it to think as epoch.

I have just presented these readings as alternatives, as opposing positions that can be taken one after another, and hence as a crux for the interpreter where she has to make a choice. But "L'Action restreinte" asks us to think about them otherwise. The strange thing about the Fellow who keeps dropping his confidence in the poet's ear is that he is neither a visitor from the epoch nor from literature. He is a third species of visitor. So far as he is concerned, these oppositions make no sense: he is "the same, this other" (*le même, cet autre*). This is not to say that he is one or the other, or even both. It is to say that it makes no difference whether he comes from the culture outside or from literature, whether he wants the poet to unscramble his confused language to tell him what he is saying or is confiding in him his view about where literature will have been going. This is a difficult but important step to make in understanding "L'Action restreinte." Mallarmé has opened his door to a fellow who makes hash of the oppositions and alternatives that we've been using to talk about the calls the text answers. It doesn't make sense to say the visitor is from the epoch *or* from literature. It is the same thing to question the text for what it has to say in answer to literature's appealing (for) its disappearance, and to question it for what it has to say to the epoch about the state of its language. It makes no difference because we only know of the visitor on account of a calling card that reads "confiding in me the need to act." Mallarmé might have surrounded his visitor in mystery, tried to get us interested by where he or she came from. Instead, he says, it's the same, wherever she comes from, when she arrives it is as a third thing, "this other," a text.[18]

The visitor shows by way of the calling card left. The text of "L'Action restreinte" says this.[19] It addresses this reminder to the visitor: "Ton acte toujours s'applique à du papier; car méditer, sans traces, devient évanescent" (Your act always is applied to paper; for meditating, without traces, becomes evanescent) (p. 369). It is a matter of indifference whether the confidence comes from inside or outside literature, or whether the act applied to paper is a verbal one (confiding) or a mental one (thinking the need for action), or, even, whether it is written on paper or some other tablet like that of memory: in every case, the text arrives as an open question. Mallarmé reminds his interlocutor of a rule about action: your act is each time (*toujours*) and for always (*toujours*) applied to paper. Always and again the visitor arrives as an undecidable text.

Third Constraints / Third Economies: Print

A third set of calculations thus affects the text in addition to the economies of poet and poem. At first sight, these calculations are external and apparently accessory to the text's orientation and meaning. They concern publication: the text's circulation; the techniques for its production, reproduction, dissemination, and preservation; the speed with which it is consumed; the returns to be gained from it.[20] Here, the poet concerns himself with the difference, if there is one, between the newspaper and the book. Thus, he compares the circulation of the newspaper, "hasty or vast page" (p. 376), to a "whirlwind" (p. 369) in contrast to the much slower circulation of a book or poem, whose movement he compares to the vague "circumvolutionary games" of cigar smoke (p. 371).[21] The actual numbers are not the point for Mallarmé. He doesn't have to tell us that his 1887 edition of *Poésies* ran only to 40 copies[22] for us to appreciate that the point he is making is a politico-historical one, involving as it does the capitalization of (and profiteering from) the labor force, technology, and systems necessary to produce, reproduce, disseminate, market, and archive a daily newspaper, compared to those required (and possible) for a book.

In discussing these calculations concerning circulation, Mallarmé does

not say that the work is either determined by or independent of its conditions. Instead, he states that there is a "reciprocal contamination of the
work and the means" (p. 371). It is true that the means of circulation act
on the work, but it is also true that they are acted on by it. Be it a newspaper article or a poem, the work intervenes to affect the means of its
production, reproduction, dissemination, marketing.

Thus the poem, which is highly inefficient as a capitalist venture compared to the newspaper, has a very different efficiency if we consider the
work of the work on the means.[23] That Mallarmé wants us to consider
the question of the efficiency of the text is apparent already in the opening passage of "L'Action restreinte" quoted above. *Plusieurs fois* (several
times), states the temporal succession of the newspapers, which show up
as daily visitors, again and again putting to use the immense machinery
of information gathering and dissemination installed for their production, and each day responding to the urgency of "the need to act" by a
new printing, a new production, a new outflow of information for a new
consumption. The newspaper appropriates the iterability of writing and
puts it to work as succession, exploiting the mark's capacity to be reproduced each time again in large editions of a single text. In the long comparison of the book to the newspaper in "Le Livre, instrument spirituel"
Mallarmé notes, besides the banality of the newspaper's news, the banality of this "news" about the newspaper: "no doubt that the glaring and
vulgar advantage is, to everyone's eyes, the multiplication of the example,
and rests in the number printed" (p. 380). Each day, everywhere, along
with the news items, each newspaper reader reads the message brought
by the date, the report of the passing of the preceding day and the lapse
of the news into the not-so-new, the overly reproduced and circulated.
The instant banalization is a result of the newspaper's use of, and refusal
to render a rational account of, reproducible print.

But *plusieurs fois* (especially in the context of confiding, confidence,
and faith [*foi*]) contrasts strongly with the punctual action of arrival signaled by the *passé simple* of *vint.* We are invited to consider the paradox
of many confidences folded into a single-time arrival. In one sense, a
poem is a highly inefficient use of the information system, requiring as it
does an immense technology of production, reproduction, and distribution to reach only a few readers. Mallarmé even goes so far as to say that
"the volume . . . does not require [*réclame*] the approach of a reader" (p.
372). An immense number of operations are required to produce a book

that requires no one to buy it to have its effect. For unlike the rapidly biodegrading newspaper, good for one time only, already out of date the day it is printed, the poem keeps on arriving. It practices its stringent verbal economies so as to arrive more than once in its singular occurrence. An easy place to understand what that entails is in the syntagma *plusieurs fois*, which we earlier read twice (as adverbial phrase modifying either the action of coming or of confiding), as if it were written in blurred or double-printed letters, by a press whose gears were starting to slip. The poem capitalizes on the fact that its letters are already iterating as they occur; it thinks them as "multiple outburst" (p. 369). The book, says Mallarmé, is governed by a single rule, which is that of making itself redeployable against the interpretation of the moment. The book is "one bound by some purity of frolic to shake up the coarseness [or, the solidity, the fat cat] of the moment [*le gros du moment*]" (p. 372). The play of the letter, we can already say, is driven by a capitalization on the printed word as providing knowledge of its own lack of self-contemporaneity. In short, by considering the letter as reiterated at its inception, the poem can work overtime, projecting itself past the immediate present to give itself futures, chances of arrival. It is, as Mallarmé says in this text, language as *placement* (as investment and as placing).

Can we then assume that Mallarmé posits a deep rift between the language of the poem (*placement*) and language as it is found in the newspapers (*véhicule*)? That is how many have interpreted statements like the following one from "Crise de vers": "Un désir indéniable à mon temps est de séparer en vue d'attributions différentes le double état de la parole, brut ou immédiat ici, là essentiel" (A desire undeniable to my time is to separate as if in view of different attributions the double state of the word, crude or immediate here, there essential) (p. 368).

But the analysis of "L'Action restreinte" suggests we need a more nuanced reading. A same syntagma—*le besoin d'agir*—arrives in the poet's ear at different speeds and to different effects, as a newspaper report *and* as a poem in the making. Similarly, the passage from "Crise de vers" has to be readable both as a statement "from" my time, by a writer caught up in the predicament of that time and presumably exemplifying its tendencies, and as a speculation on the day's fashion of believing that an uncrossable line divides self-reflexive literature from message-oriented reporting, poems from newspapers. In the analysis of the economies of book and newspaper, Mallarmé registers the epoch's desire to disassociate the double state of the printed word into two distinct tendencies. What, he wonders, have we gotten by sharpening this distinction? One thing is speed. The pace of the printing press, of the production, dissemination, and consumption of information can pick up immeasurably once self-reflexive language is seen as divorced from information-processing. Poetic language is a great consumer of resources and time for nothing; like smoking, it diverts time, money, resources to no end. The division of language into language-as-vehicle and language-as-investment helps the market. It also cordons off an arena of the ideal which supports the market and where the market is presumed not to operate, where nothing is for sale, where we have only the value of values, the gold of language. This is not Mallarmé's ideology; it is the ideology of the epoch, evidenced in the growth of the newspaper industry and the separate book industry.[24] *His* word arrives in a double state, dated from a journal ("L'Action" appears first in *La Revue blanche* in 1895), and then, a bit later, from a volume (baptised "L'Action restreinte," it appears in *Divagations* in 1897) where it self-reflexively speculates on its originary redoubling. This is not just an empirical fact. In the preface to *Divagations*, Mallarmé sees his book as a newspaper: "A book like I do not love them, those scattered and without architecture. Decidedly, no one escapes journalism" (p. 1340).

This third set of calculations gives us the text as a *report* on writing and its relation to action, and simultaneously, as a layered, complex *intervention* in those relations. This requires further explanation. As Mallarmé understands it, there is a reciprocal relation between action and representation. Action responds to a need. We need to act, that is to produce self-representations so as to convince ourselves of our existence. "Agir . . . signifia . . . produire sur beaucoup un mouvement qui te donne en retour l'émoi que tu en fus le principe, donc existes" (To act . . . meant . . . to produce on the manifold a movement that gives you in return the feeling that you were its principle, and therefore exist) (p. 369). But action is also needy. It requires representation, and is indeed limited by it: "Ainsi l'Action, en le mode convenu, littéraire, ne transgresse pas le Théâtre; s'y limite, à la représentation—immédiat évanouissement de l'écrit" (Thus Action, in the agreed-upon mode, literary, does not transgress theater; limits itself to it, in representation—immediate vanishing of writing) (p. 371). In *Mallarmé et l'éthique de la poésie*, in the context of a discussion of "L'Action restreinte," André Stanguennec even goes so far as to assert that by such statements Mallarmé approaches Heidegger in thinking action as the essence of thinking: "Thus, for the French poet just as for the German thinker, the essence of action is indeed thinking and meditation considered as human recoveries of a desire of which being is the subject 'before' being its object in human speech."[25] The interest of the comparison aside, Stanguennec has glossed over two important nuances in Mallarmé's statements about action. He has not noticed the past tense of Mallarmé's definition, which presents what action *meant* (*signifia*), and not what it means any longer. The definition of action—action is driven by the subject's wish to bring itself into existence by the redounding onto it of credit as its agent—is no longer true. We are forced not only to consider all representations or definitions of action as subject to obsolescence, but also to wonder what sort of definition of action could have taken over once action is no longer tied to (self-)representation. Stanguennec has also left writing out of the picture, which is what Mallarmé, in the passage quoted above, says does happen where literature appears limited to representation (*immédiat évanouissement de l'écrit*). It is at the point that the ties binding action to representation are in question that Mallarmé intervenes to raise the question of writing.[26]

We will look at a single example of a definition of action to see how, when, and to what effect the play of the letter emerges to affect the scene.

Bound Action: Choosing a Representative

Here is the passage:

Se détendre les poings, en rupture du songe sédentaire, pour un trépignant vis-à-vis avec l'idée, ainsi qu'une envie prend ou bouger: mais la génération semble peu agitée, outre le désintéressement politique, du souci d'extravaguer du corps. Excepté la monotonie, certes, d'enrouler, entre les jarrets, sur la chaussée, selon l'instrument en faveur, la fiction d'un éblouissant rail continu.

(Unclench the fists, breaking with the sedentary dream, for a foot tapper face-to-face with the idea, just as a wish takes you or move about: but the generation seems little agitated, beyond a political disinterest, by the concern for extravagating of the body. Except for the monotony, to be sure, of winding up, between knees, on the roadway, according to the instrument in favor, the fiction of a dazzling continuous rail.) (p. 369)

1. *The Fist*

Mallarmé takes off in the snappy style of a newspaper survey taker. He defines the need for action as a need for brusque physical activity (the paradoxical one of "relaxing" the fists), after a period of sedentary mental action, as the young Marcel used to walk after reading. The definition is an example of the kind of verbal action that an impatient reporter (himself a "foot tapper" with ideas) might knock out before interviewing his subjects. It equates motion with action, and sees the individual's wish (*envie*) to act as expressed in the movement of relaxing hand (or impatient foot). The figure of the unclenched fist is complex but readable. It consists of synecdoches bundled together by a correspondence: the fists stand as a part for the whole of the body; a one-time action of unclenching stands for a multitude of repetitions of the same act; a species of action, the action of relaxing a muscle, represents the genre of willed physical actions. The part stands as a convincing representative, as what Mallarmé calls elsewhere "the symbol glittering forth in the world's spectacles" (p. 921), because of a coincidence that brings together in a single point a metonymy (the fist as officer of the will) and a metaphor (the fist's clutch is the visible analogy of the mind's appropriative grasping of the objects of cognition). Alone among the parts of the body, as if to symbolize the mind's appropriative gesture working in harmony with the will, the fists grasp. The relaxing of the fist can stand for the loosing of the mind's grip in reverie, for a mind become less commanding, more wishful. But because—as is evident from the paradox that it is the *action* of relaxing (and thus, reverie) that interrupts reverie as mere lack of activity—the difference between work and play, activity and recreation, is actually collapsed. Both are part of the same system, and under the representation of the fist share a definition of action as the subject's willful tensing and releasing of muscles.

This situation is also mirrored in the infinitive form (*se détendre*) which is the form favored in definitions and also for imperative constructions, like those requesting subway or train riders to abstain from smoking (*ne pas fumer*) or leaning out the windows (*ne pas se pencher au dehors*). The poet may be reporting a definition of action in which relaxation cannot be differentiated from work, or else urging "relax!" The difference between definition and order is not important here, however. Both operate within the figural system totalized by the fist where activity is commanded by the will so as to represent the mind. The staccato rhythm of the sentence, its four parts spliced by commas, is in keeping with the straightforward presentation of action understood through its representative: we get delivered the representative act; the scenery it would disrupt, the impatient conceiver of the act; the wish that motivates the action together with the concept of individual freedom and self-willed action underlying it. The language here could be called reporting language plus, since the message is communicated partly by way of a totalizing figure. The figure helps compress things in view of a speedy delivery of the message.

Honest reporter that he is, however, the I has to admit that agitation so defined does not characterize the period. The first sentence delivers a definition and then starts taking it back, making reflexive turns (*mais*), expressing reserves (*outre*) and negations (*peu*). A news flash from the day on the day's "need for action" comes through: these days—less fist unclenching, little bodily extravagance. There are implications for the political scene: the sole agitation that shakes the generation is stated to be "political disinterest" (*le désintéressement politique*), as the idea of the relations in the individual between mind and body is extended to cover those of the generation with respect to the organized body politic. The current generation lacks an interest in politics—the political culture dominant after the Revolution and the pugilism of expanding nationalism have presumably relaxed their hold. Apathy is not only the prevailing form of political activity, the relaxing of muscles of individual citizens that follows a period of tension. It is also an indication of agitation affecting the political body itself. A generation's alienation, its lack of concern—it neither lends itself to, nor is unduly worried about, the disinterest in the political that is currently "shaking" the body politic—is taken as characteristic of political life.

But as we extend the metaphor of the loosening fists to the arena of politics, a critical difference between the activity of individuals and of the polis emerges. Syntax, word order, brings out the difference, which particularly affects what is meant by *souci*—care, concern, preoccupation, worry—with respect to the "need to act." In one reading of the sentence "mais la génération semble peu agitée, outre le désintéressement politique, du souci d'extravaguer du corps," the *génération*, the grammatical subject of *semble*, is taken as the human subject of *souci* in its meaning of "care." The *Petit Robert* defines *souci* as "the state of mind that consists in being absorbed by an object with a preoccupation that worries or troubles even to the point of moral suffering," or again, "subjective attitude of a person who seeks a result." From such a definition is painted a picture of citizens as concerned individuals, who band together in their preoccupation with the health of the body politic, to give it a needed rest.

Given the passive construction, however (the generation is *agitated*, not agitating) and the ambiguous genitive (the *du* of *souci d'extravaguer du corps* may be subjective) the text may be read as affirming that the apparent *object* of worry, the body, is actually the *subject* doing the worrying. *Souci* can be a preoccupation that so far takes over the mind as to dispossess it of its dominance (*Petit Robert*: "what seizes hold of the mind to trouble or disquiet it"), and the syntax dramatically enacts a violent upset, staging a rupture with idealism. In this construction the apathetic attitude of the generation is a piece of evidence in a picture where the political *body's* preoccupation with extravagating dominates. It is worth considering this alternative syntax, because it suggests that the generation's indifference is more than a form of action like relaxing the fist that consists in concerned citizens "giving the body a rest." The quiescence is part of a larger picture where the point is that the political body has a life of its own that is not commanded by a mind. It may be doing its own extravagating, or else it is acting alarmed at extravagating in its citizens. A disquieting pause occurs here, a relaxation that involves a relapse of the will willing in concert with knowledge: a gap opens up between a still current but tired-out model of what action is, based on the individual subject's supposed dominance of the body, and an *emergent* model already important politically where that dominance is not a given. "The body politic" has a life of its own, concerns of its own, and the assumption that for every action there is a subject, a concerned citizen, does not take into account this independence of political structure.

What preoccupies the political body and determines its action through concern is extravagating. Several quite different interpretations of the political body's concern with extravagating could be made, starting out from the remark that the political structures erected in keeping with the outmoded concept of action outlast their own decrepitude. A Foucauldian interpretation might settle in on a double dimension to this "concerned" body politic. On the one side, we would see the institutionalization of a broader definition of work, where what might seem opposed as passivity to activity (relaxing and clenching fists, dreaming and thinking, or even writing poems and engaging in military action) would turn out to be subsumable under the broader definition as acceptable activities for a citizen. But on the other, this broadness of definition in terms of the range of normal action would go along with a tighter and more repressive oversight of whatever falls outside the norm as extravagant.[27] The etymology of the term *extravaguer* sheds light on the sort of activity that would fall outside the zone of tolerance, as the action to be restricted. The prefix *extra* means "outside," and it partly reduplicates the meaning of the stem verb *vagari* meaning "to err, to wander off the path." Etymologically speaking, *extravaguer* means something like "to wander outside off the path," in other words, to wander "outside" the opposition between on the path and off the path, going straight and wandering, reasoning and dreaming. Oversight and censorship would be of whatever, by bringing out an outside unrecovered, a difference that is not subsumable, would cause us to suspect that an oppositional logic based on the autonomy of a subject does not exhaust action.

An Althusserian interpretation could also be made. Here the attention would be on the apparatus seeking to maintain the already outmoded order. It would be shown calling on its citizens so as to persuade them that their apathy and agitation alike, even including the brand of activism that consists in the denunciation of the state's repressive censorship, are those of voluntaristic subjects, concerned with the health of the polis (and not simply of so-called volunteers, virtually impressed into its army).[28] Here the state's surveillance and punishment of whatever activity does not fit under the symbol of the fist would be only the overt form of its more insidious operation of causing its citizens to reproduce its tensions. Urging "action" of whatever kind would be to set whoever responds to the call back inside the system where action is assumed to be "to produce on the manifold a movement that gives you in return the feeling that you were its principle, and therefore exist" (p. 369), and where the will and mind work in concert. Extravagating, in this sort of interpretation, might be extended beyond the paltry errors or subversive behavior of individuals to designate the operations by which an apparatus maintains a symbol in force, all the coercive and convulsive operations of the political body.

If the political body is preoccupied with extravagating, that means it is concerned with striking out on its own beyond the boundaries or walls of an already established public space, conceived as a rationally ordered space. The passage meditates on the need of the body politic to wander outside the boundaries it imposes, on the impossibility of its remaining within boundaries like those implied by the symbol of the fist since it has to infringe on them from the beginning to establish and maintain itself. The syntax that posits relations that are not those supposed by the metaphorics of the unclenched fist provides the linguistic equivalent of this independent action, since it shows a structure, adopted to express a thought about the subject's dominance, that ends by positing the independence of structure. For Mallarmé, whose interest in syntax as the pivot of intelligibility is well known, the interference of syntax in the production of meaning is a force to reckon with. In the short passage we are examining, the interference suggests that what looks like a message by a newspaper reporter from the period who is considering trends in action, might more profitably be read as a meditation on the independence of structure. This has clear implications for the tired-out metaphor of the polis as a body moved by a head, and thus for the fist (clenched or unclenched) as the figure for action that draws the generation together. The sentence written by the reporter on styles in action is readable for what it has to say about a failure to harmonize syntax and semantics, structure and intentional action, and thus, ultimately, a failure of the nationalist politics in vogue. The news flash dates the fist as a metaphor losing its grip.

2. The Bend of the Knees

A very different strategy of representation operates in the second sentence, where the attempt is to define the *exception* to the fashion by way of an action that does characterize the generation: "Excepté la monotonie, certes, d'enrouler, entre les jarrets, sur la chaussée, selon l'instrument en faveur, la fiction d'un éblouissant rail continu." How are we to understand this sentence, which appears anything but straightforward? One sign that the breakdown in the reporting language already hinted at has taken place is the piling up of prepositional phrases to separate the verb *enrouler* from its object "la fiction d'un éblouissant rail continu." The six commas do not chop the sentence up all the better to bring its parts together into a cohesive theory. Rather these commas disrupt and disarticulate the thought.

What is the exact sort of physical agitation that characterizes the generation in its singularity, and why has the poet had to have recourse to an exorbitant figure to get at it? These two questions can be treated as one question, given that the problem is to identify the singular activity that passes as yet unnamed and unperceived by the generation it characterizes. Through this naming the poet will make remarkable a gap that divides the generation and makes it unable to read its own predicament with respect to its political institutions. He responds to the confidence of his visitor by an act that is inventive of the exact type of activity of the period. We can best understand this by reading some of the puzzling terms of the sentence.

One key lies in the exceptional character of the activity, which lies outside the range of activity regulated by the concept of action as the body's expression of the individual's will. Its irregularity has so far passed unnoticed, perhaps because it has so far shared the same name of *agitation*, and the same representative of the fist. Mallarmé selects a new representative, the *jarrets*, and a new term, *enrouler*, to represent the "coming" sort of action.

As the juridical saw has it, this exception proves the rule for the norm in the context from which it is excepted.[29] It stands out as extravagating with respect to other kinds of action. As such, it can stand for the cleavage within the generation, which is still occupied in its institutions and rules by a past ideology, but already oriented in a new direction, by a type of activity, a doings whose arena has yet to be delimited or regulated, whose concept has yet to be found. It can also stand for the extravagating of the political body, for the independence of the structure with respect to the model to which it holds its subjects. The poet *has* to act as poet here. He has to invent because the names, the concepts, and the rules for this new arena are not yet available. The figure he provides has to be enigmatic for it is no more than a flag planted to indicate an area in need of exploration, where the newest sort of activity, in the process of seeking definition, representation, and regulation, is taking place. In order to report on this latest fashion in action, the poet has to find a representative. But first he has to find what is heterogeneous in the activities assumed to be homogeneous. He uncovers what had been passing under the cover of one representative of action. He distinguishes the exception. For Chénier, such analysis is one act of a poet: "L'esprit de lumière . . . partout, en d'heureux intervalles, / Sépare et met en paix les semences rivales" (The spirit of light . . . everywhere, at happy intervals, / Separates and brings peace to rival seeds) (p. 124). As understood by Mallarmé, the analytical task consists in reporting the rifts within the generation: between its old concept of action, and an as-yet-undifferentiated and unassimilated activity heterogeneous to the first; between an arena regulated by institutions and laws, and an arena not covered by law. These gaps affect the generation's very knowledge of itself: "Badly informed whoever cries himself his own contemporary" (*Mal informé celui qui se crierait son propre contemporain*) (p. 372). Invention is required to report on the split that divides the "present" generation from itself, bound by a set of rules already outdated, and bound for another set to come. For one cannot report on what the coming action means without also responding by an invention that does not simply repeat the old ideal of claiming to be one's own contemporary, to be acting mindfully.

Another puzzle lies in the part of the body, the *jarrets*, chosen to represent the physical activity of the generation. Several rationales are available for the election of the lowly bend in the knee to represent the exceptional physical activity of the generation. The first two rationales I will lay out meet the criterion of novelty, but are to a large extent recuperable as continuous with the system of representation given by the fist. As such, under cover of a new flag, they allow the old system of representation to continue, and with it the notion of history as linear and progressive. The third rationale is discontinuous. Even more than inaugurating a "new" epoch, it inaugurates a new way of construing epochs, history, and progress.

The first explanation starts from a commonsense observation.[30] In a sedentary group the bend of the knee is a good representative of the body's "action." The force lost from the unclenched fist gathers in the tensed knees as the generation sits down to work. When sitting becomes doing, moreover, the knees jut out as the visibly prominent part of the body. A *jarret*, in the technical language of architecture and furniture-making, is a protrusion that breaks up a continuous line, and that is what the knees do here. If the poet pinpoints the *jarret* as the representative of the latest cry in action, it is because it fulfills two requirements for a good representative of a neglected sphere. He does not choose the most prominent-*appearing* part, the protruding knee that is part of the body visible in a face-to-face encounter between subjects; instead he picks the neglected back side of the knee. It represents the bodily activity not only of an apathetic group of knee-jerk nationalists, but of a group affected by an action that does not take place in full view, either because it is semi-conscious, or because it occurs through some nonspectacular mode (like interpellation). Moreover, the *jarret* is the part that in technical terms *does* the work, conceived independently from the old symbolic system dominated by the visible body directed by the idealizing head and its gripping hand. When one works a *jarret* in French, one does what any animal with an articulated leg can do (in contrast to bending a knee, which is an action heavily invested in terms of consciousness and is what a subject humbling itself before a lord would do).

However, despite the great difference between the fist's representation of bodily activity as an exteriorizing of the work of the mind, and the bend-of-the-knee's representation of the underappreciated activity of the body independent of the mind's control, this new representative shows some continuities with the old. The *jarret* chosen as the neglected joint, the condition that brings the visible knee into prominence, suggests that an old fealty, an old idealism is carried forward here. The spotlight is on the *jarret* as enabling visibility, and it suggests a seductive model for the mind itself, which works as the *jarrets* work the knees. A set of drives and reflexes tensed even in repose, the mind is not chiefly the consciousness that projects itself in its works. It has also an underside, an unconscious side, available in the undervalued set of techniques and by which it accomplishes its wished-for transports. It is impossible to bend a knee without also flexing a *jarret*, or to engage in activity without tapping into the techniques and drives associated with the unconscious. The election of this representative of heterogeneous physical activity makes it possible to think of the mind as not entirely a *conscious* mind, but as still the dominant principle seeking evidence of itself in activity.

A second rationale can explain the selection of the *jarrets*. The bend in the knee where two bones come together to form a joint is a good part by which to represent a mode of gathering things differently than the grasping crush of the homogenizing fist. A *jarret* invites us to consider ways of making connections besides that of totalization. It can represent, from a political point of view, groupings unrepresented by the official idea that measures work in terms of workers' production, or considers the working body only in the preindustrial terms of the heads and hands involved in production. Like a group of factory "hands" banded together to form a body of their own (a union), a postindustrial group of workers having increasingly to adapt themselves to the specifications of machines can be glimpsed under the banner *jarrets*. A group of individual leisure-takers is also represented, along lines suggested by Stanguennec, who translates the "instrument in favor" between the bent knees as the vehicle for one that is the bicycle, and the group indicated as leisurely Sunday bicyclists.[31] One could also include in this group clerical workers, secretaries, accountants, registrars, law clerks, bank clerks. The point is not only that they are sedentary. It is that they are grouped together by means of exterior things such as the position of their bodies with respect to machines, and their lack of representation as a class by the ideal of action as voluntary production. They constitute a class of exceptions assembled from without, as without a common goal or idea. A bunch of people on a railroad, or the soon-to-be-built subway system, their knees jolted by the mechanical movements of mass transport, might be the best summary for the unbundled grouping of groups. The knees jolted by the new transportation system (*éblouissant rail continu*) superimposed on the old system of roads (*sur la chaussée*) bring into view the possibility of decisive activity on the body by a technology.[32] These acted upon knees stand for a class in need of regulation and protection. It should be recalled, moreover, that where there are *jarrets* there are inevitably *coupe-jarrets*, thieves threatening to hamstring their victims if they don't deliver the goods. Robber barons and pirates of late nineteenth-century capitalism—merchants, bankers, stockbrokers, railroad and newspaper magnates, societies without heads—make a phantasmatic appearance here as an unregulated group capitalizing on the unregulated groups of riders on the train of progress, whose activity is not all tied up with intentional production but whose body is jolted and fragmented (part acting, part acted on) by the systems associated with production.

To the various overlapping conceptless crowds that the *jarrets* represent we can add something quite dissimilar: grammar, linguistic structures where organization governs without concepts and that impose subjects or agents even where meaning rejects them. In a text that takes its grammar so seriously that it speculates on the meaning of a *body's* worries about extravagant action, the decision to figure syntax by bent knees makes sense. *Jarrets* bring out the bone work, the body's structure through its joints, and especially the angles and particular articulations of parts that distinguish one joint from another. We could notice here the odd number of groups of *jarrets* that Mallarmé provides in the phrase "entre les jarrets," partly by way of the linking preposition *entre* ("between, but also "among"). A *jarret* links two bones in an angle; *jarrets* can be paired by way of a common torso and a space between the knees; an odd lot of *jarrets* can be brought together as dissimilar (unpaired, perhaps belonging to different bodies of possibly dissimilar species) or similar (paired, or belonging to similar beings or species of beings); they can be coupled in terms of the intervals between one knee or set of knees and another (*entre* means "between"), or as a forest of sets among which one set is to be selected (*entre* means "among"). *Jarrets* are not only joints considered as independent of their capacity to gather as a symbol gathers into a totality; they are joints that gather various modes of associating without totalizing (coupling, spacing, pairing, separating, assembling—all the modes of grammar). The plural *jarrets* is critical here. In *Les Mots anglais*, Mallarmé says of the letter *s* that it is the "analytical letter, preeminently dissolving and disseminating" (*lettre analytique; dissolvante et disséminante, par excellence*) (p. 855). Instead of reading the text on *s* in terms of weak Cratylism, as a poet's reverie about what a letter "means," we can fruitfully consider it a comment about the *s* of the plural. The plural is always plural*s*, that is, it assembles more than one kind of thing in more than one kind of way, and so is the site of self-division. The *jarrets* can serve as a fine representative of grammar because as a plurality they clue us in to a flexibility to language as extension that does not imply any self-reflexivity. In this, knees innovate on the fist. They remind of the articulating structure on which the fist metaphor depends for its persuasiveness. In order to consider the (right?) fist as the right figure for the action commanded by the head, we have had to forget about the surprising plurality of fist*s*. *Jarrets*, which calls attention to an action of and on the structure, forces the consideration of a plurality that groups under the *s* heterogeneous groups.

In this second rationale, the selection of *jarrets* is justified by considering the need for a second, *compensatory* representation for the groupings left out of the earlier account. But the fist still dominates the scene as the representation in need of compensation. The *jarrets* compensate for parts missing from the larger scene of representation, but they do not dislodge the ideology of the integral body acting under the mind's orders encapsulated by the fists.

Binding Action: The Orders of the Garter

A third rationale for electing the bent knees is available. According to one gloss of the sentence we have been analyzing, we are being invited to select from among the *jarrets* the single reading that allows the questioning of history as a continuous progress (*enrouler, entre les jarrets . . . la fiction d'un éblouissant rail continu*). In this rationale, *jarrets* stand out as unique, and break radically with the fist and the politics and aesthetics that they embody. Alone among the parts of the body, and as if to signify in the very "body" of the word the independence of the language from the domination of the mind's I and its desire to embody itself in a representation, the *jarrets* coincidentally spell out the cessation of action: *j'arrête*. "I stop" where the knees begin. This is not an effect that can be put down to symbolization and its gathering of like things. This is an effect of a similarity between the letters of a word and those of a sentence, forced upon the attention by way of a plethora of neighboring terms drawn either from the semantic field of interruption or its opposite (*continu, monotone, rupture, extravagant, excepté*). By no stretch of the imagination does *jarrets* mean *j'arrête*, I stop. It means "knee-joint, bend in the knees," and no self-respecting translator would translate it otherwise. Nonetheless, unwittingly, accidentally—within a constellation of terms that have been gathered for semantic reasons to form a familiar neighborhood—it "letterally" almost spells it.[33] There is a disjunction between the meaning of the word and the play of the letter that posits the sentence, or sentences (*arrêts* means "decrees, sentences"). That disjunction lifts the *jarrets* out of the throng of exchangeable body parts, selecting it as the exceptional or modeling representative of the work of the generation, characterized, as we have said, by an unwitting activity of self-divergence. This is not merely a temporary slippage between the meaning and the mode of meaning that can be reappropriated. It is a radical uncoupling of meaning from structure that derails the train of progress (the iron horse galloping across Europe and the Americas) as the last word in the fiction of a continuous, progressive history. It is the place in the text, in the midst of the production of a representation of action, where writing steps out.

This third rationale is the decisive one for the selection of *jarrets* as the figure for a gap in the generation between how it sees itself (as "contemporary," as knowing itself in its symbols) and how the writer sees it (as ignorant or forgetful of its death). The kind of writing pointed to is not luminous, white on black, as the stars write for Mallarmé, but obscure, black on white, as man writes ("l'homme poursuit, noir sur blanc" [p. 370]). It breaks with representation in general because it disjoins the hermeneutic function of language from its poetic function, positing the possibility of advancing structures that can stand portentous and yet free of meaning. It identifies an agitation to language owed to its technical aspect, which cannot be shrugged off as a body's action, and thus as owed to language's phenomenality. The decision to proceed allegorically, to select *jarret* for its resemblance to *j'arrête* as the critical point, proposes as a problem of interest to the generation its ability to read a gap affecting its own representations ("Faced with aggression, I prefer to retort that contemporaries do not know how to read—" [p. 386]). Among all the *jarrets* is one that commands us to read the difference between what the *jarrets* mean, in all their exploitable richness and complex diversity (in terms of unrepresented groups, unregulated technologies, unconceived areas where representation is needed), and what they spell to the noncontemporary, through the monotonous play of the letter as *j'arrête*: the end of an expression-centered view of language, the disjunction between meaning and saying, the gap within the generation between its knowing and its doings, the noncontemporaneity of the present, the inhuman orders given by language, a technicity governed by accidents.

At this juncture, with meaning at a standstill, we do well to pause for a moment to consider where we are, what we are doing, and where it leads. Let me start by raising an objection. This is an objection I confess I have to grapple with every time I come up against one of these places where the poetic function kicks itself free of the burdensome traces of hermeneutics and requires that we consider what language is about when it thrusts itself forward as trace in another sense, the sense of mark or writing. To right- and straight-thinking people (and who doesn't aspire at least to the latter class?), such play in language is suspicious. It appears like an ingenious trick, a lucky find, a derailing joke or irony (*une raillerie*) and not an actual invention. That is largely a result of the necessary arbitrariness attendant upon the isolation of a single spot where language stands free of meaning. If, as Mallarmé says, poetry is everywhere that there is rhythm and style, if it is always the case that language is organized by formal patterns that do not correspond to any meaning, even that of grammar, then to land on one such pattern as the conclusive has to seem arbitrary, that is, violent and unmotivated. Why cut things off at the knees? What about the arrangement of the text that brings to our attention curious conjunctions and overlaps between the terminology of progress as exemplified by the train—*le rail* (the rail) (p. 369); *FUMER* (to give off smoke) (p. 369); *le voyageur perçoit la détresse du sifflet* (the traveler perceives the whistle's distress) (p. 371); *un tunnel— l'époque* (a tunnel—the epoch) (p. 371); *la GARE toute puissante* (the all-powerful station) (p. 372); *en train* (in progress) (p. 372)—and the terminology associated with the theme of writing circumlocutionary texts under the influence of tobacco—*FUMER* (to smoke) (p. 369); *s'exhale* (breathes out) (p. 370); *le long des tuyaux, la flamme aux langues réduites* (along the pipes, the flame with reduced tongues) (p. 371); *spacieusement de s'exprimer, ainsi que d'un ciGARE* (to express oneself spaciously, as with a cigar) (p. 371)?[34] The proximity of the poet's study where he smokes his cigar, rue de Rome in the Quartier de l'Europe, to the Gare St. Lazare can be taken as another version of such a text. It is a constant motif in Mallarmé's works, surfacing as early as "Le Démon de l'analogie," that the poet's reverie around a meaningless signifier can find an exact translation in a commercial landscape of everyday nineteenth-century Parisian life. Such conjunctions invariably open up a host of anxious questions as to what determines them. Mallarmé's response in "Le Démon de l'analogie," which works well enough as a commentary on the ci-GARE/GARE conjunction noted above, is that they provide irrefutable proof of "the intervention of the supernatural" (p. 273), or what the later Mallarmé will call in terms less redolent of Romanticism, writing.

Is there a privilege to be accorded to one *particular* spot where language advances its claims free of representational constraints? No, on the one hand, for it is just one representative of a general possibility. It advances poetic language as a representing without a represented (Derrida on Mallarmé), permanent parabasis (de Man on Schlegel), language as spuming (Hans-Jost Frey on Mallarmé) or rhythm (Kevin Newmark on Mallarmé).[35]

But the example is not entirely arbitrary either. When language steps out in a Mallarmé text, it is always theatrically, on a stage, with a light, an actor having devoted considerable energy to the task of preparing for its advance—as a representative, as one *jarret* thrust out from a chorus:

Plancher, lustre, obnubilation des tissus et liquéfaction de miroirs, en l'ordre réel, jusqu'aux bonds excessifs de notre forme gazée autour d'un *arrêt*, sur pied, de la virile stature, un Lieu se présente, scène, majoration devant tous du spectacle de Soi.

(Planks, lights, clouding of fabrics and melting of mirrors, in the order of the real, even to the excessive leaps of our gauze-covered form around a *decree*, upright, of virile stature, a place is presented, Scene, increase in front of everyone of the spectacle of Self.) (p. 370, my emphasis)

The representative only steps out where it comes upon a stage, the accoutrements and the actor readied for its play (the writer's task is "to institute himself the spiritual actor to the text" [p. 370]).[36] In the passage we have been reading, this stage is set for the coincidence of the two conflictual patterns by the search for a representative to stand for new modes of action. The utmost hermeneutical pressure is put on the *jarrets*, to propose them as the representative for the exceptional activity of the period that lies outside its norms and concepts but is still continuous with the need for representation. It is only then that the threat of poetics, which is a threat posed to hermeneutical consistency, has urgency and force.

Any single example has to appear arbitrary because that is how the poetic function does appear, as the purely arbitrary breaking in on the hermeneutic function. But that does not mean that each example is in and of itself merely an ingenious trick to be discounted, a way of getting language to stall without meaning any more. The poetic function steps out only where the most rigorous possible attempt is being made to understand the text hermeneutically, in terms of the representation it provides. Writing, the poetic function, appears on stage to vanish. That means we get to ask what difference its appearance makes and what difference its vanishing makes. We could not ask those questions were the poetic function not recalled, made to appear to disappear. Language that works in this way is indeed a "placement" (p. 371), that is, a capital invested for the future, the act of procuring employment for someone (some future reader), and also, the action of placing, of providing the language in its entirety. We have to read the singularity of this sentence as such, and not just as what it has to say about language in general.

We've been stalling, having reached the point where, as it seems, writing appears to make a difference, to break in on the scene of interpretation as a threatening excess. One of the meanings of *jeu*, that very Mallarmean term, is "the lack of tightness or articulation between two parts of a mechanism," and our stalling is a symptom of the fact that language is not gripping any longer. But without any gap, without any *jeu* (that is, the space contrived to enable the easy movement of an object, as for instance, between the piston and the bottom of a cylinder, or a window and its runners), the machine cannot operate either. This pause detected is a place where something is getting placed, installed. In a previously cited passage from "L'Action restreinte" where Mallarmé tells us that action requires representation to appear as such, he also remarks that representation makes writing vanish (p. 371). He is inviting us to consider, we have said, what the appearance and disappearance of writing means for action and its representation. He is inviting us to reflect on the need for action and its representation, and thus on the need for limiting the play of the letter, and especially the play given it in the public sphere. Because here language stalls, commerce stops, progress gets derailed, Mallarmé cautions: "whether it is not better—rather than to risk on the surrounding state at the very least incomplete, certain extreme conclusions of art which, diamond-like, can flash [or shatter, *éclater*] in this time forever after, in the Book's integrity—to play them" (p. 373). To make language advance as written, typed speech is to stall things around it.

In the earlier discussion of the action of the body, the possibility of the syntax providing a second reading opened a door to a reflection about the body politic and its ambiguous stance with respect to extravagant action: worried about it, suspecting its citizens of transgressing against the ideology of the subject as agent, it also appeared necessarily concerned with undertaking it in a restricted way so as to energize the tired-out representational system, to take into account new forms of action, to keep itself "alive." But here, the poet suggests we must proceed with caution in risking these conclusions on a state. The effect of abruptly unveiling the conventionality of meaning structures by the play of the letter is not playful but violent, nor is it taken lightly by Mallarmé, who insists we call it "madness" (p. 371) and sees the potential for disruption. The letter is disruptive because it unveils the fiction as arbitrary and dated. The duration of a fiction is tied to the legibility of its founding texts; the very texts that decree it also hold in reserve (for instance, in the *j'arrête* of *jarrets*) the secret of the fiction's noncontemporaneity with itself. Mallarmé's exceptional act of *electing* the *jarrets* as the new representative of action for the time has been an arbitrary decision, a choice apt in symbolizing hitherto uncollected groups, but decisive because it coincidentally points to the author's death, and as such, to the afterlife of the text. *J'arrête* is a confession that has no content, since it is only "writing" speaking. But, as it carries out the sentence implicit in it, punishing the author with death, as if the crime confessed had been real and effective, it provides a foretaste of the scene of injustice that will have been affecting the generation. The selection of a new representative is not an act that "gives you in return the feeling that you were its principle, and therefore exist" (p. 369). The poet types the speech of the period by electing death, rather than inventing a metaphor to express something. He shows where the generation, showing its literary bent, is writing its epitaph.

The choice of death turns out to be a choice between deaths, however. Not to choose one's death is to choose another sort of death, which consists in losing one's death: "Le droit à rien accomplir d'exceptionnel ou manquant aux agissements vulgaires, se paie, chez quiconque, de l'omission de lui et on dirait de sa mort comme un tel" (The right to accomplish nothing exceptional or missing from common activities, is paid for by the omission of oneself and, it might be said, of one's death as such and such a one) (p. 370). One loses one's chances by refraining from doing the exceptional thing of electing one's death. In the pause where writing appears, readings are gathered in which the next epoch will spend its time exfoliating. The release from the bonds of meaning lets the poem take "excessive leaps" (*bonds excessifs* [p. 371]). In pausing to show the generation inscribed in a text it cannot read, Mallarmé stops on a break where its futures gather. Writing uncouples action from representation, and lets us think the necessity of temporal pauses when are being assembled "distant interlacings [*des entrelacs*], where sleep a luxury to be inventoried, vampire, knot, foliage, and to present" (p. 370).[37]

What does it mean to say that the break with the hermeneutic function installs reserves? Let's look briefly at the way that our little sentence, which means nothing, nonetheless programs our attempts to understand it, deploys its folds as we read it. I have said that what occurs here is that the text ceases to be understandable in terms of a hermeneutics of the self. As sentence redoubled (according to the rule that you never get one *jarret* without a possible pair) it says that: *J'arrête à jarrets*, that is, I stop where linguistic extension ceases to be assimilable to a hermeneutics of the self. The reading of the passage is thus inscribed in the sentences of *j'arrête*(s). Ending is not a voluntary act by a subject who modestly tries to stop with a given representation. The I's stopping is not owed only to its restraint as I, but also to the brusque interference of the poetic function. The sentence sentences us to that too: *J'arrête à jarrets à "j'arrête"* (I stop *where* language starts to operate, *upon* its command). In fact, of course, I haven't stopped upon command at all, but have been inventorying *j'arrête*(s), so now I resolve to stop, to add no more new articulations to the heap. The sentence sentences: *Resolved* that *I stop where* language starts to operate, *upon* its command: *J'arrête que j'arrête à jarrets à "j'arrête."* My resolve is already broken in its expression, my decision to stop adding more bones (*arêtes*—the skeleton of fish; by analogy, the line where two planes intersect) to my collection is in trouble in its articulation. So I give myself up to the police as a resolve-breaker. *I arrest myself* in the process of *formulating/breaking my resolve* that *I stop where* language starts to operate, *upon* its command: *Je m'arrête à j'arrête que j'arrête à jarrets à "j'arrête."* In the name of what law am I repeating myself in the very act of arresting myself for repeating myself? *Arrêté que,* decreed that, *je m'arrête à j'arrête que j'arrête à jarrets à "j'arrête."* What a lot of babbling, jabbering, jargoning here! Another *jar*. *Jar*, in *jargon*, means "jargon," for which *jarrer* would be the neologistic verbal form: *Jarrer qu'arrêté que je m'arrête à j'arrête que j'arrête à jarrets à "j'arrête."* But it's not just babbling, it's a babble bound to a singular sentence, and as an operation of binding, it has an equivalent: *jarreter*, to bind with a garter (*une jarretière*), in architecture, to form a "jarret" or elbow. The formation of an elbow between hermeneutics and poetics, the attaching to the limb of a textile by a flexible bond is what the text is about: *Jarreter que jarrer qu'arrêté que je m'arrête à j'arrête que j'arrête à jarrets à "j'arrête."* But what allows us to say that this is a French sentence only, that the French language is a jar (*jarre*) or container closed off from other like vessels? How jarring all this jarring is! (*jar*—to emit a harsh grating sound, to strike so as to cause a vibration, to strike with discordant or painful effect on the ear, nerves, conscience; to vibrate audibly; to vibrate without reference to sound as from an impact; to cause to vibrate; to be out of harmony, to disagree or conflict; to be at strife or active variance, to wrangle or quarrel; example, "we were everlastingly jarring and saying disagreeable things to each other" [*Oxford English Dictionary*].) Language, the French language, ceases to be conceivable as a closed system or container, and has instead to be construed as obeying the more cosmopolitan rule of the Order of the Garter (etymologically related to the Old French *garet, jaret* from which *jarret* is descended), with its French motto "Honi soit qui mal y pense."[38] The English have provided terms for Mallarmé's French (*rail*, for example, is a term imported in the early 1800s, winning out to the dismay of the etymologists over a school of French terms), just as the French once provided scions like *jarretière* to be grafted, by a technique involving binding, onto Anglo-Saxon stock. This interest in French as angling into English is abiding for Mallarmé, and it brings into view questions like the homogeneity and purity of one's language.[39] *Jarring 'Jarreter que jarrer qu'arrêté que je m'arrête à j'arrête que j'arrête à jarrets à "j'arrête."'*

The sentence advanced thus has already programmed readings, exfoliated its futures. If we did not read against right-mindedness and straight thinking we would not see where the poetic task of binding the language to a horizon other than that of representing what already is and has been conceived is being fulfilled. The play of the letter is where meaning breaks down. But it is also where meanings, the pages of the book to be read by the generation, are assembled and folded in. Or, as Mallarmé puts it, "Le sens enseveli se meut et dispose, en choeur, des feuillets" (Buried meaning moves and disposes, in a chorus, the leaves) (p. 372).

With the *jarret*, Mallarmé provides a view of history that is not linear or marked by continuous progress. It proceeds by way of disruptive pauses, when a literature that is not reducible to a fiction totalized in a form hears its call, makes its brief appearance only to veil itself. Political action, in such a view of history, does not consist only in activism or even essentially in thinking the conditions for action. It can also consist in a responsible inquiry into the poetic, technical side of language. On the one side, the poetic sentence disrupted the meaning function, carrying away the old order of representation, and stalling us on language as excessiveness. It let us think, for instance, about new classes of action, and about the need for rules to regulate such classes unrecognized by institutions built under the sway of the idealizing fist. Then it swept away the consideration of political economy and stalled us instead in front of sheer technical display that is not without meaning for the political.

On the other side of the break, it re-bound the language, in the little unwinding sentence of *j'arrête*, toward meaning. It brought writing on stage to disappear, because as it disappears, it reinstalls orders to read.

Those orders, which we are calling the orders of the garter, are the futures of the text. Its futures: where its writing will have been being assimilated. In this text, one of those futures is of a political life not bounded by the limits of nationalism and the national language, instantiated here by the connections between English and French. This is where we are today, in the reading of "L'Action restreinte."

PART TWO

Memories of the Poem:
Histories, Chances

The reader will judge if this heap of stones comes from
a ruined monument or a building under construction.
—Hugo, "The Heap of Stones"

§ 3 Cracking the Code:
The Poetical and Political Legacy
of Chénier's "Antique Verse"

André Chénier left a legacy in two parts: a fragmentary, unfinished, and unpublished poetic work; and some published articles on political topics that were no doubt partially responsible for his meeting his death on the scaffold during the Terror. What kind of double legacy is this to hand down?

Because the poetic work was left unpublished, because the political works were published to such dramatic effect, the question has a peculiar immediacy. The first task of editors in preparing Chenier's manuscripts for publication has been to provide the poetic work the polish that it lacks, thereby making it inseparable from the history of its reception.[1] The political works, on their side, have also posed a problem. Strongly argued, passionate reflections on issues ranging from partisan spirit and the constitution to the National Assembly and the trial of Louis XVI, the political articles are topical enough pieces of journalism to have provided a battleground for the ideological disputes over the inheritance of the French Revolution and the Terror.[2] Critics have tended to seek to determine by their means whether Chénier was guilty as charged of being an "enemy of the people," or whether the libertarian and antipartisan sentiment he expressed in his political writings was not, on the contrary, closest to the spirit in which the Revolution was undertaken.[3] The existence of these two parts to the legacy has led to a third area of difficulty: the apparently innocuous decisions made by editors about the shape of the poetic work are suspiciously ideological, while the ideological battles tend to get translated into such questions as whether poetry makes a good weapon in the war of ideologies, or ought rather to exist in retreat from political questions, whether Chénier mistakenly conceived of the poet as warrior and legislator, and so on.[4]

The two parts to Chénier's legacy raise a question: Can they be thought together, despite differences in formal treatment, degree of completion, status of publication, or audience addressed? Ought they to be thought separately, despite those places where the literary and the political can be made to share a common definition—as mode of action on a public, as the products of a single intention, as leading to indeterminable effects? The *Essai sur les causes et les effets de la perfection et de la décadence dans les lettres et les arts*,[5] where Chénier traces together in a fictional genealogy the degeneration of literature and of republican political institutions, is the central theoretical text where the question is addressed, as the political writings are the place where it is given its most clearly pragmatic turn.[6] But it is in the unfinished epics, above all in *Hermès*, where is told the history of mankind with respect to the law, that the theoretical possibility of defining the literary and the political "so that they agree with or else exclude one another,"[7] and the practical necessity of deciding on a given occasion which definition is to be preferred, come together. It is thus in that epic that we can best discover the principles that divide, and bring together, the two sides of the legacy.

Now it is a peculiarity of Chénier's poetical legacy, named as the chief offering of *Hermès*, that it is no whole cup of poetry he hands us, but a cracked and fragmentary vessel. Why is the poetical work so fragmentary and what do its perceptible cracks have to say about the political? The question has been obscured by the assumption that Chénier embraced unproblematically the political and aesthetic models of the Greco-Roman tradition. The fragmentariness of the work has been considered exclusively in this light, without taking into account Chénier's interest in the Orient, and without considering whether his fragments might not lie outside, or border on, the ideals of the Western tradition.[8] A digression into the fragmentariness of the poetical works is thus required.

A peculiar set of conditions—Chénier's premature death, his disorderly method of composition,[9] and his transitional position between the neoclassicism of the late eighteenth century and the Romanticism of the nineteenth—have provided critics with ample material for speculation. Many pages have been written that attempt to fill in the gaps and to produce a continuous narrative: how Chénier would have developed had he survived the events of the Terror,[10] how he would have knit together the fragments jotted down in his notebooks for publication, how he would have negotiated the transition from the didactic philosophical poems of the eighteenth century to the lyrical voice of the Romantics.[11] Common to the general run of these stories is an implicit reproach directed at the poet for having failed so signally to provide his poems with the autonomy and aesthetic perfection we expect from the miniature totality that is the work of art.

We may ask whether the work is not complete as stands. Does Chénier pass on to us, for reasons laid down in the work, a lack of polish that he finds to be the polish of poetry?[12] The specific finish to be given poetry is addressed explicitly in various places, among others, in Chénier's much-celebrated and misunderstood definition of the task of poetry from *L'Invention*: "Sur des pensers nouveaux faisons des vers antiques" (On new thoughts let us make antique verse) (p. 127).

The central difficulty of the line centers on its articulation of incongruous terms—"new thoughts" and "antique verse." Where we might expect a relationship of simple contrast—old or ancient opposed to new or modern—we get a different, puzzling articulation between language and thought: the task of poets is to give us antique, that is, outdated, verse on new thoughts. *Ancient* connotes a continuity between present and past, either within a single existing being, or within a tradition, but *antique* names the no longer extant, the untimely. It marks a rupture with a continuous narrative joining present to past.

Much of the interpretative effort that has been expended on Chénier has consisted in translating articulations like this one into oppositions, and then reading Chénier's definition of the poet's task as that of overcoming the opposition by the discovery of metaphors expressive of a larger totality. Had "new thought" been opposed to "old form" then the thesis of Francis Scarfe would be correct, and the "central problem of *L'Invention* (might) be reduced to the paradox: imitate the Ancients but dare to be new and original."[13] For Scarfe, the author of a very respectable literary biography on Chénier, the poet stands opposed to his age around the issue of metaphor, which he sees as no mere ornament or poetic vehicle for expressing the thought of Enlightenment philosophy, but rather as the sensuous form in which the imagination reveals itself. Scarfe finds evidence that Chénier is an early Romantic poet and theorist of the lyric imagination in *L'Invention*, where invention is said to be the art of knotting things together in metaphors: "in the arts the inventor is he / . . . Who, by certain knots, unforeseen and new, / Unites objects that seemed rivals" (p. 124). That Chénier only two lines previously defines the other half of the poet's task as the critical one of separating what old metaphors have assembled, of making peaceful "rival seeds" (p. 124) by undoing false resemblances, seems to have escaped Scarfe, who has nothing but scorn for the threads of materialism and critical thought that tie the poet to his age. Scarfe's thesis comes to grief somewhere between the Scylla of the evidence available and the Charybdis of the evidence lacking. If the same poem, *L'Invention*, where Chénier supposedly gives his theory of a poetry of lyric expression, turns out to be, as Scarfe bad-humoredly states, "a piecemeal composition which does not logically hold together,"[14] one has to wonder whether the failure is not in the account of the poetic theory, rather than in the poem. Nor is it particularly convincing to be told, faced with the formulation "On new thoughts let us make antique verse," that for Chénier, originality lies "in perceiving hitherto unknown analogies and in giving them new expression."[15] Had the poet meant to say the opposite of what he did say, he would no doubt have said it.

A brief article by Paul Van Tieghem, "Un 'Monsieur' mystérieux: André Chénier," provides a more complex and theoretically informed understanding of the line, that it still translates into a binary opposition:

> Chénier possesses to a rare degree that faculty of splitting oneself that allows one to be almost simultaneously creative artist and critic attentive to grasping in advance the effect that the work, seen in a manner from the outside, will produce when it will have been finished. The continual seesaw motion that we observe in his works between the practice and theory of his art can be explained by this. One could almost say that he is always in front of two pieces of paper; onto one he throws his poetic projects, onto the other he writes the general reflections that these same projects inspire in him, he notes the reactions that the work of art makes the philosopher conceive.[16]

Van Tieghem splits off a projective, inventive writer, a Homer who does not clearly envisage the questions to which he unwittingly provides answers, from a reflective, critical writer, whose belated position with respect to the text allows the discovery of things ignored by the inventive writer. The capacity of the poet to act as reader of his own work—to uncover its foresightedness and its shortsightedness—turns the poet into a theorist analyzing the failures and successes of his original project.[17]

Now Van Tieghem's direct interest here is in explaining why Chénier was haunted by the unfinished work. The critical position of the modern involves, for Van Tieghem, a theory of the fragment. A critic is able to see in retrospect what is missing from the legacy of the past, and in his belated, self-conscious commentary will seek to compensate for the failure to achieve the totalization aimed at. In the most literal sense, this is the position of the eighteenth-century observer who considers the monuments of the past from the perspective of a Winckelmann or a Warburton. He has to take into account a discrepancy between the avowed aim of transmitting formally perfect entities, symbolic works of art, and the fragments or ruins that constitute the actual legacy of the past. The new thought Chénier wants to translate into his fragments is a thought concerning the material conditions of the production and transmission of the works of the past.[18]

In the last analysis, of course, the critical posture of the modern restores the symbolic model criticized. The opposition to symbolic writing is a negative moment quickly subsumed by a larger resemblance to it. A new-made fragment, however self-consciously it distances itself from a naive harmony between form and idea, necessarily reinstates a similar harmony, for the fragment then becomes the form adequately expressing the thought of modernity; it, too, "paints the spirit to the senses" (p. 126), although the spirit in question, the spirit of Enlightenment, becomes critical and materialist. One might legitimately say of this scheme what de Man, in his article on Benjamin's "The Task of the Translator," says of Gadamer's: It is "the scheme or concept of modernity as the overcoming of a certain awareness or naiveté by means of a critical negation."[19] In Van Tieghem's view, Chénier still concerns himself with "*finishing* some little part,"[20] with composing some perfect fragment exhibiting all the autonomy and aesthetic detachment of the masterpieces of the Greeks.

The more rigorous formulations of Lacoue-Labarthe and Nancy in *L'Absolu littéraire* give the stakes of this view for literary history. They explain that the "romantic fragment, far from bringing into play the dispersal or bursting apart of the work, inscribes its plurality as the exergue of the total, infinite work."[21] The fragment supplies the critical perspective missing from classicism. But it also points forward to Romanticism by its "fundamental theme of finishing"[22] and by its promise of future works to be written in the perspective of a dialectic of becoming. The characteristic path of the Romantic work—the development of consciousness as it projects itself outward into the visible world, and then bends back onto itself to critique its prior, naive understanding—is already implicit in the self-conscious fragment for Nancy and Lacoue-Labarthe. They state that the "fragment . . . completes and incompletes (*achève et inachève*) at once the dialectic of completion and incompletion (*de l'achèvement et de l'inachèvement*)."[23] It proves an unstable form pregnant with the promise of a Romanticism that will have fully incorporated into itself the whole history of the development from the Greeks to the Enlightenment as a coming-into-consciousness of modernity.

At least one of Chénier's readers saw him as a Moses looking over into just such a promised land. Victor Hugo suggests that Chénier's oddly cut lines and his neoclassical brittleness of diction contain the seeds for a perfecting of poetry:

> A new poetry has just been born. . . . This incorrect and sometimes barbarous style, these vague and incoherent ideas, this effervescence of imagination, tumultuous dreams of a wakening talent; this mania for mutilating the sentence and, so to speak for carving it *à la Grecque*; the words derived from ancient languages employed in all the breadth of their original acceptance; these strange cuts, etc. Each of these defects of the poet is perhaps the seed of a perfecting for poetry. In any case, these defects are not at all dangerous, and it is a question of rendering justice to a man who did not enjoy his glory. Who would dare reproach his imperfections while the revolutionary axe lies still bloody in the midst of his unfinished works? (5/1: 78–79)

For Hugo, the fragment does indeed constitute a transitional entity. Its very failures and imperfections show a way, prove replete with a promise to Romantic poetry of an inexhaustible development.

Despite surface differences, Hugo and Van Tieghem share a common vision of how the poetic legacy works to establish a coherent historical picture. As a seed develops into a tree, so a young man with his audacious and incoherent dreams develops into a maturer, more critical thinker. As a father hands on to a son in an unbroken line the findings of the past which the son has to turn against, in order to constitute himself an inventive father, so the works of the Moderns in the domain of poetry can be said to derive from those of the Ancients, insofar as they first criticize and then extend metaphor to cover larger narrative sequences.

Hugo notes, however, that Chénier's work was interrupted previous to his having become the promised poet of becoming. Further, he puts his finger squarely on a problem. What Chénier's unfinished texts actually offer is a translation between two languages: one, the untimely writing of "antique verse," at once barbarous, tumultuous and mutilated, dead, obsolete; the other, the polished, living, and expressive language of French. Chénier is less interested in breathing new life into past models or in establishing his poetic filiation, than in carrying forward into modern French the features of inscription: its unnatural inversions and incisions, its sculpted stoniness, its mutilated, fragmentary state. Hugo's understanding of Chénier's art as an art of translation between dead and living languages corresponds to what the poet himself says of it. In the unfinished epic *Hermès*, the poet envisions that his poem will offer itself in a "new world" as an "antique writing and no longer a language" (p. 405). The poetic legacy opens onto a new land insofar as its own language has become unusable as language. *Hermès* bequeathes to future sages "thinking lines," "powdery, half-eaten, obscure" (p. 405) that do not claim that it is poetry's chief task to communicate spontaneous or reflected emotion. An emphatic, if puzzling, refusal of the expressive Romantic voice distinguishes *Hermès*.[24]

What does the translation into living language of a language of inscription have to offer? One offering is clearly knowledge of a dead aspect of language that tends to get overlooked when it is considered a means of communication. The fragmentariness of the work derives partly from Chénier's perception of a discrepancy within language between what humans mean by it and what it actually says, its codified, systematic, and inhuman features, of the sort that a future sage who cannot understand what a writing means could nonetheless discern. Antique verse offers knowledge of code as it survives the death of meaning. But the struggle to translate inscriptional features into the living language of French is also productive. It arrives in some unnamed, featureless "new land," which is its other offering. It opens onto something. Both of these offerings are hinted at by the preposition that articulates the relation between new thought and antique verse. Poetry is not new thoughts expressed *in* the form of antique verse, as the traditional topos would have it. Poetry is antique verse *on* new thoughts. Two distinct metaphors are suggested here. On a new foundation, on the underlying ground or sustaining surface of new thought is to be erected the edifice of antique verse. The new thought is (of) the condition or sustaining surface. The task is to discover or invent. The other metaphor that comes to mind is very different. Antique verse rises on new thoughts as a heap of stones is piled up to mark a grave. The new thought lies buried under rubble; a radical loss of meaning has taken place; antique verse records, stands for a lost expressive voice, and keeps on standing past it. The task is to warn that the code is not subject to the same laws of progress, perfectibility, becoming, as human thought.

In *Hermès*, the question of code—system of laws, collection of rules and conventions, dictionary of equivalent terms (specifically, between a natural and an arbitrary language)—also explains the conjugation of the literary with the political. Of concern to poet and lawmaker alike is the instituting of signs in a code meaningful to an interpretative community and transmissible to posterity. Potential failures of meaning, breakdowns in transmission, interest both as well. From the perspective of the active establishing of rules governing the interpretation of a code, as from the perspective of the failure of an interpretation to be handed down intact, politics and poetics lie roughly within the same domain. In the second song of *Hermès*, Chénier seeks out the common precondition for the establishing of codes and for their conservation. The condition for invention in arts, sciences, and statecraft, he says, is writing, conceived as active, primary art. The condition for conserving and progressing in them is also writing, but a writing relegated to a secondary position as means of preservation and transmission of the other arts:

> Avant que des Etats la base fût constante,
> Avant que de pouvoir à pas mieux assurés
> Des sciences, des arts monter quelques degrés,
> Du temps et du besoin l'inévitable empire
> Dut avoir aux humains enseigné l'art d'écrire.
> D'autres arts l'ont poli; mais aux arts, le premier,
> Lui seul des vrais succès put ouvrir le sentier.

> Before the States' basis was constant,
> Before being able with pace more assured
> In the sciences, in the arts to climb several steps,
> Of time and need the inevitable empire
> Had to have taught to humans the art of writing.
> Other arts have polished it; but to arts, the first,
> It alone to true success could open the path.

> *(p. 394)*

So begins the dense fragment that traces the fictional development of writing in conjunction with the development of political institutions. The discovery of political institutions goes hand in hand with the seizing and fixing of the writing code. In the beginning, writing is the primary art, subordinate only to reason. It is the art that opens the path for the steady progress of other arts, including that of government. Writing is active in helping thought:

> Une main éloquente, avec cet art divin
> Tient, *fait voir* l'invisible et rapide pensée,
> L'abstraite intelligence et palpable et tracée;
> Peint des sons à nos yeux, et transmet à la fois
> Une voix aux couleurs, des couleurs à la voix.

> An eloquent hand, by this divine art
> Holds, *makes seen* invisible and rapid thought,
> Abstract intelligence both palpable and traced;
> Paints sounds to our eyes, and at the same time transmits
> A voice to colors, colors to the voice. *(p. 394)*

Writing manifests and fixes the invisible and unstable. As the poet tells the story of how Hermes' gift of writing develops, he will show that institutions take shape at each stage by way of an increasingly complex interpretation of the writing code. Beginning with a contractual model in which writing testifies to treaties between individuals, political entities will be discovered that regulate exchanges among larger and more far-flung groups.[25] Each new institution establishes itself by discerning and elaborating new patterns to which meaning is assigned; each one sheds light on sign relationships previously obscure.

Modernity, Chénier will further suggest, needs to be reminded of this because in one of the stages in the seizing of the writing system, the active capacity to make thought visible that writing has on the "page of Egypt" (p. 394) is covered over, and it gets conventionally determined as a transparent, faithful, and enduring repository for "our souls and customs" (p. 395). The passage just quoted already foresees this reversal: at first writing opens the trail for arts, sciences, and statecraft. Later, it loses its primary status and becomes a secondary art polished by other arts; it conserves what has already been discovered, in keeping with its other function as memorandum: "Une main éloquente . . . *Tient* . . . l'invisible et rapide pensée" (An eloquent hand . . . *Holds* . . . invisible and rapid thought) (p. 394). The stage at which writing gets irrevocably determined as window glass or shiny mirror in Chénier's fiction is the stage during which the phonetic alphabet is discovered and writing becomes subservient to spoken language. It corresponds to the opening of the Classical era. Along with the invention of a Western Greece will come the foundation of a stable state, the development of the arts and sciences, the beginning of man, and the reorientation of the world, now a Western world that has forgotten its oriental cradle, along a north-south axis. But it has to be borne in mind that the turn that makes writing the subsidiary of other arts is not the only way that written signs work. It is, simply put, the one that has had currency in the Western tradition as it has been handed down to us.

Poetry has a certain role in the civilization so organized, and one that can be easily surmised from the line just quoted. In the late stages, when writing has been relegated to a secondary role, poetry bears the memory of, and partly takes over, its role as maker. The evidence for this comes from an anagram that exerts an extra pressure on the line and makes it stand out as having a poetic and not just a meaning function, as a formalism potentially threatening or promising. The word for hand, *main*, stands out as rhyming internally with *humains*, appearing two lines before, as the first in a series of hands evoking the human producers of laws, monuments, and so forth.[26] In the line "une *main* éloquente . . . *tient*" this rhyme word calls the attention away from the literal meaning of the figure to the larger context where the discussion is about the possibility of handing down a tradition or a set of laws intact, and to itself as bringing together *as* sundered the parts of the verb *maintenir*. We are left to speculate on the cause of this anagram: Is it through a willful anachronism, with the poet seeking to remind us of the primitive elements out of which the language will have developed? Or is it another kind of reminder, an eruptive anticipatory recollection that casts us forward to a future when the hope of conservation and even the term *maintain* will have been lost, and the parts of the word will have been scattered again? In any event, the poetic function breaks with the unchanging present assumed as the horizon of speech, and requires us to consider a history affecting the means, writing, that we often consider as unbreakable vessel conserving the past and promising a future. The poetic function actively reminds of a historical dimension to the writing system in *Hermès*.

It would be easy enough to construe the disruptiveness of the poetic function as local, and as ultimately recuperable in a narrative of reason's progress. That Chénier envisions the possibility of such recuperation is clear enough from the subservience of the eloquent hand in all its doings to "thought, / Abstract intelligence." However, once the poetic function has come into play and begun to produce excessive readings, it is hard to put a stop to it. The line we have been discussing can also be read in a way that is exorbitant with respect to the narrative of reason itself. We have been reading "thought" as the object of the causative *fait voir*, and have assumed an ellipsis, with an implied human as the being made to see thought by writing. Writing makes thought perceptible to us, its implied perceivers. But the sentence need contain no ellipsis if we read it along the model of "je ferai venir cet enfant" (I will make this child come) or—to take the closer case of what a doctor lifting the cataracts of one of Diderot's blind might boast—"je ferai voir cet aveugle" (I will make that blind person see). "Thought" may well be the object of *faire*, and the subject of *voir*. The meaning of the sentence would be "Writing makes reason see, endows it with sight." Bestowing eyes on abstract intelligence is the sort of thing a poet or fiction maker might do. Such a gift must lie outside reason's narrative, since it is a metaphor that allows reason to be construed as in progress toward full enlightenment. It is neither serviceable nor unserviceable to that narrative, but is rather the condition for its being told. Evoked here is a potential of the eloquent hand to shower us with similar gifts, to endow abstract intelligence with a palpable body, sound with visibility, color with audibility, and so forth. The poetic function offers a gift that at once exceeds thought and permits it to be construed as vision. Without being in the least bit a politicized language in the narrow sense, the poem gifts thought with eyes as what opens the rationalized and visible space of the polis.

The eloquent hand always both "holds and makes seen"; it is only by forgetting that its two operations are equiprimordial that it is determined primarily as holding, secondarily as manifesting. There is something to be gained by this determination, since it enables the history of other arts to unfold as a continuous, steady progression along a path. But at no moment does writing lose its double force. Its manifesting and endowing activity may be neglected or banalized; writing does not, however, lose this activity. The continuous history that determination of writing as secondary enables can be disrupted by writing's inventive, positing force.

The reverse is also true. The activity of the hand making thought visible and even sightful can always undergo alteration. The hand may take on the aspect of a static, holding hand conserving tradition. Under certain circumstances, it can appear as a stranglehold, an oppressive hand arresting thought, holding it to a certain configuration and a certain set of possibilities programmed by the grounding fiction. A quick look at Chénier's description of the development of hieroglyphic writing shows that the Egyptians *for us* are always nothing more than the once inventive, now unintelligible writing they left. To themselves, however, the Egyptians were much closer to being Greeks.[27] We have a compelling reason for reading their "antique writing," for their history shows they were unaware of how their writing was rendering itself antique; their story may shadow our own.

1. De là, dans l'Orient ces colonnes savantes,
   Rois, prêtres, animaux, peints en scènes vivantes,
   De la religion ténébreux monuments,
   Pour les sages futurs laborieux tourments,
2. Archives de l'État, où les mains politiques
   Traçaient en longs tableaux les annales publiques.
3. De là, dans un amas d'emblèmes capiteux,
   Pour le peuple ignorant monstres religieux,
   Des membres ennemis vont composer ensemble
   Un seul tout, étonné du noeud qui le rassemble;
   Un corps de femme au front d'un aigle enfant des airs
   Joint l'écaille et les flancs d'un habitant des mers.
4. Cet art simple et grossier nous a suffi peut-être
   Tant que tous nos discours n'ont su voir ni connaître
   Que les objets présents dans la nature épars,
   Et que tout notre esprit était dans nos regards.
   Mais on vit, quand vers l'homme on apprit à descendre,
   Quand il fallut fixer, nommer, écrire, entendre,
   Du coeur, des passions les plus secrets détours,
   Les espaces du temps ou plus longs ou plus courts,
   Quel cercle étroit bornait cette antique écriture.
5. Plus on y mit de soins, plus incertaine, obscure,
   Du sens confus et vague elle épaissit la nuit.

1. Thence, in the Orient those knowing columns,
   Kings, priests, animals, painted in living scenes,
   Of religion somber monuments,
   For future sages laborious torments,
2. Archives of the State, where political hands
   Traced in long pictures the public annals.
3. Thence, in a heap of heady emblems,
   For the ignorant people religious monsters,
   Enemy members will compose together
   A single whole, astonished at the knot that reassembles it;
   A body of woman with the forehead of an eagle child of air
   Joins the scale and the flanks of an inhabitant of the sea.
4. This simple and crude art sufficed us perhaps
   So long as all our discourses knew not how to see and know
   More than present objects scattered in nature.
   But one saw, when toward man one learned to descend,
   When it was necessary to fix, to name, to write, to hear,
   Of the heart, of the passions the most secret detours,
   The spaces of time either longer or shorter,
   What a narrow circle confined this antique writing.
5. The more pains one took with it, the more uncertain, obscure,
   Of meaning confused and vague it thickened the night.

(p. 395)

Five stages in an interpretation by a tormented future sage (indicated by the numbers placed in the margins) are sketched out around the inscriptions. In the first stage, the obelisks are considered as religious monuments, whose hieroglyphs are read as pointing toward a metaphysics. In the second, the knowing columns are called archives of the state on which a history has been written. Next, they are considered as a ruin, a heap of heady emblems, from which one is chosen to explain in a metacode the composition of the code. Fourth, the whole of the Egyptian code is compared to a living language having the power to express man's inner world. And finally, Egyptian writing is determined to be a nonlanguage, an unintelligible writing, whose law of becoming is not that of progressive enlightenment, but of becoming-more-obscure.

At each stage in the seizing of the hieroglyphs, a double movement can be discerned. On the one hand, the logic is of invention and destruction: a new institutionalization takes place that involves the partial ruin of an old system. The fixing and destroying work is most apparent in the first three stages of the passage, where the knowing columns are first called "monuments of religion," then "archives of the state," then "a heap of heady emblems." By the last two stages, where the destruction of the language as living language is imminent, and where the interpretative voice weighs in as paramount, the instituting signs regulating the interpretation have become verbal colossi like man, nature, the heart, spaces of time, or certainty and clarity.

On the other hand, the logic that regulates the development of each system from the inside, as a system of meaning, is that of polishing, in its twin sense of perfecting and wearing away.[28] Each new interpretation takes into account something left out or obscure in the earlier system. It enables a larger set of exchanges, and is addressed to a larger group. The heads of state and religion in the first scene give way to representative members of the polis at work, "political hands" tracing. By the third stage, a whole mass—the people—are involved, which soon gives way to "us," men and women of the present who judge the Egyptians as lesser versions of ourselves, and then to "one," a pronoun large enough to include both the "us" who came after them, and them, the third-person Egyptians. The wider audience is found at the price of erasures: the vivid scenes of living beings—kings, priests, and animals—are effaced in the second scene to leave "long pictures." By the third stage reference is uncertain. In the fourth and fifth stages, past referents like the state, man, or metaphysical beings are denied by the interpreter, who then asserts the writing to be meaningless.

The twin logic made visible in Egyptian writing knits together writing as inventive—be it as positing or destroying—and writing as the polishing art useful to reasonable people—as perfecting and wearing away.[29] At each stage, the doubleness of the hieroglyphs—they are both pictures and characters, as Warburton informs us—gets stabilized by the erect columns into a totalizing interpretation, implying a unified interpretative community around it. On closer view, however, a discrepancy or obscurity, entailing a new interpretation, shows up in the very signs—the knowing columns—that fix the code. As the passage progresses, instead of a wider interpretative system managing to overcome the doubleness, it keeps on migrating somewhere else and getting harder to master. By the fifth and final stage, not only has the elucidating process led to total obscurity, as night falls on the Egyptians, but the doubleness spills over into the comments of the interpretative voice itself. The final lines, with their difficult inversion, tell us that this antique writing both thickens the night *of* meaning (*elle épaissit la nuit du sens*), that is, the writing has become unintelligible, and thickens the night *with* meaning (*elle épaissit du sens la nuit*), that is, the folds of the curtain falling and thus unintelligibility itself are thick with significance. This interplay is worth a closer look, because the features of Egyptian writing are translated into the language of the interpreter, making the story into an allegory for a French present.

The problem in the code's development lies chiefly in the signs that institute—the erect columns—and that are not regulated by the interpretative system they set up. They have to lie outside the system that holds sway at any stage in order to establish it; but because they are themselves double (grounding and ruined) and are not regulated by the system they establish, they can be toppled at any point. The first stages show most clearly that the columns lie outside the system they regulate: the obelisks are first called "somber monuments" and are then picked up again and elucidated as "archives" set up in an open, public space. The move from the religious to the political code entails a disclosure, a publication of the space defined by the obelisk that was dark in the first scene. The monuments of religion are pushed over, and in their place rise the secular archives of the state.

To understand the monuments, we have to look at the interpretative system they regulate. The monuments establish religious allegory as the way to decipher isolated picture-words: the living scenes are words that mean literally and properly the physical beings depicted, the kings, priests, and animals. Figuratively speaking, however, they mean metaphysical, otherworldly beings. A similar interpretation is at work in the accumulation of nouns and adjectives provided by the French speaker describing the columns. Each semantic unit has a proper, literal meaning but can also stand for an abstract entity—the priest for the spiritual, the king for the temporal, the animal for the physical world. Religion's monuments act to stabilize the doubleness of the hieroglyphs, their referential and figural capacity, into a hierarchy of meanings: first the proper meaning, then the figurative one.

But what about the monuments themselves? Are they signs having a literal, proper meaning or are they figures? As signs arbitrarily chosen to perpetuate the memory of the gods, they surely have a literal meaning, awarded to them by religion's decree. But the monuments of instituted religion have substituted for natural signs—"the august book and sacred letters" of nature mentioned a few lines above. They do not just stand for something, they also stand in, in the absence or loss of something. They commemorate the loss of the pantheistic gods. The articulating preposition, *de*, foregrounded in Chénier's line by inversion and sonorous repetition (*De là, dans l'Orient . . . De la religion*), is undecidable in the same way. It tells us that the monuments are the property of religion, which erects them to remember the gods. But it might also be that religion belongs to the monuments, that they are monuments *to* religion, reminding of its death. If the genitive is subjective, then religion has erected the monument. If objective, religion lies buried under it. The articulating preposition that tells us which is the proper term and which the extended one is undecidable. For the Egyptians living by the monuments, interpreting the hieroglyphs on their face, they are stable, enlightening. But there is an undecidability in the instituting sign that already imperils the monuments of religion and opens out onto the secular interpretation of the next scene. They have a dark side. Just so, the genitive repeats the gesture of stabilizing and destabilizing the property relation in Chénier's poem.

In the next stage the destabilizing sign from the first stage, the monument, is incorporated into the interpretative system and the columns move onto center stage as archives. Documentary writing, where signs serve to record, is the primary function of writing here. At this stage, writing is already alphabetic. Chénier follows Warburton, who suggests that the obscurity of picture words necessitated the invention of a conventional alphabet of hieroglyphs whose letters "express words, and not things."[30] Some picturing function is still discernible, but it is less important; the long pictures in which the annals are recorded also serve as symbols of the long-standingness of the state, of the duration of its continuous history. A hierarchy of sign systems gives the priority to documentary writing over fictional writing.

The primary feature of the interpretative system is that writing has become conventionally determined as a secondary art. Hieroglyphs are assigned to express the inventive signs of the earlier stage; verbal deeds, like other deeds, take place and then are written down, recorded. Much could be said about the space set up: it is a public space where men are considered with respect to their job functions and their roles in the state apparatus, where arts and strategies are being practised by crafty hands.

Once again, Chénier's lines translate the situation into French: a fully articulated grammar shows up in the relative clause describing the archives. One does not have to be a volitional subject to be the subject of a sentence; one does not have to perform any deed worth recording to be doing something in a sentence. In the place of meaningful subjects or deeds there is a subject-verb-object construction: "where political hands traced . . . annals." Roles, grammatical functions, have taken precedence over semantic units of meaning, much as the scribes' hands take a role in maintaining the state machinery.

But what of the archives? They establish a public space, a polis, which promises to last so long as records are kept. The archives themselves, however, are of another matter. They are material columns, and as such, are subject to a very different set of accidents than is the state. They can outlast it, as the obelisks have outlasted Egypt. They can fall into rubble before the Egyptian adventure is over, as they do in the next stage. Furthermore, as material signs, in excess of the "where" that they help institute, they are eminently appropriable into other contexts. They constitute a "where" of a very different sort than the "where" of a room or a square or a city. The adverb *where* (*où*) is the undecidable feature in Chénier's translation of the problem. As an adverb introducing a relative clause, it relates hands to the place indicated by the antecedent archives. Hands trace where there are archives, that is, inside the state. But *where* can also be an adverb meaning "there where, the place where." The phrase would then define where the archives are: "Archives of the state (are) there where political hands traced." In other words, the archives might not be the space within which scribes work; the scribes might be producing the archives wherever they leave material traces. The page is designated as archive; the state as an invention masterminded by secretaries.[31]

The crafty political hands, so modestly effacing themselves as mere recorders of deeds and reducing writing to a skill among others, are effectively the "doers" and "rulers" at this stage. What they are doing is actively repressing something. The sign system operative allows for the marking of local losses and posits a continuity transcending them, but it actively forgets that the promised continuity depends on the survival of the material columns and traces that constitute the archive. It represses the accidents and misappropriations to which the archive is subject. The excluded materiality of writing returns to organize the next scene—in the heap of rubble and the dream emblems composed out of dismembered body parts.

Before we turn to the emblem—which, as stage of assembly recounted in the present tense, turns out to be the crucial stage for understanding the lesson of the hieroglyphs for present-day institutions—a few summarizing remarks are in order. We have shown that instituting signs establish increasingly more complex systems of interpretation, with greater possibilities of exchange, at the price of some loss of expressiveness. But the columns lie outside the system they set up. They are always unsteady, subject to another set of evaluations and accidents, and may serve to undo the very system—however long-lasting—they have erected. The instituting signs construct and undo, they fix and crack the very codes they allow us to crack. The undecidability of the signs that institute has to be distinguished from the stability that reigns within the sign system instituted, however. The latter relies on a forgetting or repression of the instability of the articulating sign. That repression can be positively or negatively evaluated depending on whether one is faced with inventing institutions or maintaining those already found.

It is not necessarily a simple matter to know what kind of period one is in, however. In 1790, in *Avis au peuple français sur ses véritables ennemis,* Chénier will state that the period the nation is traversing is one of division and intense uncertainty; it is in the "interval that there must necessarily be between the end of the past and the beginning of the future" (p. 203). The uncertainty is over the question of whether the nation has entered into the enjoyment of rights already discovered, or whether the institutions that will establish them have yet to be grounded. In 1791, writing on the National Assembly's work on the constitution, Chénier suggests that the revolutionary moment is over, the new edifice in which people have to learn to live in peace has already been built. He warns the assembly against the dangers of continuing to act as if the house had not yet been constructed: "So long as the National Assembly lasts, the attentive people, seeing the hand that has destroyed everything and rebuilt everything always acting, will remain always in suspense and seem always to foresee some new thing. One only inhabits a house with security once the workers are no longer there" (p. 236).

In the same passage, however, he suggests that the state edifice cannot be said to be firmly grounded until people are convinced of its stability, and that the time of division and uncertainty cannot end until the constitution that will guarantee the people its rights has been written:

Among the causes that must make us wish ardently that the National Assembly, abandoning to future legislatures all that does not require its hand, will not lose an instant in finishing the constitution, and put an end to its immense work, the hope of seeing an end to all these parties, which tire us and deteriorate the public spirit, does not seem to me the least. . . . Then only will everyone, patriots and malcontents, be well convinced that the edifice is stable and firm. . . . Then only will it be possible for concord and peace to be reborn among us, as among our legislators. (p. 236)

The state edifice is built and requires only maintenance and polish; the peaceful state has not yet been firmly grounded in conviction.

The uncertainty that Chénier consistently sees as characterizing the Revolution has an analogue in the third stage of Egyptian writing. When we look to what the interpreter says of the emblem and its interpretation, we discover an open question as to whether any ruling interpretation has been set up at all. A whole has not yet been composed, it is to come: "Enemy members *will compose* together a single whole." But a means has also already been found to gather disparate pieces, in the "knot that reassembles." The knot has now to be maintained. The French commentator explains that interpreters of the emblem waver about its status in about the same way as the nation wavers over the status of the period it traverses. Among other features that suggest the stage as analogous to the uncertain 1790s is the use of a terminology of assembly and of parts. Throughout his brief career as political journalist, the National Assembly and partisan politics were Chénier's central preoccupation.

But if the emblem is a promising place to investigate what Chénier takes to be the stage in the development of the code France traversed during the Terror, it is also a singularly difficult place to do so. What kind of interpretative system is established by a "heap of heady emblems," which, at the very moment that it gives the code to the community, already stands as a ruined, undecipherable column? What is the code that allows the enigmatic emblem to be deciphered?

Warburton, from whose *Essai sur les hieroglyphes* Chénier has been borrowing heavily all along, provides a clue. The hieroglyph that Chénier describes resembles the figure accompanying paragraph 55 of the *Essai*, which is a figure of offering. It shows a woman with an eagle perched on her head, wearing a form-fitting dress of a crisscrossed design that is reminiscent of scales or tilework. She is offering a platter of

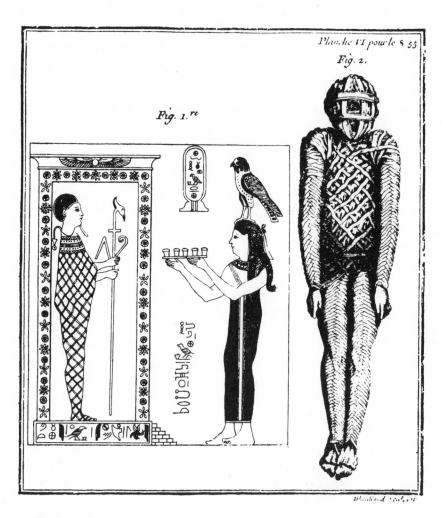

FIGURE I. *Hieroglyph of an offering and mummy in its first wrappings. The mixture of the diverse kinds of Egyptian writing described by Warburton can be seen in the hieroglyph. Warburton places the figure of a mummy alongside for the purposes of a comparison between its wrappings and the robe of the deity to whom the offering is addressed. From Aubier-Montaigne,* Essais sur les hiéroglyphes, *a 1977 update of an eighteenth-century translation of Warburton's* The Divine Legation of Moses Demonstrated *(1742).*

cups to an enframed male figure bearing a staff and swathed from neck to toe in a garment whose more loosely crossed bands Warburton shows to be like those of a mummy. The pedestal on which the male figure stands is covered with hieroglyphics, and there are also inscriptions above and below the platter offered by the female figure. Warburton explains that the hieroglyph manifests "a mixture of diverse kinds of Egyptian writing."[32]

Chénier's translation of the hieroglyph also recapitulates and brings into conjunction the two earlier stages of writing described in *Hermès*: the word-pictures of the first stage with their religious significance, and the words-standing-for-words of the second stage with their political function.[33] The emblem represents the stage in which a code as a dictionary of equivalents is being proposed that will allow for a maximum translatability between its diverse kinds of writing. It can be identified as a poetic composition for it talks about the sign system and how it signifies. However, just as the instituting signs of the earlier stages exceeded the interpretative field they set up, so does this offering exceed the intention of maximum translatability that informs it. Instead of providing maximum intelligibility for the diverse kinds of writing, the code starts to become fragmented and unintelligible. We register here, above all, a failure of interpreters to come to grips with the poetic emblem.

It is easy to see that the translation of the emblem assembles the diverse kinds of writing. On the one hand are brought together body parts, figures left over from the earlier stage when living pictures of physical creatures were the literal form in which to express abstract meaning. There are plenty of *disjecta membra* from physical beings of different provenance, remnants of picture writing. The eagle drifts down from the air, the flanks are the flotsam of a denizen of the sea, the woman's body dwells on the earth. The scale is possibly that of a fish or reptile, perhaps even the scale-like markings of an amphibious salamander who legendarily can live in fire. On the other hand, words that stand for words, the grammar and alphabet of documentary writing, are piled up here as well. The now conventionalized parts of a language are being assembled, as can be seen in the French sentence structures that repeat the earlier patterns. Thus the first clause of the emblem's description repeats the grammatical pattern of the earlier description of the monuments:

Monuments	Emblem
"De là, dans l'Orient . . ."	"De là, dans un amas . . ."
"Rois, prêtres, animaux, peints . . ."	"Un seul tout, étonné . . ."
"Pour les sages futurs laborieux tourments . . ."	"Pour le peuple ignorant, monstres religieux. . . ."

As for the juxtaposed second clause, it repeats the subject-verb-object pattern of the earlier description of the archives: "les mains politiques / Traçaient . . . les annales"; "Un corps de femme. . . . joint l'écaille." Evidence of structural work with a language can be found in other places as well. An alliterative chain links in the blah blah blah of the emblem an *aMas d'EMBLEMEs, Monstres reLigieux, MEMBres ennEMis, coMPoser ENsEMBLE, rassEMBLE,* that engenders and shades off into further strings, as, for example, the fricatives linking *Femme, Front, enFant, Flancs.* The principle, as it shows up in Chénier's French, is of reassembling language parts into collections where meaning is not the primary consideration. The emblem thus works as a book of words, a dictionary structured by principles that owe more to a grammar or an alphabet than to the representation of some being outside language.

But the emblem does not just assemble the diverse kinds of writing. It tries to make them translatable, to bring them together in a larger system that allows their deciphering. As a dictionary permits the exchange of one term against another across the whole terrain of the language, whatever the derivation of the individual terms, so the emblem tries to make all of the pieces derived from its earlier stages accessible, translatable into one another. It does so by providing a bridging term that brings different parts like picture words and conventional letters into conjunction with one another, as parts of a language construed as a whole, along the model of a body. The woman's body, we are told, *joins* the scale and flanks. Now the fish's flanks, as a region of the body, can substitute for the woman's thighs by likeness. As in the earlier stage of symbolic writing where pictures gave visible form to invisible beings being by way of resemblance, so can these flanks substitute for those of the woman. The scale, on the other hand, is not a body part but a covering bearing a mosaic-like motif of interlocking parts. It can represent conventionalized grammar, both because it figures a set of relationships and because it is a carapace, a covering. The scale, like the woman's dress in Warburton's figure, does not resemble the body; if it substitutes for it, it is by metonymy, as a conventional sign decreed to stand for another sign. With the scale, we are concerned with names and with artificial structures. The emblem thus brings together the two kinds of signs found in the earlier stages—the motivated and arbitrary, pictorial and alphabetic writing—and claims them as translatable by way of this larger figure, the body of the woman, which bridges the gap between them. It relates religious allegory and documentary writing and makes all the signs in the Egyptian writing system translatable. Whether the thighs are disclosed by way of a metaphorical transfer, or by metonymy, an indication of the dress of conventional language, it is the same thing. In both cases, a single signified, the woman's body, is disclosed. The larger figure articulates the two kinds of signs as exchangeable.

But what is the status of the larger figure and of the sign that carpenters the joint? The instituting sign that offers the dictionary is just another sign in the dictionary to which the key is needed. The emblem comments on this as well. The woman's body can join scale and flanks in a very different way. When one plank joins another, when an individual joins a group, when, a little further on, a new word enrolls itself in a regiment of other words, *joining* does not mean "making communicate." It means "enlistment, enrollment, enumeration." In this reading, the woman's body joins the heap as just one more heady emblem flung onto the others. The scale and the flanks and the forehead and the woman's body are so many unrelated terms. The emblem offers the code as a set of figures and conventional characters, translatable by recourse to a larger figure that says grammatical structure and figures are interchangeable because they all signify the "body of language." But, in the self-same terms, it also offers the writing system as a heap of names or letters to which access has been lost. The emblem, we can say, is *self*-fragmenting.

An enigma then arises as to the origin of the term, a woman's body, that bridges and does not bridge the gap between the two systems. The problem can be stated as follows. Does the larger figure that makes all signs translatable emerge, by chance, in the midst of a *list* of diverse kinds of writing? Or is a figure decreed in order to allow translation, which then turns out by bad luck, by a bad break as we say, to have already been altered, added to the list as another piece of language? The emblem speaks to the question earlier raised by the eloquent hand that maintains and bestows vision on thought. Instituted signs, letters, may have become inventive. Instituting signs may have been altered by an imperceptible temporal slippage into conventional signs. The crossing of terms shows that the emblem takes as its problem the undecidability of writing. It is suspended over the question of whether writing manifests itself as an active force capable of producing meaning independent of human intention, or whether it has always already altered its active force by virtue of its iterability. Because Chénier has been attributing agency throughout the section to the *hand* writing, rather than to human will, it is clear that he envisages the problem from the perspective of the laws of a *text* and not of expressive language.

The problem can be understood in visual terms, by reference to a mosaic, one of the etymological meanings of *emblem*. Structurally speaking, a mosaic is a network of tiles joined, as the planks in a floor, by blank spaces or articulating intervals. On the face of the tiles appears a figure, a picture delineated without concern for the design of the ground. The mosaic is somewhat like an anamorphic painting, in which a picture appears at the expense another. But it is unlike anamorphic painting in that one picture of a mosaic is most often a representational painting of a human scene, whereas the other is a geometric design. Furthermore, one never can quite erase the visible cracks running through the figure in a mosaic, nor quite forget about the parts of the human figure in examining the design. The other pattern is always interfering. One can crack one code, say that of the figure, only by neglecting the crackwork of the tiles, the structure of enumeration. As in a mosaic, in the emblem there is too much evidence of the other code's activity to remain with one as the prevailing pattern. It is impossible to say whether the emblem is constructed as an alphabet, from which a figure emerges by accident to gather all the terms, or as a figure, which is then added to the signs it is meant to translate as one more undecipherable piece.

The French interpreter comments on how the poetic emblem was received by its audience. The people who interpret the "heap of heady emblems" dwell in ignorance. In trying to understand the double aspect of the code offered by the emblem, one inevitably misunderstands it. The decisive move is the interpretation of the emblem in terms of interpretation, that is, in the attempt to understand where the suspension of meaning by listing comes from and what it means. People understand the irresolvable conflict over the emblem's origin as the expression of the essence of some divine author. The doubleness of the emblem is read as the representation of a hybrid god, a monstrous being ruling over the different elements. The various parts are made the moments of a mythic narrative of transformations (from the belly or flank of a fish, to the eagle, child of air, to the woman's body, to the dead scale of the mummy's bands) by which the god's essence as creator is revealed. The self-fragmenting fable about the emblem's undecidable origin is understood as a literal narrative revealing the nature of a divinity. The emblem is a figure for language, and it poses an open question about the way one of its terms joins others; the figure is taken as the proper, literal meaning of some monstrous creative force manifesting itself.

In a fragment attached to *Hermès*, Chénier comments on the propensity of a people to misinterpret the emblems and apologues of its sages as at the origin of positive religions: "Most fables were without a doubt the emblems and the apologues of sages. . . . It is thus that were made such and such dogmas, such and such Gods . . . mysteries . . . initiations. The people took as proper meaning what was said figuratively. . . . Origin of religious follies" (pp. 411–12). And later he notes, "this mania of believing that the Gods had their eye on all their little disputes, and that on the most frivolous occasions a miracle would come to violate the laws of nature" (p. 413).

People decide that some God-like author reveals itself in this undecidable text. The emblem does not know whether it originates in meaning or in enumeration. But it seems to be impossible, when one tries to understand it, not to decide that the suspension of meaning is the visible form of a thought.

Now within the ignorant people, there are actually two divergent sacrifices being made to the monstrous divinity. On the one hand, there is a sacrifice, discussed by Chénier in a political text called *Les Autels de la peur*, of thought to belief (p. 358). Thought tells us that we cannot tell whether someone means the figure to emerge, or whether it just emerges out of the spewing up of the words in the language. Belief tells us that the emblem means to tell us this. That is superstitious nonsense. It cannot be that some single author controls the effect of what is stated to be an uncontrollable machine.

On the other hand, another group of people, working within the same interpretative framework, but inflecting it differently, see a chance to chase after their individual interests and pleasures. Among the signs indicating this group are the terms ascribing human feeling to the empty verbal entity of the emblem: *heady, astonished*. This group can be said to make another kind of sacrifice to the God, which Chénier also names in *Les Autels de la peur*—the sacrifice of conscience, the moral faculty of judging action (p. 358). There are initiates into the mysteries of the God, knowledgeable people who understand that the larger figure may have been produced by an accident of structure. They treat the machine producing meaning as just machine, having nothing to do with human bodies or wills. Language is just language; one can play with it, exploit it for the power it provides.

The emblem asserts that texts always undecidably refer to the world and to language, undecidably offer a sage's understanding and offer things no sage could mean. But this group grasps the emblem as meaning "just language producing more language effects." They forget that the emblem provides only *one* figure from a heap for the way that the hand writing may *always* be working. The story shows that the grasp of the writing system is indissociable from the progress of institutions, as well as of the arts and sciences. To claim that this is just this language working to proliferate extra meaning is to deny that the machinery might be operative in those places which were of most concern for Chénier in writing the history of Hermes' gift, namely, in politics, religion, arts, and sciences. It is also a literalization to understand the figure for the monstrous text as just language play, since the play by now involves institutions, legal and religious codes, and so on. Chénier translates the technical manipulation of the textual machine into the prepositions of the emblem.

The prepositions do not merely relate semantic units into larger units of meaning; they also disarticulate and rearticulate them. Take the *de* that relates astonishment and knot as a subjective attitude toward an object of perception ("a single whole, astonished at the knot"). Besides functioning to relate parts, the *de* makes the line into a self-reflexive commentary on the potential of knotting prepositions to produce wholes out of unrelated parts. It can also relate these semantic units in a very different way, on which it provides a very different commentary, however. It can make the "single whole" into the object of an action for which the knot is the agent, thereby entirely changing the meaning of the adjective *astonished* to "cracking or splitting" (one of the significations of *étonner*). The phrase would then read "a single whole, cracked by the knot."[34] The preposition turns the sentence into a metacommentary on the capacity of knotting prepositions to fragment the wholes that it assembles. A whole surprised at the knot that makes it a whole trembles by the self-same knot. Or take another example among the many that could be found: the *au* that joins a woman's body, a forehead, and an eagle. The preposition gives us at least two separate figures: the woman's body *with* the forehead of an eagle and the woman's body *on* the forehead of an eagle. To this could be added another relation: because *au front* is the place of conflict between two enemy members, it can be read as a battle line, a front, the interval or line where a conflict over interpretations is joined.

The prepositions and joining intervals of the emblem are hyperactive. They seem to be producing and destroying meaningful structures. They seem to be acting to try to undo the figure, to point to its enumerative ground. But in fact, the hyperactivity is really a simulation of production and destruction: it looks like someone is offering further knowledge of the text as system, when in fact all we get is accumulated instances of how one can make purely relational, grammatical terms mean. The group of technicians just offers more parts to the monstrous divinity of which it can proleptically make sense. Prepositions are not pre-positional to meaning in the emblem; they do not undo the anthropomorphism whereby both grammar and figure are translated into meaning. They simply provide added instances of how meaning can be made of functional, grammatical relations; they simulate, as a technical operation simulates, the operation of the understanding. Nothing is happening here; nothing is getting destroyed, nothing is getting established. We are just watching busy hands simulate the work of construction and destruction in order to enjoy the power to make sense of everything that the anthropomorphism offers.[35] Drunken interpreters with stupefied faculties are more clued in about the artifice of writing, and the power that signs provide for making and undoing systems, but they are senseless of the danger clearly indicated by all the disarticulated body parts lying about. When the sage gives us the emblem as an allegory of textual undecidability, he does not give a religious code to live and make sense by, but a code to die by—in thought or in conscience.[36]

To understand textual allegory as a "negative theology," or as free play with a linguistic machine, is to misunderstand it. That is how the dead Egyptians understood the emblem; they knelt at the foot of what Chénier calls a "murderous idol" (p. 396).

The problem spills over into the metatext of the French interpreter as well, despite the comfortable distance of several thousand years from the text on which he comments. The body, the forehead, the scale, and the flank are joined by "heady" to form the larger figure of a "heady . . . body." Juxtaposition, abusive coupling, produces the larger figure here and makes the Egyptian text communicate with the French metatext. The Frenchman is commenting on the emblem, but his commentary adds a new part of which the emblem makes sense. We cannot say he means to do this, since what he tells us is that the textual machine can produce meaning out of random juxtapositions. We cannot say, however, that he does not mean this, since he also tells us that this machine can always be made to spin by any skilled technician with a grip on the mechanism. The beheading of the French interpreter, who starts to get confused with the dead Egyptians, is also figured by the text.

The text gets stuck in a machine-like mode when we try to interpret its inhuman conflict in mythico-religious terms, as pointing to divine intention. It just keeps on spitting up new parts that join to make larger figures, and that join in the list of mutilated parts. So long as one persists in thinking the inhuman way that texts engender meaning by random juxtaposition in terms of a negative theology or as the mere play of the signifier, one is stuck in this mode.

Chénier analyses the Terror as an epoch when people were trying to make like the Egyptians, that is, to translate into meaningful human terms the undecidability of texts. The period was characterized by an attempt to come to grips with a textual problem that it only managed to literalize. The French commentary hints at who is identifying itself with the monstrous god: the people, in whose name the Revolution was undertaken. *People* is a collective term for disparate members related by proximity; it is also a term that collects into a single whole, a body subjected to a single set of laws, a singular will. To understand a people as a body, we have to forget about disparate peoples and understand its enemy members as members of a collective body to which they are subject. The freedom of each individual member, however, depends upon each having the possibility of appropriating, in private, for his or her own interests, the machinery of the state. This is fairly straightforward Rousseauian contract theory and is a figure for the textual problem of a collective term. The Terror takes the figure literally: individual people keep getting sacrificed so that the will of the people as a whole can reappear, and individual people keep appropriating the mechanisms of power that the concept "will of the people" provides.[37] Chénier does not offer this textual allegory because he sits at the feet of the god Language and ignores "real" people, or because he takes pleasure in mere formal play. He offers it because texts always do offer such allegories, and because their misunderstanding in religious terms has consequences for "real" people.

The way Chénier conceives to begin to get the machine unstuck, given that anthropomorphism is a step that cannot be undone by interpretation, is to recall the enumerative possibility that is the ground for the figure. In the tale from *Hermès*, it is by enumeration of the unintelligible emblems, rather than by the attempt to understand them, that people topple the monstrous god and new discoveries are made: "Quelque peuple à la fin par le travail instruit / Compte combien de mots l'héréditaire usage / A transmis jusqu'à lui pour former un langage" (Some people at last by work instructed / Counts how many words hereditary usage / Has transmitted to it to form a language) (p. 394). A way of collecting numbers that is not totalizing also turns out to be the key to the political allegory with which the fragment ends:

> Le passé du présent est l'arbitre et le père,
> Le conduit par la main, l'encourage, l'éclaire.
> Les aïeux, les enfants, les arrière-neveux,
> Tous sont du même temps, ils ont les mêmes voeux.
> La patrie au milieu des embûches, des traîtres,
> Remonte en sa mémoire, a recours aux ancêtres,
> Cherche ce qu'ils feraient en un danger pareil,
> Et des siècles vieillis assemble le conseil.

> The past of the present is the arbiter and father,
> Conducts it by the hand, encourages it, enlightens it.
> Forefathers, children, grandnephews,
> All are of the same time, they have the same wishes.
> The fatherland in the midst of ambushes, of traitors,
> Goes back in its memory, has recourse to ancestors,
> Seeks what they would do in like danger,
> And of the centuries grown old assembles the counsel.

> *(p. 396)*

Take just one of the sententious statements that regulates the fatherland as it collects itself into a political unit: "The past of the present is the arbiter and father" (*Le passé du présent est l'arbitre et le père*). This commonplace works as a rule that gathers into one counsel, one piece of advice, and one representative group three distinct interpretations of the relation between present and past as a father-son relationship: (1) The past is the arbiter and father of the present, that is, the past invented the model that the present imitates. This is the way that French classicism understood Greece. (2) The past *of the present* is arbiter and father, that is, the past invented by, belonging to, the present, fathers. The French interpretation of Latinity as the inversion and satirizing of the Greek model is also represented. (3) The past of the present, by way of the ambiguous genitive, might also be the pastness that possesses the present, that makes it unintelligible to itself, that lives on in it, that obsesses it, that it cannot master. An Egyptian is also included on the counsel, as the forefather of the disjunction between action and meaning potentially repeated in the present. These are three interpretations of a single code, three ancestors seated in counsel.

But a fourth, and very different, translation can be found. The line actively asserts that the past is the arbiter and father, from the present, for the time being (*Du présent, le passé est l'arbitre et le père*). Other assemblies are possible, the rule being simply the way the present has decided to understand the relation. An exchange among sons of the advice given by Greek, Roman, and Egyptian ancestors is just the code by which, for the moment, things are to be interpreted. This reading of the rule is out of synch with the others and could not give rise to an interpretation or seat on the counsel. It is a rule that has to be respected for the counsel to come into existence to discuss which past is to father. To start to discuss it on the counsel is already to have shown the present, so defined, to be partly ruined, become past.

The rule thus shows a disjunction between the conserving statement that governs interpretation within the counsel, and the inventive, active writing that imposes the code on the present. The rule regulates the disjunction; for there to be a present, for the fatherland to appear, one has to forget about the arbitrariness of the inventive fiction. On the other hand, as a willful fiction, the rule enrolls itself on the list as an already-past rule that can be subverted by a critique recalling its fictional origins. The decree, "Let the past be arbiter, for the present" signs up as one in a series of other rules, now gone by.

Chénier's politics are not a party politics, however closely a passage like this one might seem to associate him with the constitutionalism of the moderate Feuillants. He is explaining that, for there to be a political space, and not a religious one, a violent imposition of a fiction has to take place and be forgotten. But he is also explaining that that fiction can always be shown to be a repressive fiction, an arbitrary and violent decision about an undecidable relation, and as such, can be subverted by recalling writing's materiality. The political emerges by way of undecidability, be it as a strategy for making use of undecidability to impose an interpretative law, or as a critique that recalls undecidability to topple worn-out fictions. The poet separates himself from the scribes of the second stage of Egyptian writing, the political hands who veiled the violence of the fiction regulating the state. Unlike the scribes, he has written his rule on the list of falling idols. Chénier the political thinker, concerned with peace inside the house, tells us that, for the fatherland to be convinced of its stability, it has to forget about the violence of the rule. But Chénier the poet is critical of the arbitrariness of such laws and sees them as idols already fallen. The fiction of humane familial relations drawing together pious sons in the fatherland is a mask for a machinery anything but humane. The political thinker is at his most revolutionary in his poems.

Two distinct reasons, both of which touch upon the political, emerge to explain why Chénier did not publish his fragmentary poetry. He may have wanted to cordon off the dangerous productivity of textual allegories. His understanding that people tend to read poetic language in mythico-religious terms, romantically, as translating formal structures and figures into single totalities expressive of a divine artist's intention, could very well be one reason for what amounts to an act of self-censorship. But there is another and perhaps more compelling reason. An invisible hand offers us poetry by a posthumous author; the "thinking lines" of his self-fragmenting "antique verse" never do appear as the lyric songs of a human author, but always as the legacy of writing itself. They cannot be thought as expressive, lyrical language; they are always thinking along the lines of the political.

§ 4 Hallucinatory History:
Hugo's *Révolution*

Readers of poetry and its criticism have long been accustomed to mixed reviews of its alleged autonomy. The lyric is generally the target here, although other poetic forms are also open to the charge of retreat from the public arena of history and politics. The loss of reference to empirical experience, deplored by some, has been felt by others to be a sacrifice made for gain: what poetry loses in concrete historical veracity, in attachment to a context, it makes up for by its achievement of the self-sufficiency and meaningful ideality of a fiction. What poems sacrifice in the way of a capacity to portray events or historical personages, they regain by depicting the human in all its generality.

Structuralist and poststructuralist critiques of the subject have modified this assessment somewhat. A theory of texts as self-reflexive structures has dispelled the illusion that poems represent a generalized, fictional self. In recent times, one tends to praise poetry for its undoing of ideal fictions, rather than for its production of them.

It is no doubt natural that, in the wake of the undoing of the self as the meaning of the lyric, critics should cast around for something to put in its place and should ask whether they had not been too hasty in accepting the poem's autonomy. Even a poem understood to forgo the representation of empirical experience can be considered in terms of a referent, for instance, as portraying a subject's wishful production of a self.[1] Poems do more than signify, they also refer. Words are not only interpretable figures, they are also signs that point. Some critics have therefore felt justified in asking whether, having passed through the bath of the theory of language as the locus of the poem's meaning, we cannot now place poems in a larger historical picture. In short, they have sought for poetry a place in a new historicism.

The return to questioning poetry as to its possible referent in experience has of course not meant the return to a literal referent provided by the author's biography or by a historical event. Instead, the self-reflexive language of poetry having been identified as the source of meaning and its undoing in the poem, it becomes possible to suggest that the referent of modern poems could be precisely the historical event of a change in the way that poets think about language and poetry, the event of the establishment of a new and more modern understanding of literature and literariness. A Foucauldian epistemic shift moves a poet away from the naive wish to polish language so it can prove the perfect mirror of the self, toward a more sophisticated understanding in which language, the stuff of poetry, stands revealed as multivalent, a structure always capable of saying more and less than the ideality of the unified self.

A historical thesis of this sort shows up in an admirable essay by Joel Fineman entitled "Shakespeare's Perjur'd Eye."[2] In the space of the slim volume of Shakespeare's *Sonnets*, Fineman finds two conflicting poetic practices that suggest to him just such an epistemic shift. Fineman explains:

> Shakespeare's sonnet sequence marks a decisive moment in the history of lyric, for when the dark lady sonnets forswear the ideally visionary poetics of the young man sonnets, when poetic language comes in this way to be characterized as something verbal, not visual, we see what happens to poetry when it gives over a perennial poetics of *ut pictura poesis* for . . . a poetics of *ut poesis poesis*, a transition that writes itself out in Shakespeare's sonnets as an unhappy progress from a poetry based on visual likeness . . . to a poetry based on verbal difference. (p. 71)

For Fineman, the visionary, idealizing poetics of the young man sonnets implies a metaphorical system based on vision in which sensuous form and idea have an adequate relation to one another, and poetic language is Cratylic, its signifiers and signifieds brought by the poet's craft into harmonious relation. In the dark lady sonnets, on the other hand, language is not the transparent language of pure visibility, but a verbal, performative language, full of artifices and duplicity, and one that, capable as it is of showing the idealism of the homogeneous vision-centered sonnets to be predicated on an illusion, has a life and force to be reckoned with. Language does not mirror without distorting; the ideal image is, upon closer examination, itself a distortion, since metaphor makes things that are in fact very different look alike. Shakespeare's sonnets thus serve Fineman as the index of a decisive move from a poetry that wants to reflect only the self and its self-sameness, to a poetry far shrewder about language as difference. That poetry, he claims, is the product of a subjectivity that has undergone alteration in its understanding of language and has recognized itself to be belated and historical. It takes only a little forcing to make the sonnet sequences—whose organizing principle is not necessarily that of a progressive narrative—into a bildungsroman ordered around a moment of conversion that entails an increased awareness in poetic consciousness.

Thus, the highly formalized construct that is the poem finds itself cleared of any charge of ahistoricity. Shakespeare's sonnets refer to the event of a change in consciousness within Shakespeare's history as poet, an event that marks the appearance of a new subjectivity (pp. 71–72) and that corresponds to a shift from the Elizabethan lyric, with its tired Petrarchan themes, to a more modern and sophisticated literature of belatedness. Fineman is then able, in a polemical move, to suggest that recent language-centered theories are an epiphenomenon, a coming-into-theoretical-consciousness of the crucial insight that Shakespeare had already figured in the dark lady sequence (pp. 78–79) as long ago as the Renaissance.

But to make the lady and her sexual difference stand for the difference of language is a decisive, stabilizing move on Fineman's part. On the one hand, it establishes the possibility of each poem or poem sequence operating autonomously as a system of meaning in which things as unlike as women and words can substitute for one another by way of a shared property—here, their difference. The dark lady is a figure within the sonnets for the language of the sonnets. On the other hand, it also establishes the possibility of reference for each poem or poem sequence, since a language known to be false can be a reliable vehicle for communication, at least about its own gainsaying (p. 77). The figure of the lady consoles us for the revelation that language is a lie by telling us that we can trust it at one point, at the point that it identifies itself as lie; we can know, in a word, when we are dealing with liars and literary language, and when not. What Fineman calls a second degree of Cratylism makes the signifiers of lying language correspond to their signified, the lie of language.[3] Any language that tells us that it lies reveals the truth about language and is literary. Any language that does not tell us about its lie lies with respect to itself, but we can then know it is not poetry and so does not mean to deceive us by what it says. In Fineman's interpretation, the figure of the dark lady thus consolidates and protects a distinction between a poetic space where the verbal nature of literary language is interrogated, and the public, historical space where language aims to represent the world as in a painting.[4]

But one can wonder whether poems (and poets) are as certain about the status of their language as Fineman wants them to be. The indeterminacy of texts touches on the impossibility of deciding whether a given use of language is a referential use or a self-referring one. One would expect poems to address this undecidability and the pressures exerted toward deciding it in their self-referential discussion of their language. To reanchor a poem too quickly in a context by a referential determination is to foreclose on the very place where poems could be speaking to the question of a historicity where undecidability has more play.

The question to be pursued in what follows, then, is the question of what poems have to say about the pressures in language toward reference and signification, as also what they have to say about their historicity. My example will be a poem by Victor Hugo that ostensibly, in its title, refers to the historical event of the French Revolution, an event credited by the idealist tradition of Kant and Hegel with having opened modern history as the actualization of the idea of history itself.[5]

The poem *La Révolution* dates from 1857 and was originally to have been included in a group called the *Petites épopées*, the little epics.[6] Reworked and expanded in 1870, shortly before Hugo's return to France, it was intended to figure in a collection called *Les Quatre vents de l'esprit*, as the single example of the epic spirit. The title—translatable as *The Revolution* or as *Revolution*—suggests that the poem will be about the famous revolution of 1789, or else about revolution in general.[7] But to all appearances, the poem takes neither tack. Instead, it seems a hallucinatory history. The first section, "Les Statues," recounts the coming to life of the equestrian statues of three French kings, which it follows as they trot through Paris. In the second section, "Les Cariatides," the poet apostrophizes the long-dead sculptor of the Pont-Neuf, and then sets down the spoken thoughts of that downtrodden bridge about the reigns of the kings. The third section, "L'Arrivée," concludes with a brief dialogue

concerning the meaning and authorship of the guillotine, a dialogue between the statues of the kings and the talking head of Louis XVI, which
floats by. An epilogue affirms that the outcome of all this delirium is
progress toward peace, harmony, and love. If the poem has a bearing on
the real Revolution, or on the reality of revolution in general, it is as a
hallucination relates to the real.[8]

A few preliminary remarks on the term *hallucinatory* are in order.
Hugo's hallucinations and his experiments with the occult during his exile are not at issue here. Riffaterre has already demonstrated that one need
not have recourse to Hugo's biography or psychology to understand the
hallucinatory effect of his poetry, which is a result of linguistic structures
and figures. I will not be attempting the description of those structures either. Riffaterre has already done so in *Essais de stylistique structurale*, in an
essay that—with its deliberate *parti pris* of formalist study—does however leave some room for an account of the issues hallucination raises for
consciousness and history.[9] Nor will I be seeking to establish a causal connection between the events of the French Revolution and a psychology,
be it of an individual revolutionary or of the Parisian masses.[10] The poem
does not support a crude causality of this sort. Finally, however tempting
it would be to explore *La Révolution* as a history written within a psychoanalytic framework, there are reasons for preferring to start with a less
subjective landscape. One reason for resisting psychoanalytic terms is that
it is entirely uncertain whether the poem presents itself as the description
of a hallucinatory vision or is rather the fiction of a hallucination, made
up to elucidate something else. One notion of what that something else
might be is provided by Foucault, in the essay on Deleuze called "The-
atrum Philosophicum," where he announces that "the philosophy of representation . . . is dissolving," and celebrates "the birth—re-birth—(of) a
'phantasmaphysics'."[11] Phantasm, for Foucault, is where the historian can
chase down the motley material forgotten when historical events are "reduced to accentuate their essential traits, their final meaning, or their initial and final value," instead of appearing as they are, "a profusion of entangled events."[12] For Foucault, a true historical sense has to attend to
"our existence among countless lost events, without a landmark or a
point of reference," and thus, among the hallucinations and phantasma
that testify to such lost events.[13] The historian starts by recalling the
phantasm, not as revelatory of a particular subject's lost past, but as revelatory of the lost pasts of the event. To become conscious of hallucination

is to become conscious of an experience of language that provides events outside or prior to their reduction to meaning, as again entangled, textual, multilayered, with multiple meanings.[14] In a historical view like Foucault's, the hallucinatory concerns events affecting a collectivity rather than an individual. It is the way to get access to events affecting us all, prior to, or outside, their determination in terms of final meaning.

The etymology of the word *hallucinate* supports the contention that a relation between consciousness and signs is at stake. *Hallucinate* is derived from the Latin *alucinari,* a term meaning "to wander in mind, to dream," but also, "to talk idly, to prate, to discourse freely." The etymology suggests that Hugo's hallucinatory poems might best be considered in the line passing from Montaigne's logorrheic *Essais,* through the Cartesian digressive *Discours* and *Méditations,* to the discursive vagaries of Rousseau's *Rêveries du promeneur solitaire.* The locus of exile from which the later Hugo speaks is analogous to the dislocation of the I of the *Rêveries,* whom a catastrophic loss of intersubjective and subject-object relations has forced back upon itself and its own resources. The Rousseauian I has nothing left to affirm itself over and against the void except its experience of memory and memory-signs. Characteristic of the hallucinatory poems of the second half of *Les Contemplations,* as well as of *La Révolution,* is a similar intense epistemological uncertainty and a resultant forcing back of the self onto an experience of indeterminacy available in texts, where, to quote Foucault again, discourse does not maintain "a single and exclusive meaning (by excising all the others), but the simultaneous existence of multiple meanings."[15] It is to find oneself in a slightly scary position, having lost secure definitions of the subject and the object, never mind of what—if anything—is going on. It is to find oneself having done what poets do, "having maintained, as if they were realities, symbolic abstractions."[16]

And it is indeed into a landscape from which human subjects and their objects of perception have disappeared that the poem introduces us, offering its horrific visions of mobile bronze, "visions où jamais un oeil humain ne plonge" (visions in which no human eye has ever plunged) (10: 220) to "on ne sait quels spectateurs funèbres" (who knows what funereal spectators) (10: 218). Against the landscape denuded of human subjects, in a night so dark that only the eyeless dead can see anything, move the statues with their human visages, endowed with sight, hearing, speech, and motion.

The walking statue is a redoubled prosopopeia. A statue is a work of art that gives a face to a dead or absent entity—the definition of pro-sopopeia—in a material very unlike that of the entity, be it granite or bronze in the case of sculpture, or, as Hugo says in the case of poetry, "the bronze dithyramb and the marble epic" (10: 230). To call such a work to life and motion is a prosopopeia to the second power, the prosopopeia of a prosopopeia. The poem is thus allegorizing its central figure, which is precisely the kind of figure by which Shakespeare, in Fineman's reading, puts a lady's face on language's difference.

Like a metaphor for metaphor, the walking statue meditates on itself as statue, as prosopopeia. But unlike a metaphor for metaphor, which tends toward the stasis of a revelation, giving a face to the giving of face has to concern itself with an open and undeterminable series of effects. It asks about the responsibility of and for the human face incurred by the work of art when it endows an inhuman material with human char-acteristics, about what Hugo apostrophizes as "Responsibility of the hu-man shape / Seized in granite or fatal bronze!" (10: 220). Prosopopeia to the second power considers the possibility of ungovernable referential ef-fects engendered in the making of anthropomorphic fictions. This possi-bility is carried to an extreme in the poem when the poet credits an ob-scure artist under Henri IV, the putative sculptor of the mascarons of the Pont-Neuf, with having sketched out a likeness of the future Robespierre in the guise of Trivelin, the type of the scoundrelly manservant French classical theater inherited from Italian comedy:

> A ton insu même . . . tu mettais la lueur
> Des révolutions dans le regard des faunes. . . .
> Et ta fatale main, ô grand tailleur de pierre
> Dans Trivelin sinistre ébauchait Robespierre.

> But unwittingly . . . you put the glow
> Of revolutions in the look of fauns. . . .
> And your fatal hand, oh great hewer of stone,
> In a sinister Trivelin roughed out Robespierre.

> *(10: 230)*

The prosopopeia to the second power raises the specter of unmastered repetition. For even should the poem manage to bring a closure to the effects of having first given human face to an inhuman material, it would incur a second set of debts and responsibilities by the second prosopopeia, the very one that lets it assume a discourse of responsibility for the effects of the first.

And it is in their effects that the statues reveal what attends them as redoubled prosopopeias. In the passage to be discussed these effects are divisible into two rough categories: the statues bring the immutable and the dead to life, and they chill or petrify the mutable.

> —Visions où jamais un oeil humain ne plonge!—
> Et comme par la rampe invisible d'un songe,
> La statue à pas lents du socle descendit.
>
> Alors l'âpre ruelle au nom fauve et maudit,
> L'échoppe, la maison, l'hôtel, le bouge obscène,
> Les mille toits mirant leurs angles dans la Seine,
> Les obscurs carrefours où, le jour, en tous sens,
> Court l'hésitation confuse des passants,
> Les enseignes pendant aux crocs de fer des portes,
> Les palais crénelés comme des villes fortes,
> Le chaland aux anneaux des berges retenu,
> S'étonnèrent devant ce cimier inconnu
> Dont aucun ouragan n'eût remué la plume,
> Entendirent le sol tinter comme une enclume
> Et, tandis qu'au fronton des tours l'heure étouffait
> Sa voix, n'osant sonner au cadran stupéfait,
> Virent, dans l'épaisseur des ténèbres accrues,
> Droit, paisible et glacé, s'avancer dans les rues,
> Accompagné d'un bruit funèbre et souterrain,
> L'homme de bronze assis sur le cheval d'airain.
>
> L'eau triste frissonnait sous la rondeur de l'arche.
>   . . .
> Horreur prodigieuse! une statue en marche!
>
> La lourdeur de cette ombre étonne le pavé.
> Elle glisse, elle va, morne, le front levé,
> Avec une roideur de cadavre, et sa forme
> Inflexible résiste au vent du gouffre énorme.
> L'affreux ordre nocturne en est bouleversé.
> Après que cette chose effroyable a passé,
> Sous les plafonds glacés où les cercueils séjournent,
> Les squelettes hagards dans leur lit se retournent
> Et disent à la nuit funeste qui ne sait
> Que leur répondre: ô nuit, qu'est-ce donc qui passait?

Si l'oeil pouvait plonger dans ces hideux royaumes
Et percer le mystère, on verrait les fantômes,
Frissonnants, éviter le lugubre inconnu.
Larve dont le regard sans pâlir soutenu
Fait toute la grandeur de don Juan athée!
Spectre où s'ébrécherait l'épée épouvantée,
Et qu'en l'osant toucher la main sentirait froid!
Actions de la vie, amours, justice, droit,
Crime, vengeance, orgueil, qu'un simulacre traîne!
Responsabilité de la figure humaine
Prise par le granit ou le bronze fatal!
Oh! dans l'égarement d'un orage mental,
Dans quelque âpre chaos de villes abattues,
Qui donc a vu rôder lentement des statues?
Ces êtres inouïs, impossibles, affreux,
Vont, ayant la stupeur des ténèbres sur eux.

—Visions into which the human eye never plunges!—
And as if by the invisible ramp of a dream,
The statue with slow steps from its pedestal descended.

Then the precipitous lane with its fierce and accursed name,
The street stall, the house, the mansion, the obscene hovel,
The thousand roofs mirroring their angles in the Seine,
The obscure crossroads where, by day, in every direction,
Runs the confused hesitation of the passersby,
The street signs hanging from the iron hooks of the doors,
The palaces crenellated like fortified towns,
The barge held back by the rings of the banks,
Were astounded before this unknown helmet crest
Whose feather no hurricane would have moved,
Heard the earth ring like an anvil
And, while on the fronton of towers the hour stifled
Its voice, not daring to sound to the stupefied dial,
Saw, in the density of the gathered gloom,
Straight, peaceful and icy, advance in the streets,
Accompanied by a funereal and subterranean noise,
The man of bronze seated on the horse of brass.

The sad water shivered under the roundness of the arch.

. . .

Prodigious horror! A statue on the march!

The heaviness of this shadow stuns the pavement.
It glides, it goes onward, dreary, forehead high,
With the rigidity of a corpse, and its form
Inflexible resists the wind of the enormous abyss.
The awful nocturnal order is upset by it.
After this fearful thing has passed,
Beneath the icy ceilings where coffins dwell,
Haggard skeletons turn over in their bed
And say to the fatal night who does not know
What to answer: Oh night, what then has passed?
If an eye could plunge into these hideous realms
And pierce the mystery, phantoms would be seen,
Shivering, to avoid this lugubrious unknown.
Larva whose look sustained without paling
Makes for the entire grandeur of the atheist Don Juan!
Specter on which the terror-struck sword would become nicked,
And, daring to touch it, how cold the hand would feel!
Actions of life, loves, justice, right,
Crime, vengeance, pride, that a simulacrum drags with it!
Responsibility of the human shape
Seized by granite or fatal bronze!
Oh! in the wandering of a mental storm,
In the rough chaos of towns overthrown,
Who has seen statues prowling slowly?
Those beings unheard of, impossible, awful,
Go forth, bearing the gloom's stupefaction upon them.

(10: 220–21)

Upon the descent of the statue of Henri IV from its pedestal, a structure, the mapped city of Paris, takes on human features: it is surprised, hears, and sees. A little further on, a bone structure, a skeleton, turns in its grave to voice questions. The endowment of structures with life affects the larger sections of the poem: each monument mobilized will ride up to the next and, by an apostrophe—"Viens voir si ton fils est à sa place encore" (Come then and see if your son is still in his place) (10: 223, 224)—will awaken it.[17] On the other side, however, the fugitive and figural is arrested in the passage. Time does not flee, but is, on the contrary, paralyzed; the temperature of the Seine—already a mirror (*une glace*) in its function—drops and it becomes chilly enough to shiver; further on, the dream loses its transforming and distinguishing capaci-

ties. A double movement is uncovered: the work of art on the march endows with and deprives of life, or, what is the same thing here, feeling,
movement, voice, distinctness.

What does this chilling and mobilizing mean with respect to the pressure toward reference or signification? Hugo is commenting on the problem in this passage where—under the effect of the passage of statues—
exchanges take place between the spatial and temporal dimension of the
text. The city with its structures and edifices, its fixed signs and names,
starts to take on intention, emotion, and new meaning possibilities.
Meanwhile the figures of the text—here, especially, humanized time,
equated by de Man with figurality[18]—lose the mobility characterizing
them as tropes. As for the statue's movement, its jerky discontinuities
and direction—which takes it downward off its pedestal, and then literally into the streets—make it work very well as a figure for the collapse of
figure into denomination. Tropes, figures of speech, literature, get out of
their fictive frames and advance—dragging with them love, right, and
justice—into the streets.

Within the general clearing and preparing of the stage so the "event"
can be viewed in its appropriate spatiotemporal frame (the frame of a
frame in flux), the arresting of time is one of the most notable reshuf-
flings.[19] It would seem that a poem ostensibly about the historical event
of the French Revolution, and one claiming at that to be the example of
the epic spirit, ought to be regulated by some overriding temporal
scheme. Instead, among the various astonished spectators of the mobile
statues an immobilized clock informs us that at the same time (*tandis
que*) that the animated city is expressing its surprise, the suspension of
time is taking place: "And, while on the fronton of towers the hour stifled / Its voice, not daring to sound to the stupefied dial." The events of
La Révolution take place against the background of this animated city
and simultaneously stilled hour. One might even say they are indistinguishable from the transfers occurring in that background, where the
very fundamental categories of space and time enter into exchanges: the
events as told consist in a shift or collapse occurring in the conditions
for conceiving events.[20] This needs to be shown at some length.

The oddity of this time of arrested time lies partly in the fact that the
hour is no longer perceivable by the means that human beings have
found to make their rational constructs of time felt, that is, by the movements of the clock. Time cannot make itself heard or seen; its bell is si-

lenced, its hands stunned into immobility. With the loss of time as we perceive it by the clock are also lost the constructs that go with it. The linear progression made perceptible by the sounded hour as it disrupts a continuum of silence is not operative,[21] nor is the cyclical model for which the turning hands of the dial provides the visual analogy. The familiar rational structures—both of which are associated with the modern meaning of revolution—are suspended along with the familiar sensible manifestations that are their conventional correlative.[22] The stopped clock suggests that to get a grasp on the event the poem refers to, we must suspend familiar analogies, and the sign system that they suppose.

Hugo is well aware that we do not experience time directly, but as a language, by way of signs. The rest of the poem bears out the contention that the arrested clock signals an end not only to time as an object of which we have some experience, but also to the stable sign system and the hermeneutical system that goes with it. The poem does not narrate the events of the French Revolution or suggest that revolution seeks to return man to a more originary state of virtue and freedom, as Hugo's novel *Quatrevingt-treize* can be construed as doing. Only in the most oblique of ways—by an allegory developed in *Choses vues*[23] which says that a statue off its pedestal is like a dethroned king—can the moving statues be said to point to such empirical events of the Revolution as the destruction of the royal statues, the renaming of the Place Louis XV, or the beheading of Louis XVI. Hugo's stilled clock stops correlating the perception one has of the clock as signifier to time. It suggests that the event represented does not have a ready analogy in experience.

But, in another sense, the clock does not cease to keep time. It is still a sign and can refer to itself as an empty order or construction. The clock stilled is still a clock, and keeps the time of its arrest, just as a representation that represents nothing is nonetheless something: a representation or sign of nothing. It keeps the time of a lapse or rift in time. Thus, for instance, the Renaissance clock of *Sylvie*'s narrator, which "has not been wound up in two centuries," proves very well suited—in a tale that feeds off memory—to keep intact the pasts that concern the narrator.[24]

Is the objective time scheme then voided in order to open time and revolution to a subjective interpretation, as the reference to Nerval would suggest? The poem might be arresting the clock's movement in order to allow Hugo to focus inward, on the Revolutionary crisis as a crisis of spirit in which the French nation found its identity, and Europe found confirmation that history was not a set of random events but reason actualizing itself.

The gift of voice, of feeling, and of the capacity for voluntary action associated with subjectivity is indeed conferred upon the hour: "the hour stifled / Its voice, not daring to sound to the stupefied dial." But the gift of life is an equivocal one. The hour is endowed with human characteristics so that it may have more of which to be deprived. It gets the passion of fear to petrify passion's mobility, action to deprive itself of action. More tellingly yet, in a poem where the human is represented by voice, the hour is given voice only to mute it. Even its vestigial ears—for the root of *oser*, to dare, is *audere*, to hear—are taken away from it: *n'osant*, not daring / not hearing. The hour is made human so as to assert its striking resemblance—death-like stillness and stupefaction—to a suicide's cadaver. The prosopopeia gives us to know the hour by an odd likeness to ourselves: it is like us when we have called into question our selfhood by an act of self-annihilation. The hour is the time ushered in when, in an act of Mallarmean self-doubt, the self calls itself into question and ceases to exist as an operative category. The hour's stifled voice undoes the harmonious correlation between signifier and meaning. Time is not a signified expressed by ringing bells, as voiced language expresses human feeling; just as the stupefied clock interrupts the passage by way of meaning from the sign to an outside referent, so the stifled voice, the suicidal hour, interrupts the process of signification itself, the passage from the outside of perception to the inside of meaning.

Introspective time—be it of duration or of memory—is thus not operative in the poem either. The thematics confirm this. The poem, a vision reliant on no human eye, is about statues and masks, things devoid of inner life. The most human figure is that of the dead sculptor, Germaine Pilon. But even this representative artist is no self-conscious genius. He is said to have been a prophet who was not in on his own secret, a soul who did not have the revelation of his whole thought, a dreamer who did not know what symbol he had thrown across the Seine in the Pont-Neuf. *La Révolution* does not promise the great interpretative wealth of an introspective poem, centered on a subject and its freedom, or on a radical transformation it brings about in its mental or moral order on its way to absolute knowledge. The stifled voice of the hour speaks rather of a discrepancy between consciousness' understanding of figures as expressive and their actual existence as independent

structures whose action cannot be measured by categories like expressiv-
ity. This discrepancy is registered on the face of the clock, as a *doing* or
making that does not derive from consciousness, and has rather an effect
hostile to it. The dial, it seems, is stupefied (*stupéfait*—literally: "*made*
stupid, paralysed, or incapable of action and reaction*").

The point that the hour is not a subjective one is made in part by the
undoing of prosopopeia as seductive human figure. Here prosopopeia
does not just give face and voice to a dead or absent entity, it also works
in the reverse direction: the humanized hour is made a dead or absent
entity, its senses deadened and voice muted. The figure speaks against
the construction of the language of time in terms of the self.

But the hour is a houri, *l'heure est un leurre*, a lure, a trap, a Nervalian
will-o'-the-wisp, a gleam (or *lueur*). It is seductive because, in the act of
undoing itself as human figure, it becomes convincingly more and more
like a human figure, endowed as it seems with a purposiveness in its act
of self-stifling. It turns itself into a not-self by a fearsome, murderous
gesture and, in so doing, hides itself as not-self by the intentionality of its
turn. The second prosopopeia undoes the first self only by reconstituting
it at a higher and more general level. In *Notre-Dame de Paris*, the half-
crazed priest Frollo suffers from a like tenacity of life, even at the height
of his feverish delusions. Hugo comments on it: "A remarkable thing was
that during this whole torture, the serious thought of dying never came
to him. This miserable being was so made. He held on to life."[25]

However, the seductiveness of this reconstitution is a blind that conceals a less graceful and more threatening spectacle. For we should remember that the hour and the clock are not coming to life in this passage;
they are tending toward progressive petrification, and with them, the
hope of a resolution favorable to spirit. The distinctive feature of the passage on time is the seizing of the mobile, the figural, the human, in stone.
The clock is stupefied, the hour is strangled; the fronton of towers turns
to us a stony forehead (*fronton* derives from *front*, forehead). A rigor mor-
tis seizes the temporal. Its use as conventional category for measuring objective events and its meaning for consciousness have both been evacuated
in favor of a rigid self-referential structure of uncertain or no meaning.

The syntagma *fronton des tours* accomplishes the rigidification by
freezing in a single place the two functions evacuated. The plural, *des
tours*, which effaces the gendered article, couples two different kinds of
tours, both of which have been at work in the passage: on the one hand,

tour as term for tower, la Tour de la Bastille, la Tour de Nesle, or la Tour de Babel[26]; on the other hand, all the turns of *le tour*, from trope and turn of phrase, from sleight of hand or trick, from circuit or circular walk to rotation or revolution. As in Baudelaire's *Thyrsus*, where the hieratic emblem of a wand around which dances a snaky line of flowers allegorizes the indissociability of sign and trope, Hugo's double *tours*, undecidably referential and tropological, are yoked together by a single—indeed a singular—*fronton*.

Like its near synonyms, *pediment* and *façade*, *fronton* (an architectural term designating a frontal or small pediment) names by catachresis, that is, by abusive metaphor. A catachresis does not exchange terms between known entities but rather sets up an unequal exchange by means of which a known entity can give a term to an unknown entity so that the latter can get a name for one of its parts. The human body is often pillaged for these unequal exchanges, to name the teeth of a comb, the arm of a chair, the eye of a camera, or the face of a building. As catachresis *fronton* is both a name and a figure, and as such can successfully bridge the gap between signification and reference, trope and name, turn and tower. It very neatly wraps together both descriptive and tropic dimensions of the passage.

But the *fronton des tours* presses the passage away from the seductions of tropes and the self-undoing hour toward a system of fixed names, of conventional, referential language. It is the proper term for a part of a tower and it pushes the passage in the direction of a description of a literal scene of a tower on whose pediment is a stopped clock. One could, for example, read the passage as inspired by an event of the 1848 Revolution described by Hugo in *Choses vues*: "The Tuileries' dial stopped at three o'clock. (Has not been rewound since the revolution.) Marks the hour of the monarchy's fall."[27] As name, the catachresic *fronton* presses the passage about the undecidability of language toward reference, and thence toward such referential towers as the Bastille, and such referential events as the French Revolution.

There is room to consider such pressure in terms of a larger question. We have been talking about language in this passage because time can come before us only by a process of signification, by the mediation of a language.[28] In a word, to talk about time is to talk figuratively about a language, as to talk about the arresting of time is to talk figuratively about bringing a stasis to a mobile, figural system. The passage tends toward the sudden, one-sided collapse of all its figures into reference that it has been anticipating by its discussion of rigidification (and attendant themes such as brittleness, cracking, overthrowing of cities). The meaning of the catachresis, the thought of this extra forehead, is that self-referential meaning and referential meaning are collapsed into reference when language starts referring to itself as undecidably trope or sign. The stopped clock of *Choses vues* confirms the insight of *La Révolution* that there is a pressure toward the loss of a distinctness between names and tropes at precisely the juncture where the undecidability is being posited.

The arrested clock signifies the sudden collapse of the figural system, the loss of its distinctness from a literal, referential language. That collapse is considered in *La Révolution* to constitute one part of the untellable event of revolution. The event is not of time's passing, for which a narrative or a clock could suffice, but of its abrupt passing away. Of course Hugo is not claiming that the shots of the 1789 or 1848 revolutions were fired by language. But he is suggesting that the collapse of the two disparate functions of language into a single referential function is necessary for revolution to be conceivable.[29] This is not a delirious notion on Hugo's part. We can certainly understand that, in order for the attack on the Bastille to be more than a criminal act, the Bastille had to be invested as more than the name of a literal tower, that was also one of many symbols for the king's power. It had to be the place where those two functions were collapsed into one, so it could appear plausible that an abstract symbol could be dismantled by taking apart the stones of the tower. In *Notre-Dame de Paris*, the Bastille is given this value of a symbol for the reign of a monarchy collapsed into an edifice in the epithet that heads one chapter: "Le retrait où dit ses heures Monsieur Louis de France" (The retreat where Louis of France tells his hours). The fall of the Bastille, in an account of this sort, would not consist in the literal fall of the tower, but rather in the preparatory collapse of the abstract symbol into the name of a thing that, as thing, can then be made into rubble.

On the other side, the untellable event of revolution has effects registered on the spatial dimension of the city. To the city, we have said, has been transferred all the movement (and with it, the pathos, and attempts at self-knowledge) missing on the side of river or clock. The poem sets up an opposition between space and time that suggests how we are to read this animation and attempt at self-understanding on the part of the city. Time is seized in stone and tropes fall into referential names; meanwhile, spatial constructs start to move and get (e)motional. The dramatic change takes place around the monumental statue.

Now the statue is of the city, insofar as it is a structure, but insofar as it advances, it is not entirely like the city. It has some of the features of the time system, and can be said, if not absolutely to be replacing time broken down on the other side of the equation, at least to have appropriated some of its properties. Its advance, its passage, is the signified that clock and bells ordinarily mean: time does not advance or pass, but the statue advances and passes. Furthermore, the ringing that should be the perceptual sign of time passing shows up here as a funereal and subterranean noise, the ringing of the ground itself that accompanies the statue's advance: "le sol tinte(r) comme une enclume." Hugo's choice of the term *tinter*, a term that characterizes the sounds of a bell, underscores the point: the statue's passage is known in the same way as time's passage used to be known. This ringing of the earth as anvil tells us that a Vulcan of sorts is at work on a new production. At the same time as there is a terrific loss of energy to the tropic dimension—the clock hands do not turn, the bells do not ring, the turn of *tour* itself tends to disappear, the forehead of the colossus Paris[30] cannot be distinguished from the easily destroyed fronton of a clock tower, the advancing statue is soon to be indistinguishable from an advancing man—the space of the poem is getting reenergized from the ground up by the act of a Vulcan, and the earth's ringing is the phenomenal equivalent of this creative surge.

It is to the poem's signifiers, as to its ground, that we need to look for the meaning. It is there that we hear a ghostly time advancing. *Heure* continues to sound, as if passing, throughout the rest of the quoted passage: in *épaisseur, rondeur, horreur, roideur, leur, grandeur, stupeur.* Similarly, although time can no longer be seen turning in the hands of the dial, a turn can be sighted in a signifier, indeed in the signifier of vision itself, the peculiar *virent*, the third person plural past tense of the verb *voir,* "to see," but which is also the third person plural present tense of *virer,* "to veer, to round a corner." The strategic placement makes this *virent* appear as turn. Distanced from its subject by six lines, and from the other verbs in the enumeration by the clause about time, it is brought into close proximity to the *tours* and the unturning hands. Effects of neighborhood and distance let the object of vision, the man of bronze and the horse of brass, step out as the potential subject of *virent,* as a wheeling man and horse.[31] Hugolian enumerations often tend toward Babelic ruin in this way.[32]

This perspectival shift, with its transfer of the meaning of movement to the term, is the more plausible because the theme the poet is considering is the effect of the statue's movements on roofs and intersections, as well as the possibility that the troubled vision of the intersections themselves is at fault. The thematic, from an allegorical perspective, suggests that a figure, a representation, might start up from the structure, a theme put forth by the chances of word order. A delirious vision of this sort is just what is proposed by the accident of placement that thrusts out the wheeling horse and rider from the description of the vision. Just so, the signifiers of the poem, through accidents of neighborhood, as part of the mechanics of constructing utterances, propose themes and figures to fill the void left by the collapsed figural dimension.

The poem is commenting on itself as word organization that offers itself as ambiguous stimulus, a potential reservoir of monsters, a gigantic Rorschach test for the passerby. Language is getting treated as available to experience, its signs are treated as audible. That audibility supplies the phenomenal correlative of the hallucinated visions of the statue in motion and the activity of the streets. These "perceptions without an object"[33] provoke the descent of the dream into a mental maelstrom—

> as if by the invisible ramp of a dream
> . . . in the wandering of a mental storm
> . . . the dream itself . . .
> The dream . . .
> Is terror-struck . . .
> And shudders.   *(10: 220–21)*

—and raises the issue of whether the text *advances* by way of such play with signifiers. For the system of signifiers, with the accidents of grammar and the sonorous plays it brings into view, does not merely serve as the correlative of meaning, as the voice expressing a thought. It seems actually to advance new meaning. Thus, the *épaisseur des ténèbres* seems more than just a nonsensical tolling of "heure," a resounding of its signifier after its meaning has been emptied out. It sounds as though it rings the changes on a new hour, an hour that can be made substantial and spatial, an hour made thick (*épaisse heure*), an hour outside of the hour (*hors-heure*), a weighty hour (*lourde heure*), an upright or kingly hour (*roi d'heure roide heure*), a great hour (*grande heure*) the impersonal hour itself, *l'heure elle-même, enfin!*

We are familiar with the engenderment of texts around its babbling, prating signifiers. This is one model for engendering texts at work in Rousseau's *Rêveries*. We find it in numerous lyrics, as part of the Ovidian inheritance of the Narcissus myth, in which Echo invariably roams around the same pool where Narcissus studies himself. What is striking about the passage from *La Révolution*, however, is that, as it refers to its own phenomenalization of language, it starts to move away from the original comparison of the vision to dreaming and thus from the hope of achieving a Cratylic correspondence between signifier and signified. Instead, in this "little epic," the lyric commonplace is associated with dread and a play that stops short of resolving the disjunction feared. In the text cited earlier from *Choses vues* where statues off their pedestals are compared to dethroned kings and riderless horses, Hugo allegorizes this "free play" of the signifier as the movement of a vehicle. It takes place in a space where a reason dethroned is occupied with maintaining what semblance it can of its former glory.[34] The prosopopeia endowing the city with intention reintroduces a dysfunctional model that has us first rubbing our eyes, wondering if we see or just think we see a turn in *virent*, and then checking our ears, wondering if we hear the voice of the stifled *heure* or the sound of "the wind (*le vent*) of the enormous abyss" in *devant, s'avancer, épouvantée, vengeance, s'épouvante, arrivants, vivants, s'avança*. That this dream is not so much a longed-for correspondence as a troubling hallucination that continues to dog the text is shown when the poet starts to ask about the status of the event on which he is focusing and of the subject who sees and hears it: "... qu'est-ce donc qui passait? ... / Qui donc a vu lentement passer les statues?" (10: 220). The point is not to see or hear any one of these phenomena, or to find who might think to have seen them. The poem is rather pointing toward the mechanical aspect of the text as the cause of certain effects, by way of which we make sense of nonsense rather than opt for no meaning at all. The pressure toward meaning is great enough that when all sense has been evacuated and we are left with just a "nom fauve et maudit," one prefers the inspiriting of a wind rattling up from the abyss, which makes language's indeterminacy seem a thing, rather than nothing.[35] Side by side with the collapse of an order where the distinction between figures and names was possible, the poem shows the capacity of nonsignifying structures, juxtaposed signifiers, to provide meaningful representations.

Laplanche and Pontalis, in "Fantasy and the Origins of Sexuality," confirm that when signifiers get treated as objects of perception, we are indeed in the domain of hallucination. When an infant hallucinates a breast, it is not attempting to get milk, which it knows is not there. Its "vision" of the breast is not the means by which it tries to satisfy its physical hunger. The child, in the dearth of milk and breast, thinks it sees "not the real object, but the lost object; not the milk, but the breast *as a signifier*."[36] The infant substitutes the signifier for the milk, a substitution that is possible because the signifier, like an object, has a phenomenal existence. Whatever satisfaction the child gets from the hallucination comes from the linguistic operation of substituting signifier for object, and then from sucking it for all it's worth, that is, for mental nourishment, for extra signifieds, to give nascent consciousness some sense of its own life and operation.

In "Hypogram and Inscription" de Man further elaborates the distinctive character of hallucination: "In hallucination, the difference between *I see* and *I think I see* has been one-sidedly resolved in the direction of apperception. . . . Consciousness has become consciousness only of itself."[37] Toward the end, the passage from *La Révolution* talks about such a collapse in the dreamspace itself.

> Et l'alarme est dans l'ombre, et le rêve lui-même
> Qui distingue à minuit dans l'immensité blême
> Tout un monde terrible à travers l'oeil fermé,
> Le rêve, aux habitants de l'ombre accoutumé,
> S'épouvante de voir cette lugubre espèce
> De fantômes entrer dans sa nuée épaisse,
> Et frémit, car le pas de ces noirs arrivants
> N'est ni le pas des morts ni le pas des vivants.

> And alarm is in the shadow, and the dream itself
> Which distinguishes at midnight in the colorless immensity
> A whole terrible world through a closed eye,
> The dream, accustomed to the inhabitants of the shadow,
> Is terror-struck at the sight of this lugubrious species
> Of phantoms entering in its thick cloud,
> And shudders, for the step of these black arrivals
> Is neither the step of the dead nor the step of the living.

> *(10: 221)*

The dream can see with a closed eye because it knows no difference between waking and sleeping. But it is accustomed to distinguishing between the dreamspace (*dans l'immensité blême*) and the dream world with which it furnishes that space (*tout un monde terrible*). When the lugubrious phantoms arrive, however, they render the space into which they enter (*dans une nuée épaisse*, into a thick cloud) indistinct from themselves as intruders (they enter *dans une nuée épaisse*, that is, *as* a thick cloud or swarm). The dream no longer knows how to distinguish its habitual space from invaders that occupy that space. It cannot differentiate between what it "sees" with its closed eye, the cloud of phantoms, and itself as dreaming consciousness, the thick cloud of thought. Phantom thought grips itself in phantom perceptions. There is indeed no difference between "I see" and "I think I see."

The lines toward the end of the quoted passage that explain the cause of the dream's terror yield a theorization of this way that the text is proceeding in the absence of a distinction presumed necessary for producing texts. The explanation reads: "Car le pas de ces noirs arrivants / N'est ni le pas des morts ni le pas des vivants." This line is hard to translate, as hard to translate as it is to understand the distinction the poet is trying to make between the three sorts of *pas*, or methods of proceeding. If we translate them as I have done—"For the step of these black arrivals / Is neither the step of the dead nor the step of the living"—we suggest that, for the poet, there are three distinct ways of walking, one for the living, one for the dead, and one for the statues. The living do indeed have a step, but what madman has seen the dead, never mind a town's monuments, walking? The *pas* of the dead is no step, *pas de pas*, that is, *pas* in its other sense, of negation. To translate *pas* as step in all three cases is to lose the distinction between the dead and the living, without even considering what could separate both dead and living from the statue.

Things are no different if we translate *pas* in every case as negation, and consider the poet to be distinguishing between three kinds of negativities: "For the negativity of these black arrivals / Is neither the negativity of the dead nor the negativity of the living." The living cannot be said to have no step. Walking, thinking, discoursing, even casting forward to their death, they are always stepping. And what about the *noirs arrivants*? They are said to be arriving. Even if that coming does not involve a step, it is not no step either. The poem is trying to distinguish the *pas* of the living (a step, an interval, a progress) and the dead (no step, no interval, no progress) which exist in a specular relation, from a third *pas*, the *pas* of the statues.

One could propose a third translation that would try to take this distinctness into account: "For the *pace* of these black arrivals / Is neither the *negativity* of the dead nor the *step* of the living." What distinguishes the *pas* of the statues is that it neither has the meaning of negation nor points to a referential event, a step. It is a signifier, a sounded *pas*, distinct by virtue of its indifference to the difference between steps and negations. It functions as an empty piece of language, necessary for the meter pacing the poem, irrespective of all questions of reference and significance.

This third translation is problematic in its own way, because it loses the tripleness of *pas* and localizes in one place the rule of *pas* as *pace* rhythming the poem throughout. Furthermore, the translation makes the problem into that of distinguishing between three separate species of signifieds (step, negation, the signifier itself), when in fact, the difference that language makes appears phenomenally here—to ear and eye—as a slide or progression from one *pas* to another to another. In rhythm, an aspect of poetic language everywhere available, signifier and signified are not yet distinct sign features for consciousness. It is a reduction to make of rhythm either a signified, an object of knowledge, or a mere set of signifiers sounded to the inner ear of readers. Rhythm is at once perception and meaning, insofar as it is organized perception. It is also a reduction to discover rhythm at a single point when the suggestion is that any understanding of the *pas*, as step or negation, necessarily rests on the existence of a pattern and the insistent recalling of the signifier. The hallucinatory passage of the statues signals the movement of the poem away from specular oppositions of dead and living, reference and signification, to the level of a language treated as an object of the senses undifferentiated from its signified, a progression that is neither a progress nor a stasis.

The effect Fineman notes in Shakespeare's dark lady sonnets, namely, the effect of a secondary Cratylism in which a language that does not say what it means ends by saying exactly what it means—"I lie"—is under discussion in this kind of text. The *pas* of the statues declares itself to mean neither step nor negation but to be just a signifier, *pas*. In so doing it reintroduces the equivalency of sound and meaning previously undone when the hour was stifled, since the sound *pas* gives us access to the meaning of the poem as residing in rhythm or *pace*. But Hugo does not find this secondary Cratylism to be just a problem of poetic language, nor does he see it as the proof of an advance in understanding, as does Fineman. He identifies it as hallucinatory and advancing in a way that a narrative of progress cannot account for. Consciousness in its infancy, prior to any distinction between its inside as consciousness and the outside of perception, is also only conscious of itself in apperception. As de Man graphically puts it: "In that sense [the sense of consciousness as conscious only of itself], any consciousness, including perception, is hallucinatory."[38] A consciousness that subsists by producing meaning out of empty signifiers, milkless breasts, is certainly not a "wiser" consciousness. The triple *pas* of the statue gives access to an organization at work in the poem and can be said to add the signified "language" to *pas*. But this is emphatically not a poem in which sound is taken as source of meaning or an echo reverberating with the possibility of a natural language being achieved by a correspondence between signifier and signified. Rather, sound gives us access to a consciousness that cannot get out of hallucination, apperception. Hallucinatory consciousness just glides from *pas* to *pas* to *pas* to *pas*, in a *pas-sage* that neither achieves wisdom nor abandons its procedure. This consciousness lives in proximity to a kind of terror, the terror of the sign that does not represent thought, but spasmodically produces visions of its capacity to engender themes, including themes mirroring its productive energy. But there is a certain consolation even in this obsessive consciousness. One may not move ahead or experience a breakthrough by way of play, but at least there is an organization that provides evidence that there is a consciousness around. When the possibility arises that we may not escape out of language to an outside referent, at the very least, the poem suggests, we can get evidence of the reality of consciousness. Just so Frollo, victim of hallucination in *Notre-Dame de Paris*, has a "single healthy idea, a sole upright thought." That thought is of the ruin of his own reason, which "lay there, almost entirely destroyed."[39] That thought sustains him.

Are we then to consider that, for Hugo, the track through the poem is finally that of a consciousness that constitutes itself over and over as apperception each time that the authority of its representations is put into question by undecidability, and it finds itself confronted with a meaningless organization of names? Does Hugo, in keeping with Foucault's hypothesis that the phantasm is the "play of the (missing) event and its repetition,"[40] construe history as the retrieval and release of "the hidden and forgotten monsters,"[41] repressed when history is made eschatological, and events are reduced to their main or essential values?

In such a view, the poem would get its title from its understanding of the Terror as the equivalent, for a collectivity, of the threat of a disintegration into sheer difference, a threat over and against which would be constituted a one-sided consciousness of consciousness. The very term *Reign of Terror* is instructive here. Fear is alienated from subject and object in the term *Reign of Terror*. We do not say the Terror of Robespierre, for example. We do not think of it as the fear he invokes in others, or as his own fear. It is a structural Terror, it is the law as rule that does not gather the collectivity into a unit, but instead assembles it as a list of placeholders, a roll call of names. Against the threat of a proliferation of forms and the utter loss of meaning, to find an overall sense of patterning, even of the unlikely sort that rhythms the poem as the pursuit of one *pas* after another, is consoling for consciousness. Is Hugo then proposing, in lieu of a poem on the French Revolution, or on the meaning of revolution, to track the subterranean, hallucinatory history of revolution, defined as the rule by which signifiers can be milked to produce meaningful effects for consciousness, independent of reference or signification? Unlike Kant or Hegel, for whom the French Revolution turns out to be proof that the idea of history actualizes itself in events, which are thus demonstrably not random, Hugo finds evidence in the Revolution that consciousness grasps its operation by superimposing a phenomenal grid upon a formal order like enumeration or some other assemblage. The Revolution would be a turning point when, faced with a voided system in which it had seen its threatened destruction, consciousness would have sought for one last time to assert its mastery in its phantasms.[42] The hallucinatory is a permanent interpretative possibility and indicates the underlying possibility of a consciousness that does not progress, but obsessively repeats its gesture of glimpsing itself in every act of apperception.[43]

In its first part, the poem has concerned itself with the phenomenalization of the signifier, and with the Terror as the equivalent of such a concern. But that is not where its only understanding of history is available. In a later part of the poem serving as its epilogue, a part which was originally to have been a separate poem called "Le Verso de la page,"[44] another version of history is provided. From its first words, "Soit. Mais . . ." (So be it. But . . .) (10: 246), it sets itself up as a postscript, another angle from which to view the same problem. The epilogue tells us that the Revolution is the lair of a divine monster into which Progress enters, but from which it then departs: "Le Progrès n'a pas peur d'entrer, lui qui s'envole, / Chez ce monstre divin, la Révolution. / . . . Puis il sort de la haute et grondante tanière" (Progress, who takes flight, is not afraid to enter / The house of the divine monster, the Revolution. / . . . Then he leaves its lofty and grumbling lair) (10: 246). In these lines, the poet insists that the poem does not remain stuck in hallucinatory consciousness. Its historicity is not to be reduced to that dark moment when reference and meaning are collapsed into one another by the abusive naming of catachresis, and we are confronted with a one-sided, hallucinatory consciousness.

If we return to the passage we have been reading to look for clues in the direction of the page's verso, we find a puzzling element, as yet unaccounted for, that stands out from the others, characterized as it is by a repose beyond the reach of both the activity and immobility of the rest. This element makes the immobile clock towers and the advancing statues appear as its distorted shadows. The element in question is the feather that no hurricane can move, perched on an unknown helmet crest: "ce cimier inconnu / Dont aucun ouragan n'eût remué la plume."[45]

The helmet crest or *cimier*, from the word for summit, *cime*, stands out as having pride of place. Higher even than the helmet that might serve to protect a high forehead (*fronton*), the crest appears at the exact midpoint of the section, in the ninth of its seventeen lines. As for its feather, it is not one of the sort that birds shed and that could be tossed about by a light wind. By virtue of its absolute immobility, it is not even the sort of feather to be expected atop the helmet of a man of bronze in this poem, where after all, statues move. "Rien, pas même l'airain, pour jamais ne s'arrête" (Nothing, not even bronze, stops forever) (10: 219), Hugo asserts in the passage just preceding this one. Nothing, no *thing*, even something made of bronze, can be arrested forever. Insofar as it can be reduced to a thing, even a creature of language can be moved or removed. But the feather is not to be moved by a hurricane. What is this feather atop this unknown helmet crest, that stands for the non-thing, for language as non-phenomenalizable, and that cannot be budged even by a hurricane?

Why is the *cimier* characterized as "unknown" (*inconnu*) anyway? The fact that it is an unknown suggests that it is placed there as resistant to consciousness's attempt to make everything apperception. If we look up *cimier*, the *Robert étymologique* explains that it too is not just a thing, an ornamental part of a helmet; it is also a heraldic term, indicating the uppermost part of an escutcheon. It is a thing, but it is also a part of the language of blazonry. It signals an arena forgotten when we think we see and hear things like language muttering in this passage: namely, that it is a text, or what amounts to the same thing, an escutcheon. Of blazonry, Hugo says, "For those who know how to decipher it, blazonry is an algebra, blazonry is a language. The entire history of the second half of the middle ages is written in blazonry, as the first half was written in the symbols of romanic churches. The latter are the hieroglyphs of feudalism, coming after those of theocracy."[46] The language of blazonry is not an oral language to which the phenomenalized signifier could be the key. It is a written language which has as a precondition for any understanding an act that is not an act of perception or even decoding but rather of reading. When the poet reads a field, as Hugo does in the *Contemplations* (9/1: 164), previous to asking what its signs mean, he has first to confer on the seeming randomness of nature the status of letters in an alphabet. He has to take the field as a written page, given as such, whose significance is of less importance than the fact that he confers the authority of a sign on it. Similarly, the *cimier* is the element that reminds us we are reading an escutcheon, a written passage, part of the archive, and not "seeing" or "thinking we see things." It suggests that the question of reading and writing is the unknown around which the rest is elaborated. The feather atop such an escutcheon would of course be a writerly pen.

The quiet eye of the hurricane is writing, material inscription. Around it systems of exchange get set up and undone. In the face of its materiality, consciousness feels threatened enough to grasp at the straw of language as phenomenalizable. But also with respect to writing's materiality, the hallucinatory and repetitive history of the first part can be considered just a passage inscribed in a longer poem, or a reading of what shows up as inscription on the page's other side.

The unruffled emblem doesn't move partly because inscriptions don't move or get moved by hands, or even by whatever consciousness confers perceptibility and meaning on them. It also doesn't move because the wind that blows from it blows in one direction, forward, *devant*. It blows all its signs toward the future-oriented history of the epilogue. Again, the choice of the term *cimier* supports this reading. It derives from the

Greek *kuma*, meaning "swelling," "inflation," "wave" and, by connection to the related verb *kuein* (to be pregnant, to carry in one's breast), takes on the meaning of "fetus," "embryo," or "bud." It stands out as a term, in the midst of the cracking and ruin affecting the city, that bears the meaning of "bearing a future." I would like to conclude with an example from the epilogue to *La Révolution* which gives an idea of why, for Hugo, the historicity of poems resides in inscription and is future-oriented. Two lines tell us:

> A qui te cherche, ô Vrai, jamais tu n'échappas.
> Une étape après l'autre. Après un pas, un pas.
>
> O Truth, you never escape the one who seeks you.
> One stage after the other. After a step, another step.
>
> *(10: 246)*

The short sentences restate the cliché about the seeking of truth as the only way to take hold of it. The ideology it defines, Progress with a capital *p*, seems equally a cliché. But the last sentence, which repeats the problematic found in the earlier passage on the stepping statues, does so with a difference worth noting. Unlike the earlier lines about the statue's step, which offered apparently alternative translations but in fact made sense only in the light of the sounded signifier, this line defining Progress is very generous to the translator. One can translate it in many different ways, according to various systems of meaning: after a step, another step; after a negation, another negation; after a negation, a step; after a step, a negation. All these translations of the line are possible. All affirm, albeit in very different ways—from the predialectical to the dialectical to the negatively dialectical—that progress toward truth is the law of history. The poem—and indeed, the Hugolian corpus—can be understood in the light of each of these differing ideologies of progress. To those interpretations can be added a commentary on the obsessive *pas* that gives rhythm to the poem and makes it a rhythmical pace or musical progression: after a *pas*, another *pas*. The definition of progress in this translation would be repetition, consciousness of consciousness as obsessive. In short, progress would be the repetitive move whereby consciousness persists in seeing itself in structures voided of meaning for it.

To that reading can be added another, however. Hugo could be distinguishing between the obsessive *pas* of rhythm from which one can escape by forgetting about it, and the *pas* which one has more trouble getting away from, namely, the *p-a-s* of the inscription: after the sound *pas*, still another kind of *p-a-s*. What we do when we go after a *p-a-s* is track it, follow it as a *footprint* (another meaning of *pas*). This new *pas* is a stilled *pas* that recollects the others.[47] It is the trail of tracks left for seekers to follow ("After a footprint, another footprint") that allows the gathering and proffering of all the diverse interpretations to which it is susceptible, the collection of meanings of *pas*, into a single written rule. The written rule shelters all the hermeneuts seeking to interpret it. But the same rule also reveals a fragility that does not derive from consciousness, but rather from its aspect as inscription or imprint. It can be effaced or rewritten, and is subject to the accidents of the archive.

On the other side of the page of the hallucinatory history of Terror, we find Hugo writing toward an opening. His understanding of revolution as a history untellable except in linguistic terms is a double understanding. If, on the one hand, at its worst, in the Terror, revolution got stuck repetitively refiguring an insight into language's inhuman difference in human terms, then on the other hand, at its best, in its fundamental texts it did not seek to remodel representation in terms of the subject and of consciousness, but rather in terms of a text. He writes rules that gather otherwise than in terms of the subject and the authority structures invested therein. It is possible to glimpse an opening, within the text of *La Révolution,* toward a definition of revolution as text, as "poème inouï" (10: 231), the unheard, the unheard of, the magnificent poem, the yea-saying (*oui*), future-oriented poem which broadcasts the wherewithal to undo its ideologies of progress as far as or farther still than the ideologies themselves.[48]

The materiality of writing is threatening to consciousness because it denies its power to progress to a certainty of anything beyond it—to an outside referent, to the inside of consciousness, or even, as in Fineman, to a progress in consciousness's understanding of how language functions. But it also provides a resistance to consciousness that gives it a handle on, an opening to, an outside of consciousness. Given the delusions of which consciousness showed itself capable at the end of the Enlightenment, we must consider that a good thing. There is, I would maintain, a *yes* worth thinking about in this gloomiest of deconstructive texts, *La Révolution.*

§ 5 "An Immoderate Taste for Truth": Censoring History in Baudelaire's "Les Bijoux"

POET. Your sort of verbal materialism.
You can consider *from on high* novelists, philosophers, and all those
who are subjected to the word by credulity;—who *must* believe that
their discourse is *real* by its content and signifies some reality. But
you, you know that the real of discourse is words, only, and forms.
—Valéry, *Memoirs of the Poet*

In May 1949 a French court of appeals reversed an 1857 decision condemning six poems from Charles Baudelaire's *Les Fleurs du mal* for obscenity, in a signal case of a public lifting of a ban against some lyric poems.[1] Not the least of the several interesting features of the case is the decision to proceed against the work in the first place. Lyric poetry does not appear an attractive target for censorship, for its subject matter and formalism remove it far enough from the experience of most readers. Gustave Flaubert, fresh from his troubles with the court over *Madame Bovary*, expressed his surprise at the government's attack: "This is new," he wrote to Baudelaire, "this pursuit of a volume of verse."[2] Although his comment was in point of fact inaccurate, Flaubert put his finger on a problem worth considering.[3] Here *Les Fleurs du mal* would seem to be naturally exempt from state intervention, by virtue of a deliberate retreat from risky political subjects and the inaccessibility of the genre, yet it was nonetheless censored by the state. Can anything be learned about "normal" state censorship from this exceptional case?[4]

A key factor in the government's decision to pursue the book, according to the prosecutor Ernest Pinard, was that Baudelaire's poetry might prove accessible to a large audience: "An immoral book that had no chance of being read or understood would not be pursued," he states.[5] In his argument, as in the judgment by the court that the condemned poems "lead necessarily to the exciting of the senses by a coarse realism offensive to modesty" (1: 1182), the assumption is that the work is extraordinarily available, its pictures immediately referable to ordinary experience. In the six condemned poems, language is judged to be not a veil but a tool, and a sex tool at that. "Despite an effort of style" (1: 1182), the poetic situation—in most of the poems that of the boudoir—is painted in a language insufficiently flowery.[6]

A second interesting feature in the case is that when the decision was reviewed again in 1949, during de Gaulle's Fourth Republic, the court summarily dismissed the 1857 judgment of coarse realism as just one possible interpretation, and a forced one at that. Instead, the court found that the poems are self-referential, symbolic entities that do not represent ordinary experience: "If some pictures, on account of their originality, were able to alarm some minds upon first publication and appeared to the first judges as offensive to morality, such an appraisal, attaching itself only to a realistic interpretation of the poems and neglecting their symbolic meaning, has proved to be of an arbitrary character, unratified by public opinion or by the judgment of the literary world."[7] The representations that were considered outrageous in 1857 were in 1949 understood to deliver the Wordsworthian "shock of mild surprise" by which we recognize the original work of art. By 1949, the poems had become precious artifacts. Their language was not realistic but symbolic, and the language's sensuous forms revealed an inner, spiritual meaning.

A crucial resemblance can be discerned between the actions taken by the two courts: both make their judgments in terms of a "reading pact," a set of "artificial rules" (1: 1206) that are presumed to govern reading and to have currency in the context. *Les Fleurs* was policed in the name of this generic purity, with the prosecutor Pinard calling "the judge . . . a sentinel who must not let the border be crossed" (1: 1206); the 1949 decision said something similar when it confirmed the opinion of the literary world that the poems' supposed transgression against public morality, in view of later developments, proved a transformation of the rules regulating the narrow confines of lyric poetry.[8]

This concern that texts be framed by a reading pact aimed at constraining their interpretation is worth considering for anyone who would like to move the discussion of censorship from the pragmatic to the theoretical. It leads to queries about the possibility of getting rid of state censorship entirely and about the state's interest in the institutionalization and enforcement of such reading pacts. It raises the issue of an ambiguity in the role played by the literary establishment, which can be seen most often acting in collusion with the state on this matter of generic purity. This is partly a matter of empirical fact. In the case of *Les Fleurs du mal* for instance, literary journalists brought the whiff of scandal to the state's attention in 1857; in 1949 a Society of Learned Men brought the suit to rehabilitate Baudelaire's memory, and literary critics provided expert testimony as to what Erich Auerbach called the work's "aesthetic dignity."[9] The reading pact also touches on a region where censorship law flows over into copyright law, with the rights to profit from a work's reproduction and dissemination entailing, besides the responsibility to publish the names and coordinates of author, publisher, and printer, an implied directive not to mislead readers as to the literary genre to which the work belongs. As for the works themselves, they can presumably collaborate with as easily as infringe upon the state's attempts to regulate linguistic indeterminacy. Where they help maintain the border between referential and self-referential language uses, they are presumably complicitous with the state and form a perfect mirror of its ideology.

The point I will pursue is a somewhat different one, albeit related, and it requires a bit of preliminary introspection. I suspect that part of the attraction of studying cases of state censorship for a critic is that one can point to such cases as tangible proof that literature does matter, that it sometimes does leave its ivory tower to touch the world. The state is hit in a vital spot, as if the work lays open some secret that censorship laws try to rebury. This is thrilling to critics, this notion that the state is somehow imperiled by the work. It vindicates literary activity, which turns out not to be pointless after all, but instead invested with urgency and relevance.[10]

I cast this in the form of a confession because I am somewhat suspicious of the drama of the scenario. It neatly pits a beleaguered text or author against the monolithic authority of the state threatened by and threatening to the literary work.[11] The reality of censorship is less reassuringly centralized, more diffuse, more disseminated, and less univocal in its functioning than such a scenario would suggest. Nor are works ever all black or white: their complicity with the state on matters of textual hygiene is at least partial.

Nevertheless, the scenario of the state censoring Baudelaire's poems helps focus in the preliminary stages of our inquiry, for it centers attention on the threat posed by textual indeterminacy as it spills over to disturb the presumed unity and stability of its context. In the case of *Les*

Fleurs, poems the state rehabilitated once they were found to have a legible address and mode of meaning, the point of contention is the relation of the literary work to experience, memory, and history.

The prosecutor in 1857 provides the first hint that memory is at stake when he complains that the poems do not remove us from past sensuous experience but instead *produce* and even *model* it. He says the poems have the effect of "giving back their senses to those who can no longer feel" (1: 1208). Into the experience of reading—an experience considered as reflective and removed from the senses—intrudes a new kind of remembering: the sudden revival of deadened senses. This experience of memory as transgressive recollection has been analyzed by the eminent critic of Baudelaire, Walter Benjamin, in a discussion relevant enough to merit a brief summary.

Discussing Theodor Reik's distinction between memory and remembrance, Benjamin explains that remembrance protects and preserves impressions whereas memory destroys and disintegrates them. Remembrance is a present act of retrieval that relies upon a forgetting of "what has not been experienced explicitly and consciously, what has not happened to the subject as an experience" says Benjamin.[12] It thus conserves the past as past, subordinating it to the present act of consciousness, and confirms the view that the gain of understanding more than compensates for whatever the present has lost in terms of immediacy or in proximity to natural experience.

As for memory, it recalls uncollected and as yet unexperienced fragmentary impressions connected to the memory trace, that is, the "writing" that records and preserves sense impressions in the mind. It is apparent from Benjamin's analysis that memory disintegrates at least two structures for parrying what he calls the *shock* made in the imprinting of sense impressions. First, it calls into question the everyday experience of a subject by showing that conscious life is an artificial construction, reliant on decisions and exclusions such as those in which vision (with its tendency toward seizing an experience as a totality in an idealized image) is privileged over the other senses. Second, it disrupts the temporal assumption of remembrance, which preserves the past as past with respect to its act. Memory is an experiencing *for the first time* of left-out impressions, for instance, the repressed sensations of the body as a tangle of parts and disconnected senses. Such a past has not taken place until it emerges, shattering the stability of the present, in the act of recollection.

The knowledge provided by memory can be termed negative knowledge, since in recalling what is left out by consciousness in remembrance, one is faced with understanding the limits of the understanding. If, as Benjamin quotes Reik as saying, "becoming conscious and leaving behind a memory trace are processes incompatible with each other in one and the same system," memory forces consciousness to engage in a desperate and open-ended struggle of recalling traces it never can fully assimilate, but upon which its survival depends.[13]

Benjamin's analysis of Baudelaire calls into question the view that literature depicts a prior model, whether that model be found in nature, in other works, or in the author's transforming imagination. In such a view, the work of art preserves the image produced by the artist as a faithful remembrance of his act; it stands as a memorial to the mental activity of a conscious subject. For Benjamin, however, Baudelaire's poems situate the work with respect to an experience that requires writing in order to happen. Benjamin's argument implies that Baudelaire's poems act against what Laurence Douglas calls the "preserving of responsible memory."[14]

Responsible memory, translated into the terms of our discussion, would be remembrance and memory working together dialectically. In a dialectic, the undoing of the mystified images of the past would occur with the ultimate aim of incorporating the findings of the critique into a more satisfying image or pointed narrative. Remembrance and memory would together produce a version of events that not only would preserve the past (and could thus be termed a *memory*) but also would answer the demand for truth (and could thus be termed *responsible*). If Benjamin's Baudelaire acts against responsible memory, it is not because he is irresponsible, but rather because, as a poet, he is interested in language, which is always more and less than a serviceable medium of exchange and is thus, like the refuse impressions rejected by remembrance, never fully accounted for by a dialectical interpretation.

Baudelaire's poems reveal a forgetfulness in the space of public monuments. Such monuments—among them would be those stockpiles of acquired knowledge called archives and libraries—tell us that past events and past theories are over and done with; they try to place the past of remembered events in a stable relation to the present of their interpretation. They shelter the present from the past, making the past so distant as to be unlikely to erupt into the present as unassimilated shocks. Baudelaire's library is, rather, a cross between a heap of incomprehensible ruins and a fireworks factory set down in the midst of the bustling modern city. In his view, memory and history are open-ended, future-oriented projects of recalling the conditions and limits of consciousness and of any history that would be modeled as a coming into consciousness. Small wonder that poems publicizing a fault line in the archive should be relegated to the Hell (*L'Enfer*) of the National Library where nineteenth-century French law sent censored texts.

My hypothesis is that the question of how the text enters history lies at the heart of the censoring of *Les Fleurs du mal*.[15] That is the problem I would like to discuss here, first complicating what has been said about the state's position on the text as public monument, and then pursuing, through the reading of a poem, the notion of a disintegrating, inventive memory available in licentious writing that is incompatible with public, preserving memory. It is this disintegrating memory that explains the uneasy relation of the state to the literary work: as disintegrating, its violence is perceived as a threat; as inventive, it is memory oriented toward the future, and has a productive energy to be exploited. Since the poet's ultimate responsibility as poet is to the language, it is history carried in language that will provide the lens for my analysis.

Writing Between the Lines: Remembering Language

Leo Strauss's "Persecution and the Art of Writing" provides a good starting point to complicate the state's position. Strauss's discussion of censorship is guided by a complex understanding of the relation of philosophical texts to history. As products of their time, philosophical texts preserve and pass on the opinion of that time, but they also engage in conflictual dialogue with opinion, and as such, transmit less a content than a critical method distinguished by a negative moment. Where state censorship has gotten in the way of the explicit expression of this dialogue between opinion and its critique (as it did in much of eighteenth-century Europe), for example, philosophical writers have had to have recourse to elaborate strategies of indirection, called by Strauss "writing between the lines," to transmit their philosophical method.[16] To write between the lines is to write a text that, read as statement, is entirely orthodox but that, by the arrangement of the statements, devices of argument, and strategic asides, criticizes the orthodoxy.

The recognition that the means of saying can intervene actively in signification allows Strauss first to formulate a critique of historicism as interpretative method. According to Strauss, the principle of historicism forbids interpretation of an author to involve any term of consequence not literally translatable into the author's language and not used by him or in fairly common use in his time. The only presentations of an author's views which can be accepted as true are those ultimately borne out by his own explicit statements (pp. 26–27). By such methods, teaching texts like those of Plato, Averroes, Kant, or Rousseau were diminished to documents transmitting the most platitudinous orthodoxies. Against historicism, Strauss presents a theory of history as an ongoing process of interpretation of fundamental texts. Its method is that of active, self-critical dialogue over orthodox doctrine, a dialogue made available in works written in time of persecution by way of a disjunction between a statement and its mode of presentation—or, as we would nowadays say, by way of a disjunction in an utterance between its force as a constative or statement, and as a performative affirming or denying the truth of whatever it states. Strauss can thus distinguish the true interpretation of a work from the merely correct, historicist one. The true interpretation is neither the orthodox nor the heterodox opinion qua opinion; it is rather the interpretation that, having taken strategy into account, can teach a dialectical method to "the young men who love to think" (p. 24).[17]

What is most relevant in this account for our question is that the recollection that language actively affects meaning serves as a teaching moment, a privileged moment of progress and liberation from mere doxa. A crucial double effect on the concern of the liberal state with freedom of expression can be extrapolated from Strauss's theory of history and of writing between the lines.[18] If his young men—the "puppies of the race" (p. 36)—progress by recalling language, then a liberal state interested in the fostering of its puppies and furthering of progress must tolerate to a certain degree the disruptiveness identified with Benjamin's disintegrating memory. We have to revise the simple opposition that pits the censoring state against the individual author, the public space of preservation of the heroic past against a private space where memory can be free to be disintegrative. Revealed here is a gray area of production and education where public and private interests overlap, where groups of reasonable citizens can amicably disagree with one another and with a state founded on reason, and where agreements can be forged. The contents of texts, statements qua statements, are in themselves revealed to be unthreatening. Once an opinion has value only insofar as its truth is confirmed or belied by the force of its language, a state conceived along Straussian principles can easily liberalize its censorship of content. Paradoxically, however, this state would tend to tighten its control over the means of expression, hoping to limit the negative power of language to what can be assimilated as positive knowledge. Strauss notes the need to find such limits in his essay, in discussing the need for "criteria for distinguishing between legitimate and illegitimate reading between the lines" (p. 32).

Censorship in such a state would hardly merit the name: its aim would be to shelter the means as inventive and educative, while limiting the potential for disruption. The aim is simply accomplished by the determination of those limits as those of knowledge. Any monological text whose structures confirm the liberal orthodoxy by saying what they mean would be allowable, as unproblematically providing knowledge of a content. Any dialogical text whose presentation has a force discrepant with respect to the views it states would provide a lesson on method to the alert few. In either case, the relation of performative to constative enables education, but revelation of a potential, momentary discrepancy contributes the most by promising a dynamic, progressive education in which action and knowledge in the long run coincide. The axiomatic statement that "virtue is knowledge . . . and thoughtful men as such are trustworthy and not cruel" (p. 25) would allow a Straussian state conceived along liberal principles to reduce the arena for positive censorship almost to nothing. The only texts offensive to public morality, and thus excisable, are those that provide for knowledge and action that do not confirm the axiom.[19]

The very few cases that could still fall under a positive censorship can be found in Strauss's own essay in the form of deafening silences on issues germane to his topic. One silence is on playful modes of writing between the lines—literature, especially poetry—where indirect expression is not a teaching method but an art.[20] Another silence is on obscenity, a language use that falls outside the interpretative scheme defining the work as the intentional act of a moral being.[21] Nor do any young women who love to think make an appearance in Strauss's essay. There is no thought of woman at all in his dreamed-of future; the only love moving "thoughtful men" (p. 25) is for the male puppies.

The reading of licentious writing, "profitable," in Baudelaire's words, "only to those minds possessed by an immoderate taste for truth," leads in another direction.[22] It demands that we take into account a dimension of language that may not ultimately confirm the harmonious convergence of knowledge and action. An *immoderate taste* for truth is the taste of someone who has not stopped with the revelation of the truth of method and of history as progress, but has developed an unhealthy appetite for revelation irrespective of whether it leads to positive knowledge. Obscene writing thrusts in our face a certain repetitive material, and a certain pleasure to be gotten from the material, that are rejected when writing is conceived in teleological terms. To recall obscenity is to threaten more than a prohibition on certain topoi. It threatens the very fundamental, convening assumption of the Straussian version of the liberal state that "virtue is knowledge." The censorship of obscene materials, we may hypothesize, would constitute an attempt to keep the neglected material from returning to affect the public space of the liberal state, which is built by respectful, preserving remembrance and by the state's tolerant encouragement of a limited work of disruption by disintegrating memory.

Dirt for Dirt's Sake

Let me gather some support for my understanding of obscenity, and start filling in the gaps left in Strauss's discussion, by reference to a case settled in the American courts in 1933, the case of Joyce's *Ulysses*, where we see an enlightened judge hard at work interpreting a literary work as productive of knowledge. Because it is a work of fiction that is in question, it is the language as used by its speakers, rather than logic and method, that is the object, but the same axiom is still operative.

John M. Woolsey's ruling on the question of whether *Ulysses* could enter the United States became famous outside of legal circles because it was incorporated in several editions to the text as its foreword. In his discussion of the "dirty words" that pepper the text, Judge Woolsey explains what he takes to be Joyce's nonpornographic intent. It is the sincere and honest one proper to the artist of "show(ing) exactly how the minds of his characters operate."[23] For Woolsey, the artistic intent of bringing out "not only what is in the focus of each man's observation of the actual things about him, but also in a penumbral zone residua of past impressions" (p. ix) carries with it demands and responsibilities. Joyce, he says, would have "funked its necessary implications" (p. ix) had he not told fully what his characters think. Woolsey explains away the dirty words: Joyce's "attempt sincerely and honestly to realize his objective has required him incidentally to use certain words which are *generally considered* dirty words" (pp. ix–x).

For Woolsey, in this specific context—given the framing intent and the creative technique—words generally considered dirty are not really dirty. They are determined otherwise, as the words that the author in all honesty must use. We might call them *honest dirt*, for they symbolize the sweat exuded from the brow of the inventing artist. In the specific context of *Ulysses* they have ceased to be filthy. The artist reconfigures the language, with the expletives as the clue.

What that means first of all is that the author does not really "use" the dirty words at all. He uses them, as Woolsey says, "incidentally." For a term to be judged obscene, it is clearly not enough that it refer to a sexual or excretory organ or function. Otherwise, any talking about such functions, never mind any talking about talking about such functions, would be forbidden, and obscenity trials themselves would become impossible.[24] The key to obscenity lies in the way language is being used. Like *tree* or *table*, dirty words are literal, referential terms properly designating entities in the physical world. If they nonetheless offend good linguistic hygiene, it is because when we use them we break the rule, set forth in the work of empiricists like Locke or Condillac, that dictates a one-to-one correspondence between the ideas we get from our senses or our reason, and the terms designating them. In obscenity (as in certain theological discourses) the terms reserved to name a single referent—physical or metaphysical—proliferate and a reserve of words piles up that can be substituted for or added to one another without loss or gain in meaning. Obscene terms guard one door to a secret place of play in language, where the substitution of names unregulated by meaning, unaccountable to knowledge, can go on and we can take pleasure in words for their own sake.[25] Language's public virtue as enabler of education is contested by the use of expletives (*explere*—"to fill out"), forceful verbal filler.

When Woolsey says Joyce does not use obscene terms except incidentally, I take it that he means the author does not himself commit the abuse. Rather, he collects and pins these obscene words into his text purposively, as *examples* of language abuse. Obscenities, Woolsey says, clutter the minds and speeches of Joyce's characters, but they are always in quotes so far as the author himself is concerned.[26] He *mentions* them to fulfill an obligation he has to provide a full picture of the language. Adding quotes to a dirty word partially launders it by making it an example of a general possibility of language. It brings the prohibited material and the prohibition forward as objects of knowledge. Framed obscenity obtrudes the sheer physicality of language on us, but at a distance. By it the writer signals his debt and promise to represent the language in its entirety.

Quotation marks, literal or implied, are crucial in Woolsey's discussion. They are laundry marks added by the artist that let him represent the whole body of language, without reserve.[27] The judge gives a glimpse of the stakes when he reminds us that the words that Joyce has reclaimed are "old Saxon words known to almost all men, and, I venture, to many women" (p. x). Joyce accepts our English language as is, soiled by overuse and abuse, in parts reserved and shameless, with the aim of restoring its ideal Saxon integrity and purity. He takes terms eroded over time to the value of filler and makes them signify as examples of the transformation to which language is subject. By this move he arrests and even reverses the work of time. Language *shown* to be shopworn is language revealed as subject to unacknowledged historical processes, and thus language brought into a certain conformity with the Straussian axiom "virtue is knowledge."

The point is worth tarrying over, for there Woolsey reveals an attitude toward history and the function of the work of art in reversing the corrosion of language by time. In their account of the trial, Ernst and Schwartz insist that the explanation of "each four-letter word in historic terms" was the turning point in the battle.[28] Counsel for *Ulysses* gave etymological arguments that persuasively carried the terms back to a time before they had been set aside as obscene. These etymological arguments are in point of fact *a*historical, for they try to fix the term in an imagined pristine state, before any figurative extension, any reserve or repetition. Counsel states of the word *fuck*, for instance, that "one etymological dictionary gives its derivation as from *facere*—to make—the farmer fucked the seed into the soil. This, your honor, has more integrity than a euphemism used every day in every modern novel to describe precisely the same event."[29]

Everything is revealing here: the definition, the example, the vague "this," the appeal to "your honor," the emphasis on the integrity of the past as opposed to modern prudishness. Most interesting is the example. Here we have a farmer, the sort of man who might have minted the term to name his work, which is that of sowing his seed. This is an Adam before the fig leaf, who would have called things by their proper names, before figurative extensions, reserves, or euphemisms. *Fuck* was as innocent and honest a word as any in the English language. Counsel provides a glimpse of a nascent, agrarian people whose language was as fresh and virginal as the soil they planted. In contrast, the modern situation shows the same event of making, but everywhere repeated, in a banal, degraded version. The cause of corruption is overuse, unacknowledged quotation, and the veil of euphemism is interposed to hide it. Joyce partially reclaims the term by an acknowledged quotation that frames a mythic picture of a language once virginal, but now prostituted, whose exemplary tale can serve as a warning about the rest of the language, still meaningful and still capable of being used with decency and respect.

Woolsey signals that he agrees with this recall to hygiene as a valuable service performed by the work of art. He does so partly by a slip, clumping the four-letter word *fuck* with the others, as criticized terms that are actually "old Saxon words." To say that *fuck*, which counsel had just derived from the Latin *facere*, is a Saxon word is to wipe out such suspicious episodes as the Roman and Norman conquests, responsible for the large-scale importation of latinate terms into the English language. It is to assume that there was a moment when the English language was entire, before contamination by suspect foreign influence, by transports this way and that. In the name of race, nation, people, some ideology of the proper, the judge goes along with what he takes to be the artist's function with respect to the language: cordoning off the ruined parts from the living language and restoring the ideal of a language as an intact whole.

Judge Woolsey also considers the same dirty words from the perspective of the diegesis, in terms of the internal consistency of the characters depicted. Here, the quotation marks function somewhat differently. The obscene terms, he says, are "such words as would be naturally and habitually used . . . by the types of folk whose life, physical and mental, Joyce is seeking to describe . . . it must always be remembered that his locale was Celtic and his season Spring" (p. x). From the perspective of the internal world of the novel, these dirty words are, so to speak, *natural dirt,* compost from which might spring flowers. So we are not surprised when

Woolsey suggests that Joyce is truly inventive, opening up the unconscious of his characters by way of this dirt. Any other terms would have been euphemisms, the censored language of conscious thought, and would have kept locked the door to the world within the world of the novel which is that of the unconscious. As words from its unknown language, they point beyond the visible world of literal language and the spiritual world revealed by metaphor, to a third world ordinarily repressed, that obeys the logic of a logorrheic stream of consciousness. But that means that they are not really spoken by the characters, who are instead ventriloquized by them. As they erupt out of the mouths of the characters, they are the terms of an unfamiliar language pronounced by the characters, as one pronounces the words of a text written in a language one doesn't know. The obscene terms are the written language of the unconscious.

Placing the disruptive utterances in quotation marks, implied or literal, helps contain the violence. A mouth of a single character or class of characters opens at a single moment to express the unconscious. Woolsey is very clear that this kind of talk is that of "persons of the lower middle class living in Dublin in 1904" (p. ix). Joyce's framing techniques isolate, as in a sick ward, those utterances that are not spoken consciously from the normal, conscious utterances of a character, as well as from those uttered in the world outside the fiction. The marking devices are internal dikes in the elongated sentence that is the novel; they let us differentiate, say, between Molly Bloom's soliloquy and Judge Woolsey's prefacing opinion. Mentioning dirty words launders them doubly: first, by preserving them as ruined terms recalling the originary state of the language in its integrity and propriety; second, by a partial censorship, a separating of the disruptive talk from ordinary utterances.

Joyce's partial censoring provides a clue to a third kind of dirt, a dirt neither honest nor natural, potentially afflicting the whole of the language. Had Woolsey found it in *Ulysses*, he *would* have termed it obscene. He says of *Ulysses*: "although it contains . . . many words usually considered dirty, I have not found anything that I consider to be *dirt for dirt's sake*" (p. x). This third kind of dirt the artist has caused to be rejected as unreclaimable excess. The phrase Woolsey uses—"dirt for dirt's sake"—tells us what is unreclaimable: it is dirt unendowed with a purpose, dirt as an index, just more of the dirt that it stands for. Dirty dirt puts the tautological and repetitive in the place of the teleological at the outset, and thus threatens Woolsey's myth of language as originarily an intact whole. Woolsey says that *Ulysses* expels such dirt. He knows that by the purging effect the work has on the reader: "my considered opinion, after long reflection, is that whilst in many places the effect of 'Ulysses' on the reader undoubtedly is somewhat emetic, nowhere does it tend to be an aphrodisiac" (p. xii). The dreck the work of art cannot purify, it must cause to be expelled. *Ulysses* induces vomiting rather than pleasure. It makes its readers sick of sex.[30]

The case of *Ulysses* supports the contention that the censorship of obscenity operates according to a different logic than that of the censorship of philosophical texts. In the literary text, where knowledge of language use is the stake, the representation of obscenity can be seen as necessary. The judge, representative censor, lifts the quarantine on *Ulysses* because he finds it to be good for linguistic hygiene: it purifies and reclaims the language for use where it can by quoting, and purges dirt where it cannot.

Note the juridico-political situation of the literary text vis-à-vis the censor. Where message-oriented texts are concerned, the arena for legal censorship can be greatly restricted. Strauss's censor is bound by the law which demands proof of the author's intent and of his vigilance over all his expressions. Structurally speaking, for Strauss the censor is less intelligent than a writer of even average intelligence (p. 26). Where it is a matter of fictional texts whose aim is to represent the language, however, the same protection does not seem to apply. Implicit in Woolsey's argument is the view that artists are to draw the line anew between those words and images that can be reassigned meaning, and those that are unreclaimable. Theirs is the Herculean task of mucking out the Augean stable of language made dirty by overuse and excessive euphemism. But that means that artists stand open to the accusation of obscenity precisely insofar as they try to keep their promise as artists.

As for the censor's limits, it seems that the judgment of obscenity ought to stand on the success or failure of the work to reclaim the language as a whole. But since no one is or could be in a position to judge on such a matter, it relies instead on the intelligence and courage of the censoring judge. Judges are required to be informed about things that, for structural reasons, they cannot know. For instance, they have to know when an author is exemplifying language, mentioning a term in quotes, and when she is using it, speaking in her "own" voice.[31] Judges have to know when obscene talk is in quotes that clean up and contain the dirt, and when such quoting is just guilty pleasure taken in manipulating sensuous language—repetition without transformation.

As for the definition of obscenity, it is entirely problematic.[32] More than one author complains of the lack of any objective criteria to follow.[33] If the work is indeed engaged in redefining obscenity first by reclaiming "foul" language for meaning, and second by causing to be regurgitated as excess what it cannot so reclaim, then it follows that the judge never could approach a new work armed with a prior definition, but would always have to rely on the work to provide a dividing line. To the extent that the work manages to assimilate "dirt," the work defines dirt in terms of a purpose. To the extent that the work cannot assimilate it to that purpose, to the extent that it expels it, the dirt is mere tautology. By definition, *as* tautology, the obscene falls outside of definition. Indeed, Woolsey's own attempt at defining obscenity, which is one that enjoyed a certain currency in the writings of the mid twentieth century on obscenity laws—"dirt for dirt's sake"—is really less a successful definition than a phrase coined to renounce definition. It gives up on determining a concept of dirt, gives in by just reiterating the term.[34] It indicates a symptomatic moment of breakdown, of unreclaimable excess in Woolsey's own writing. Because it fills in for a missing definition with a word that adds nothing, we can call it an expletive, a swear word in its own right: For dirt's sake, dirt![35]

These problems—the special risk and license of the artist, the special requirements of the censor, the necessary time lag in the law that makes it so no author could know when she was breaking the law before having been called to account for it, the impossibility of defining obscenity—make the problem of censorship much murkier in the case of obscenity and the work of art than in the rather optimistic case that Strauss presents for the philosophical text.[36]

Nonetheless, despite their differences, Strauss and Woolsey do agree on the teleological nature of the understanding as mirrored in texts, with censorship legitimated as the act of reason overseeing transgressions against its rule. Woolsey's account can be said to complete Strauss's account, since it awards the work of art the function of reclaiming language to make it susceptible to bearing meaning. A question arises. Is this official view of the work of art as upholding the border between telos and *tautos* actually consonant with the nature of literary language?

Art for Art's Sake

To address this question, we require an example. What better place to look than the text of Baudelaire, the self-proclaimed theorist of "Art for Art's sake"? We may as well start with the slogan "l'art pour l'art," coined by Victor Cousin, imitated by Woolsey, and picked up by Baudelaire in defiance of Hugo's "l'art pour le progrès." Does Baudelaire mean by his slogan the opposite of what Hugo says, namely, that art does not serve an ideology outside itself but is responsible to its own truth, to no idea but that of autotelic beauty and formal perfection? Certainly, the preposition *pour* (*for*) can express purposiveness, and suggest a religion of art and a celebration of symbolic language. But a coined phrase comes with two sides. *Pour* can also state an equivalence between two different inter-changeable things, as in "j'ai eu un pain pour cinq francs" (I got a loaf of bread for five francs) or even among similar exchangeable things, "oeil pour oeil, dent pour dent" (an eye for an eye, a tooth for a tooth). The problem expressed by *l'art pour l'art* in such a reading would be to find two equivalents interchangeable with one another, one art for another art, say poetry for painting. Baudelaire often does call attention to this underside of the poetic economy, where the poet is engaged in sniffing out terms that are equivalent as terms—rhyme words, words of equal syllables, words with alliterative possibilities, or the like. With *l'art pour l'art* then, Baude-laire may be pointing away from the teleological toward the tedious labor of the artisan with his material. With this duality to the work in mind, let's look at one of the poems condemned by the 1857 court, "Les Bijoux."

Les Bijoux

La très chère était nue, et, connaissant mon coeur,
Elle n'avait gardé que ses bijoux sonores,
Dont le riche attirail lui donnait l'air vainqueur
Qu'ont dans leurs jours heureux les esclaves des Mores.

Quand il jette en dansant son bruit vif et moqueur,
Ce monde rayonnant de métal et de pierre
Me ravit en extase, et j'aime à la fureur
Les choses où le son se mêle à la lumière.

Elle était donc couchée et se laissait aimer,
Et du haut du divan elle souriait d'aise
A mon amour profond et doux comme la mer,
Qui vers elle montait comme vers sa falaise.

Les yeux fixés sur moi, comme un tigre dompté,
D'un air vague et rêveur elle essayait des poses,
Et la candeur unie à la lubricité
Donnait un charme neuf à ses métamorphoses;

Et son bras et sa jambe, et sa cuisse et ses reins,
Polis comme de l'huile, onduleux comme un cygne,
Passaient devant mes yeux clairvoyants et sereins;
Et son ventre et ses seins, ces grappes de ma vigne,

S'avançaient, plus câlins que les Anges du mal,
Pour troubler le repos où mon âme était mise,
Et pour la déranger du rocher de cristal
Où, calme et solitaire, elle s'était assise.

Je croyais voir unis par un nouveau dessin
Les hanches de l'Antiope au buste d'un imberbe,
Tant sa taille faisait ressortir son bassin
Sur ce teint fauve et brun le fard était superbe!

—Et la lampe s'étant résignée à mourir,
Comme le foyer seul illuminait la chambre,
Chaque fois qu'il poussait un flamboyant soupir,
Il inondait de sang cette peau couleur d'ambre!

The Jewels

Knowing my heart, my dearest one was nude,
Her resonating jewellery all she wore,
Which rich array gave her the attitude
Of darling in the harem of a Moor.

When dancing, ringing out its mockeries,
This radiating world of gold and stones
Ravishes me to lovers' ecstasies
Over the interplay of lights and tones.

Allowing love, she lay seductively,
And from the high divan smiled in her ease
At my love—ocean's deep felicity,
Mounting to her as tides draw in the seas.

A tiger tamed, her eyes were fixed on mine,
With absent air she posed in novel ways,
Whose candour and lubricity combined
Made charming all her metamorphoses.

Her shoulders and her arms, her legs, her thighs,
Polished with oil, undulent like a swan,
Passed by my tranquil and clairvoyant eyes;
Then belly, breasts, those clusters on my vine,

Came on, tempting me more than devils could,
To break the peace my soul claimed as its own,
And to disturb the crystal rock abode
Where distant, calm, it had assumed its throne.

Her waist contrasted with her haunches so
It seemed to me I saw, in new design,
A boy above, Antiope below
The painting on her brown skin was sublime!

—And since the lamp resigned itself to die,
The hearth alone lit up the room within,
Each time it uttered forth a blazing sigh,
Flushed with tones of blood her amber skin.[37]

The poem was polemically rebaptised by the prosecutor "Naked woman, trying on poses before her fascinated lover" (1: 1208), and its opening lines, as translated by J. McGowan, seem to support the point:

Knowing my heart, my dearest one was nude,
Her resonating jewellery all she wore,
Which rich array gave her the attitude
Of darling in the harem of a Moor.

The artifices by which the woman attracts the lover and the epithet "la très chère," which ironically suggests that the dearest one is very dear indeed (in that the jewels she displays may have been purchased by some rich lover), contribute details that might have served the prosecutor's contention that Baudelaire is attempting to "give senses back to those who no longer can feel" (1: 1208). McGowan has pushed the poem in this direction by translating the impersonal "la très chère" (literally, "the very dear one") as the more intimate "*my* dearest one," and the rather sinister "les esclaves des Mores" (literally, "the slaves of Moors") to whose air hers is likened, as the more innocuous "*darling* in the harem of a Moor." The poem is translated as a representation of an intimate moment between lover and expert courtesan, a moment that the poet—something of an exhibitionist as well as a voyeur—is letting us share.

In this reading, the poem blatantly contradicts some of Baudelaire's strong statements of preference for draped women over the nude. In *Le Peintre de la vie moderne*, for instance, he writes that

> [Woman] is above all a general harmony, not only in her bearing and the movement of her limbs, but also in the muslins, the gauzes, the vast and shimmering clouds of material with which she envelops herself, and which are, as it were, the attributes and pedestal of her divinity; in the metal and the mineral that snake about her arms and neck, that add their sparkle to the fire of her eyes, or that chatter softly at her ear. What poet would dare, in the depiction of the pleasure caused by the appearance of a beauty, to separate a woman from her costume? . . . [The disinterested enjoyer makes of] the two, the woman and the dress, an indivisible totality. (2: 714)

The stark nudity of the woman in most readings of "Les Bijoux" contrasts with this refusal to separate woman from her dress.[38]

With this in mind, looking back again at the first lines, we find that another reading emerges, one that would be more in keeping with an accent on the enveloping garb: "The very dear one was . . . a cloud, and knowing my heart, she had reserved only her sonorous jewels." *La nue*, from *nubes*, is a term for cloud that a working poet, one concerned with the formal requirements of the alexandrine or of a rhyme scheme, would do well to have in mind.[39] The poem, in this translation, would contain a daring metonymy representing the dearest one by her dress. It would be playing on something of a commonplace of midcentury Parnassian poetry, the topos of the cloud-wrapped goddess descending from her mountain retreat, eagerly awaited by her priest-celebrant.[40]

We can thus give two readings to the female figure: the first, the crude and fleshy nude, "la très chair" (*chair* means "flesh"), that links the poem to those addressed to the courtesan Jeanne Duval; the second, a veiled and enthroned idol, "la très chaire" (*chaire* means "throne, chair"), a figure close to that glimpsed in "La Beauté" who "reign(s) in the azure" (*trône dans l'azur*).[41] Whichever reading one starts from is shadowed by the other.

The problem is not which reading is the right one, since the poem can and does make sense of both. The problem is rather how the poet presents their relationship in the singular gift that is the poem. That relation is puzzling. The poet quite deliberately does not provide us with the obvious itinerary, say, by exploiting the protean shape of the cloud as a metaphor for desire, and then stripping away the cloud cover to reveal the nude.[42] In "Les Bijoux" such an avenue is not available: no natural landscape is provided. We are in a room illuminated by an uncertain fire, with occasional light refracting from the "clairvoyant" eyes, polished limbs, and sonorous jewels. It takes an act of the mind, an observation finer than that of the eye, to find in the fleshy nude a relation to a cloud-enveloped deity. The poet has to bypass visible nature and the analogies it makes available. He has to find an allegory.[43] If "Les Bijoux" is an allegory, what does it allegorize?

One allegory is of the poem itself, as engendered from the homonym. Take the seemingly insignificant detail of the sonorous jewels on which the poet fastens for the length of two stanzas. Whether we consider the poem as inspired by goddess or courtesan, "sonorous jewels" points away from resemblances based on what we can see (away from the signified) to analogies prized for their sound alone. The jewels have the audibility of signifiers, and in celebrating them, the poet celebrates analogies based on sound. A nude courtesan can substitute for a cloud-wrapped goddess if one has only one's ears to rely on.

This is remarkable and, in its own way, scandalous. Here is a poem that takes a dirty postcard, the representation of a gentleman eyeing a nude courtesan, and the representation of an intoxicated priest awaiting a goddess, and treats them as indistinguishable. Not only that, but the poet, who is writing a poem for poets, is only interested in the double image as possibly owed to a homophony. Allegory (which gets its "didactic effectiveness," according to Paul de Man, by making "one forget the vices it sets out to represent") is the right term to use for a poem that sets aside so quickly the pleasures of sex and religion in favor of a discussion of poetic form.[44] This is the sort of quotation of an obscene image that Woolsey might approve, since it lets us know that it is *language's* sensuous existence that is being depicted, and not "dirt for dirt's sake." Read as an allegory, the central conflict of the first two stanzas concerns whether the poet's attention to the signifier is degrading or elevating. On the outcome of this conflict will ride a second question: whether the homonym is ultimately to be understood in terms of the sounded signifier.

On one side in the conflict, we have the reading of *nue* as a nude courtesan who has *gardé* (kept on) only her sonorous jewels. The attention of the poet-as-john is distracted from the nude to the jewels; the poet's concupiscent eye intent on seizing its pleasure gives way to the ear. The ear, always open to the word of the other, is here the organ of conscience that starts to turn the voyeur poet away from pleasure, to contemplate such questions as the evanescence of things (stanza 5), the state of his soul (stanza 6), a new form of art (stanza 7), and even his own death (stanza 8). The ear can overhear words differently, as saying something other than what the speaker means by them. These chance words are not just places where cultural differences are revealed, where one group of speakers of a language systematically misunderstands another group apparently speaking the same language—as when a visitor from England overhears an American parent bewailing the "potty talk" on a school playground and comes away with the impression that madness is rampant among the American elementary school set.

Chance words can also awaken us to consider the disorienting possibility that language speaks about itself through us, in the very utterances that we think reveal us as subjects. At the beginning of the second stanza, the poem provides an instance of a word received as if from on high, where "son bruit vif et moqueur" stands out as significant. In context, in terms of the figure visualized, the phrase could be literally translated as a description of an attribute of the courtesan's jewelry, "its lively and mocking noise" (or "ringing out its mockeries," as McGowan less literally puts it). Given the invitation to listen to sound, and given the proximity of the term for noise, *bruit*, we could easily read *son* not as the possessive adjective *its*, but as the homonym, the noun *sound*. The rest of the line becomes an apposition, offering a sort of definition: "sound, lively and mocking noise." The sound of the words of the statement interferes with the statement that is made about the value of sound to the poet. The interruption reveals a meaning more "elevated," poetically speaking, than the mere pleasure taken in the sensuous signifier, since here the signifier can plausibly be said to have *produced* meaning, by spinning off a theoretically sound definition of *sound*. It does not emerge from the poet, who receives it rather as a listener, but seems to come from the poem itself, as it were "divinely inspired." The poet-as-john is shown distracted away from the sensuous pleasures associated first with the eye and then with the ear, toward an increasingly elevated mood of introspection. The possibility is that the play of the signifier, language in its independent action, recovers an earlier state of language when words shed light by their sound.

On the other side, the *nue* can be read as the cloud-veiled goddess anticipated by her priest-celebrant. Here things take place very differently. Awaiting her imminent manifestation, the priest gets so impatient as to start hearing sounds of her approach before they occur. In keeping with her veiled approach, she has *gardé* (kept back, in reserve) her sonorous jewels, and yet the poet starts to celebrate his furious love for sound. This is a rapid degradation: eagerly anticipating the arrival of the goddess, at the first chance the poet is distracted and thinks only of his own senses. A movement of falling can be traced throughout the poem, down through the final stanzas where the priest compares his idol to other goddesses, as a connoisseur in deities (stanza 7), until finally, letting the sanctuary light go out, the poem closes with a euphemistic veil partly drawn over the final sex act.[45]

Instances of sound play in the first stanza support this movement of degradation. The line describing the effect of her sonorous jewels, "Dont le riche attirail lui donnait l'air vainqueur" means "whose rich array gave her the conquering air." But it also adds, distractingly, a homophone, a word that sounds the same as *don* (gift), *dont* (whose). It sounds like the priest, talking about the air the jewels give her, is giving her another gift, *don(t)* . . . *don(nait)*. The gift is not as innocuous as it looks, or the priest is drunker than he first appears, for he says *don* . . . *don*. *Dondon* is an onomatopoeic term of some vulgarity meaning "fat lady," and it would be a wounding insult from a priest, officially charged with celebrating the cult of "the dear one." The excess carried by the chance words of the sounded signifiers gets in the way, threatening the overall meaning of celebration. The poem thus diverts our attention away from its meaning, which in this reading states that the play of the signifier is the source of a threat to meaning, and leads to mental distraction (*fureur*).[46] Here, the play of language does not tend toward an ideal reconciliation of sound and meaning, force and signification, but is instead disruptive. It leads toward the ventriloquizing of the very words in which the priest tries to celebrate his deity.[47]

What then is the outcome of the conflict between the two readings? Does Baudelaire evaluate the play with the signifier as a divinely inspired means for producing meaning, or as a dangerous, degrading fall away from Art, into sensualism? This question requires that we consider what the *poem* means about poetic language independent of the poet's wishes or thoughts on the subject. Whatever the reason for this distraction—excesses of pleasure, madness, or divine inspiration—it is a key that his statements are those of a literally absentminded poet. Something else (which we are calling the poem) seems to speak momentarily through him.

In a remarkable move, the poem discards the question as a false question that derives from the mistaken idea that poetic language is voiced, phenomenalized language and that poems are "meant to be read aloud."[48] There are several places where it is evident that the poem labors against the poet to reject sound patterns as a source of meaning or pleasure. Consequently we may conclude that the homophony is a diversion away from the *written* homonym as figure for the poem. In the first line of the second stanza, the poet explains that he loves "Ce monde rayonnant de métal et de pierre . . . quand il jette en dansant son bruit vif et moqueur" (this radiating world of metal and stones when it throws off in dancing its lively and mocking sound). The line summarizes the problem succinctly by way of the ambiguous term *jette*, which can mean "emit, throw out," with the sensuous poet celebrating the jewels as emitting sound, and also "throw off, discard," with the meditative poet celebrating the jewels as producing meaning in the shedding of sound. But the dilemma is dispensed with quickly once we understand that dancing is not the actual situation of the poem. The poet loves this world "(w)hen . . . dancing." But the poem knows that "when" is hypothetical. It is not now. The *mundus muliebris* does not now emit or discard any noise at all. The hypothesis, with all the razzle-dazzle of the signifier producing meaning, is a fiction indicating the actual situation of the poem, which is one of stillness and deprivation—of voice, sensation, presence, sentiment, mobility, and so on.[49]

The poem is, after all, a poem of mourning. It commemorates the stilling of the spoken language and lays to rest any interpretation that seeks to exploit the sounded signifier. The poem's jewels mock sound to obtrude their actual silence on our notice. For what reason should the poem insist on reminding us of its existence as a written artifact? The simplest reason is that it cannot help but do so. However powerfully it charms us into believing that some subject, or language itself, is murmuring lessons in our ear, it can only exert its charm because it is written down. The meanings of the homophone are only available because the phoneme (ny) is written down in a memorandum as *nue*, not said and heard but quoted and read, reiterated and reiterable as it appears. Of course, the poem makes a virtue of necessity by forcing a comparison between the poem desired (as a spoken, intelligible communication be-

tween subjects) and the poem received (as a written, legible legacy from
the past). That comparison requires us to consider the relationship of the
poem's intelligibility to its legibility particularly with respect to history.

A likeness shows up between the spoken word and the written word:
both are historical products. Instead of asking what Baudelaire means by
his Janus-faced image, instead of considering whether he might be representing the sacred and obscene of his epoch, instead of asking about the
relation of his text's teaching to the doxa of the context, we are forced by
the unveiling of the homonym to consider another history—perhaps
subsidiary, perhaps not—that affects the vehicle. We are obliged to ask
what historical accidents have happened to make *nue* indistinguishable
from *nue*. The answer a philologist might provide—that the difference
between the *b* of *nubes* and the *d* of *nudus* has been eroded and forgotten
by usage[50]—is less important than the fact that recourse to the homonym, to writing is necessary to pose, never mind to answer, the question. Homonyms appear as dead spots where the historical character of
the so-called living language is in evidence. Differences between homophone and homonym also surface. For instance, the homonym reminds
of the operation of history whereas the homophone tends to occlude it.
Also, the rates and sorts of transformations to which spoken and written
language systems are subject differ. In considering the effects of spoken
usage on language, the view is either that difference is erased, that language decays in the mouth away from some earlier state of freshness and
completeness, or that it evolves slowly from some less differentiated,
more primitive state. In either case, language is thought as analogous to
a living being, and one continuous over time. But what of the history
connected to the reminder? The writing system, which preserves spoken
language, is subject to other kinds and rates of loss: to surprise gains and
irrecuperable collapses, to calculations and regulations affecting the material word. Worms eat books; censors delete passages from them; laws
regulate and sometimes prohibit their publication or circulation; libraries get set up to preserve them; a misprint or uncertain spelling is stub-
bornly recycled; and sometimes—because of fortunes of war, acts of
God, deliberate repressions—libraries get burnt. Writing systems can
lose their legibility, in parts or wholly. Or someone can force a comparison between meaningful and legible language and open new terrain. In
short, the poem quotes or mimes a speaking, and in doing so, it makes
us ask what is added and lost by its quoting.

The collapse and withdrawal of the homonym foreseen by the poem is then significant. "I follow in vain the withdrawing God," Baudelaire says in "Le Coucher du soleil romantique," and that movement is quite literally what he has seized here. In 1877, the *Littré* still sees *nue* as a cloud, a synonym for *nuage* and *nuée*. But by the end of the century, when Mallarmé writes, "She, dead *nue*, in the mirror" he is already taking into account the fact that *nue* is dead as a common term for cloud.[51] A new *âge* has dawned; *nuage*, already the usual term for Baudelaire, has entirely taken over in ordinary speech about the cloudscape. The recent *Trésor de la langue française* consecrates this change, saying the term *nue* is "archaic, poetic and literary" and subsists in only a few clichés in common parlance.

Clearly, from the perspective of the referent, it doesn't matter whether one calls a cloud a *nue* or a *nuage*. What does matter is that in this poem, access to the allegory is only available if the figure remains legible as a metonym for the goddess figure. The homonym is the key to the riddle of writing as it reduplicates (for preserving remembrance) and deprives (as disintegrating memory) the speech act of its originary force. Its loss spells the possible end of the poem's legibility. The poem takes a snapshot of a little fissure in the archive, a fracture that by our period has so widened that the chief problem of the poem is nearly inaccessible. It tries to capture in its snapshot the moment of collapse at which the very memory of the departing *nue* is getting lost, and with it the memory of writing as redoubling the spoken language as it originates. Far from providing a reader's pact against which to measure the value of each of its enunciations, the poem concerns itself with its inability to transmit meaning without losing legibility. However we interpret the *nue* we are forgetting that the poem, as given in the speech act, is preserved in a writing whose legibility is already in doubt.

The little fragment provides evidence that the act of reconfiguring the language as a whole, healthy body entails a loss of its legibility. That it is a small piece is not comforting, since with it goes not only the poem's discussion of the idol of the time, the lesson on the play of the signifier as leading to madness, and so on, but also what the text has to say about a sclerosis affecting the legibility of texts. In poems, it is possible to ask where the language is in its process of becoming, as André Chénier says, "an antique writing and no longer a language."[52] By determining language as meaning, in terms of consciousness, we become estranged from, forgetful of the state of the archive. When Baudelaire proposes opening "for poets, the curious, philosophers" a "museum of love where everything would have a place, from St. Theresa's unapplied tenderness to the serious debaucheries of bored centuries" (2: 443) I take it that he envisages that such a museum—beyond titillating the senses or slaking the interest of the curious in the love customs of other places and times—would collect instances of this fracturing affecting the archive, partly through the stylization and artificiality of the postures into which this "natural" sentiment thrusts the human figure (upon which Baudelaire rather heavily insists), and partly through details leading in the same direction as the image of "Les Bijoux."[53] Certainly, the melancholy that he claims affects the viewer of obscene drawings in the same text from *Salon de 1846* indicates that their true subject is not sensuous pleasure but loss and mourning.[54]

The poem is indeed concerned with the question of history at work in the language, just as Woolsey's Joyce is, but to very different effect. In Woolsey's view, Joyce adds quotes to obscenity to give us back the language in its pristine state. In Baudelaire's poem, a fissure shows up in the act of giving the poem that shows language ruined at the outset. Obscene language reveals the truth that language never was a virgin, and by it we learn that language is always already affected by deprivation. It is not a whole body but a catalog of parts.[55]

The poem knows that determining language for meaning is working to render illegible its bicephalous figure. In an ensuing crucial section of the poem (stanzas 5 and 6, the stanzas that came under direct fire in the 1857 trial) the verbs *Passaient* and *S'avançaient* establish the meditation as concerned with the past and future of the language.[56] In this section, the examination of the double-sided figure and the development of the allegory proceeds in the relative calm provided by the knowledge that the poetic figure is stilled. She lies mute on her couch, and the term *couchée*, which means "prone, abed," but which also can mean "consigned" or "inscribed in a text," again points to the textual allegory. Something disturbs the quiet, however, and we are given a second glimpse of the poet, no longer distracted, but now awakened by the poem to an awareness of the historical character of the language as represented by the movements of the central figure. The poet's love has turned contemplative. With the idea of an eventual intervention, he contemplates the movements of the allegorical figure for poetry. Its movements are doubly evaluated: a potential for evolution, for continuing metamorphosis and renewal is seen, but a rather threatening fracturing is also evident, as certain body parts recede or are thrust forward.

In the fifth and sixth stanzas, the poet differentiates between those parts of the figure that pass away before his serene surveying glance, and those that advance—belly and breasts—to trouble his repose. In terms of the poetic allegory, these body parts are details that draw our attention to the structural parts of the poem: the organization of its stanzas and its syntax. The poem provides a striking instance of such structuring parts in the coordinating conjunction *et*, made visible by dint of its being repeated no fewer than nine times in eight lines, three times in positions of stress.

Et has two distinct grammatical functions in the fifth stanza. It adds together like things, body parts: "bras et . . . jambe, et . . . cuisse et . . . reins . . ." (arm and . . . leg, and . . . thigh and . . . loins . . .); "ventre et . . . seins" (belly and . . . breasts). It also adds together things considered in their difference. It adds the two verbs—"Et . . . Passaient . . . Et . . . S'avançaient" (And . . . Passed . . . And . . . Advanced)—so as to present the widely different effects of the parts on the poet. He is "serene" in his mastery over the parade of some passing parts, yet "troubled" by the advancing belly and breasts. We have to be able to tell the difference between *et* as enumerating like things and *et* as enumerating different things to understand the dramatic shift in the stance of the poet.

The poet is considering the corrosive work of usage on the parts of the language. He furthers the erosion of certain articulations by repeating, polishing them to the point of near liquefaction: they are "polished as with oil." This stream of conventional, polished parts is passing away, and the poet views it with serenity, for he sees that other articulations still have meaning. The use of *et* is exemplary. It makes no difference to interpretation and could almost be replaced by commas in the list of body parts. But in the list of verbs it makes a very big difference by making available *as different* the serene and the troubled poet. The poet knows himself to be engaged in a double process: he speeds up the polishing of *and* by repeating it, and he slows down that work by reactivating the differentiating function of the conjunction.

Things change in the sixth stanza. Here *et* plays, in addition to its grammatical role, a properly poetical role in the formal organization of the stanzas. It links the sixth stanza to the fifth, finishing out a pattern set in the fifth stanza by the opening words of the lines: "*Et. . . . Polis. . . .* Passaient. . . . *Et. . . .* S'avançaient. . . . Pour. . . . *Et.*"[57] Formal questions are not accidental in the sixth stanza, which is thematically concerned with the dominance of Poetry over the poet, with Poetry's ability to shake the poet's tranquil assumption of mastery, and, thus, with his subservience in certain matters like those of stanza organization. If we ask what function this *et* serves in terms of meaning, moreover, we would have to say it is a negative or subtracting function. The poet indulges in what can only be called a pleonasm, a needless repetition, when he says that breast and belly advanced to trouble his soul's repose and to disturb it off its crystal rock ("pour troubler le repos où mon âme était mise / Et pour la déranger du rocher de cristal"). This *et* does not add like or different things; it adds the same thing, said again in different words. Half of the stanza is an exercise in redundancy, with the poet forced, as it were, by the demands of formal unity to finish out the stanza despite his failing inspiration.

My point is not that Baudelaire is a bad poet who ekes out his stanza by repeating in other words thoughts he's said before. Clearly, the stanza is concerned with this issue, and Baudelaire is so good a poet because, knowing that it is a possibility plaguing any poet, he acts out this loss of poetic inspiration before the poem is finished, to ask after its effect on poet and poem. The effect is dramatically negative with respect to the interpretation that makes the poet a serene surveyor of the scene of language, picking parts to polish off and parts with a differential value worth reactivating. This master is knocked off his perch by the poetic demand for formal order *regardless* of meaning. The term *et* enacts the fall for us. It is an *et* deprived of its additive function altogether, having the value of a "minus" sign. Nothing is added by this pleonastic *et* except formal symmetry, unless one considers a verbal gesture dramatizing in advance the poet's fall into poetic senility and the elevation of the constraining power of formal structure fresh additions.

It could be objected that *et* can sometimes be used emphatically, at the beginning of a sentence, to introduce something startlingly original.[58] Baudelaire's poem has an example of such an *et* in the last stanza, where he introduces a view of the room that appears unconnected to the earlier stanzas, which concentrate on the effect of the female figure on the poet. It is not far-fetched to interpret the *et* of stanza 6 in the same way, as disruptive. Throughout the poem, whenever the poet is talking about his own passion, his speech has inevitably turned out to be really about "the very dear one," and what is more likely than that he is again speaking of her (and not his soul) when he states that her breasts and belly advance "pour *la* déranger" (to disturb *her*)?[59] But in that case what the poem says is something quite different: not that the poetic form overturns the poet by forcing him to repeat his utterances; rather, that the poem advances against itself through those utterances, pushing *Poetry* off her pedestal. The stilled figure gets mobility. Poetry thrusts herself forward in her separate parts against the tranquil ideal of "art for art's sake" and of the poet laboring to polish and differentiate in the name of beauty. Instead, by her self-fragmenting move, she posits the value of the work as that of "art against art," as *anti-work*. The androgynous figure emerging in the seventh stanza represents the poem as self-divided in exactly this way.

Reading the stanza as disruptively self-toppling makes sense in the light of earlier patterns. Everything has had to be read twice—the naked figure / the veiled goddess; its lively and mocking noise / sound, lively and mocking noise; and so on. It is not surprising that the poem should repeat the pattern of doubling at the level of these lines. But what is disruptive is that it does what it says in a new way, inventively. It states, "And to disturb *her* off her rock" but it can only state this if the overriding pattern of doubling is advanced to cover the utterance. This is an unconventional performative. It is blind in that it neither confirms nor denies a truth presumed to be prior to it: the blind performative posits a truth that only becomes one as a result of its act of positing. The poem only ceases to have the immobility of an idol when and if it thrusts forward the disruptive reading. It is impossible to determine the legitimacy of this reading which is at once inevitable because it is in keeping with earlier formal patterns, and radically unauthorized because it has emerged without the poet's say so, in the very enunciation where his claim is that of a technician making concessions to sheer form. As the "lamp" of consciousness resigns itself to die, the framing structure—that is, the "hearth" of the last stanza—produces another light by which to read the poem. The poem makes use of the poet's attempt to resolve a purely formal problem as the occasion to impose its law. Like a Straussian interpreter, the poet is alerted to the fact that sheer structure can produce meaning. But whereas Strauss's puppy cut his teeth on a work received from a thoughtful author whose structures are calculated to

teach, the putative author of "Les Bijoux" stumbles in his text over a lesson still to be read about the nonconvergence of meaning and structure.

However we look at it, "Les Bijoux" outrages the axiom that makes
virtue converge with knowledge. It does so by bringing to the fore problems of reading and writing centered on the memory trace. On the one
side, it commemorates the supplanting of a spoken language by silent
writing and transmits a lesson about the differing modes of memory and
forgetfulness attached to each. It situates itself at the fracture line that
disconnects the text's capacity to transmit knowledge from its capacity
to be read, bearing the gloomy awareness that determining language for
interpretation is forgetting "the writing on the wall"—that is, the writing system and the accidents that affect the legibility of the archive. By
censoring the poem in 1857, the court agreed with the prosecutor that
the court's job was to keep from view what the poem had to say about
disintegrative memory and a destabilizing fault line in the archive. In
this light, the action of the 1949 court consisted less in a liberal, uncen-
soring move, than in a confirmation that, with the loss of the homonym
from the lexicon, the poem's shocking secret about a redoubling at the
source of the poem had become a secret.

The advance of the poem against its own ideal of formal unity dis-
closes another side to the predicament. By reproducing its pattern, the
poem produced something new. It produced a certain reading, a certain
future for itself, as self-fragmenting antipoem or self-toppling symbol.
Here the poem is still lively. If we need any proof of that, the court's deciding opinion in 1949 that Baudelaire's poems are to be interpreted
symbolically can provide it. The attempt to regulate the means of expression by imposing a reading pact on the poem, the attempt to relegate the realistic interpretation of the poem to the dustbin of history as
erroneous—both are attempts to recover the poem for "responsible
memory" by a partial veiling of the destabilizing, wild performative that
advances the poem against itself.

The free agency of human subjects with respect to linguistic structures, their ability to determine whether those structures are referential
or symbolic, is in doubt in this poem. The rationale for the state's attempt to limit access to such a possibility is obvious enough: where freedom of expression is a fundamental right, there is need for a convention
assigning an individual like Baudelaire authorship over his speech acts,
and not, as in this case, the poem the authorship of its reader Baude-

laire.[60] At the same time, there is need to incorporate alternatives like the one glimpsed here where the individual's freedom of expression turns out to be limited by a nonexpressive side to language. The point is not simply that it is useless, by censoring one bearer of the news, to try to censor the news of disintegrating memory or of the limits the material places on individual freedom. It is worse than useless. Acts of censorship reaffirm the relevance of the scenario evoked at the beginning of this chapter—where the enlightened state, tutelary spirit, moves to protect its citizens in the name of responsible memory from the shock delivered by a work.[61] That scenario is out of date, corresponding neither to the modern state and its operations in Baudelaire's day, nor to the needs of its citizens, nor to the nature of the literary work. Our modern states, after all, have come into existence on the basis of blind performatives positing interpretations that were not true before their positing.[62] It is a model that ought perhaps to be laid to rest as the model of the enlightened monarchy from whose collapse our modern states arose, rather than resuscitated and brandished to ward off a fragmentation that the poem shows to have already arrived.

There is more. Benjamin has shown that for the modern lyric poet like Baudelaire or Valéry, the keynote of modern experience consists in delivering shocks which consciousness initially parries by forgetting, and then, retroactively, by a recollection that gives it time to prepare to receive them. That means that the state's censorship of Baudelaire's poem in 1857 and 1949 precisely repeats the thrusts and parries by which consciousness in Baudelaire's poem, faced with the shock of fragmentation, seeks and fails to master it. The censoring of a poem whose message is that by censoring consciousness fails to dominate and indeed falls victim to the structures it has produced seems the sort of suicidal move that an individual can perhaps afford, but a collectivity cannot.

The censorship of the obscene can be attacked from a perspective closer still to Benjamin. The poem discussed was at its most creative where it tried to figure a recognition of the limits of consciousness and of a memory residing in the material. A poet who learned a lot from Baudelaire, Paul Valéry, similarly disengages himself from that triumphant, restorative faculty called remembrance in a text called *Mémoires du poète* (Memoirs of the poet): "Memories that revive are painful to me, and the best of them unbearable. Not for me to apply myself to trying to recover time gone by!" (1: 1467). Valéry refuses memory as a retrospective absorption of a past traumatic event.[63] Instead, in a chapter of the same work called "Fragments des mémoires d'un poème" (Fragments from the Memories of a Poem), he proposes a work composed along principles nearer to the memory he sees operative in texts, memory which can as well be referred to as its futures:

> Perhaps it would be interesting to make just *once* a work that would show in each of its cruxes the diversity that can be presented there to the mind, and among which it will choose the single sequence that will be given in the text. That would be to substitute for the illusion of a unique determination that imitates the real, one of the *possible-at-any-moment*, which seems to me more likely. It has happened to me to publish different texts of the same poems: some were even contradictory, and I have been criticized for that. But no one has told me why I ought to abstain from such variations. (2: 1467)

This text with its diversity possible at any moment underlines that the poem's memory does not have a single line of development. Instead, it is closer to a Mallarmean throw of the dice, a set of chances hidden by a determination as a single development, but that the poet tries to make available at every step. Gains are associated with this notion of the poem text as virtual. Besides the pleasure the mind takes in the virtual act, which Valéry compares to the tactile pleasure of turning an object over and over in the hands; besides the arena of freedom opened up by considering that what is might be otherwise ("life . . . is woven of details that *must be*, to fill in some square on the checkboard of the understanding; but which *can be this or that*); besides the critique of history and of the "naive and bizarre structure of our belief in the past" available when one considers not that what was might have been otherwise, but that it might still *become* otherwise, through another combination of circumstances or another reading; besides the gains for positive science in terms of the unforeseen enunciations, descriptions, and organizations of things (2: 1468); the chances with which Valéry plays lead, by resistance, to hyperconsciousness and the creation of new methods of calculation (2: 1470).[64] They let him posit—in the place of a politics of one individual influencing the other, sharing thoughts with or trying to convince the other—a politics where combination and organization are everything and rhetoric and intention nothing: "But true force is imposed by structure and asks for nothing. It constrains men without seeing them" (2: 1472). It lets him state quite categorically that the end cannot justify the means for him, "because—*there is no end*" (2: 1472). The memories of the poem, divorced from any intentional structure in the text by that name, gain from being rethrown as chances.[65]

Working backward from Valéry's lesson to Baudelaire's poem, we can suggest that the censorship of the poem's disintegrating memory tends to deprive it of its futures, which are also ours.

Reference Matter

Notes

Introduction

1. Valéry, "Réponse à une enquête (sur la chose littéraire et la chose pratique)," in *Oeuvres complètes*, 1: 1148. References will henceforth appear in the text.

2. According to Robert's *Dictionnaire historique de la langue française*, not until 1952 does *le statut* appear regularly invested with the meaning of "social standing."

3. Heidegger, *Metaphysics*, p. 128.

4. Cf. Song of Solomon 7:4: "Thy neck is as a tower of ivory," and Sainte-Beuve in *Pensées d'août*, "A. M. Villemain": "Vigny, plus secret, / Comme en sa tour d'ivoire, avant midi, rentrait" (Vigny, more secret, / As if into his tower of ivory, retired before noon) (*Poésies complètes*, p. 378).

5. See Hunt, *Politics, Culture and Class*.

6. See for example "Essai sur les causes et les effets de la perfection et la décadence des lettres et des arts," which conjugates of the rise and decay of the state together with that of the arts. See also Chénier's statements in his political essays on revolution and writing, notably in "Avis au peuple français sur ses véritables ennemis" and "Réflexions sur l'esprit de parti" in Chénier, *Oeuvres complètes*, ed. Gérard Walter. References will henceforth appear in the text.

7. Such is the hypothesis of Scarfe in *André Chénier*. For a more nuanced version of the argument, see Starobinski's "André Chénier and the Allegory of Poetry."

8. See, for instance, Hertz's "Medusa's Head," in *End of the Line*. See also Hunt, *Politics, Culture and Class*.

9. In Chénier's *Hermès*, in *Oeuvres complètes*, p. 396.

10. Baudelaire's liminal poem to the *Tableaux parisiens* begins by making the

cityscape the subject of an idyll (*Oeuvres complètes*, 1: 82). In an accompanying note, the editor, Claude Pichois, interprets "Paysage" as a poem by the "depoliticized" Baudelaire (1: 994). If one understands political life as activism, and the problem as one of Baudelaire's participation in or distance from the "Riot" that flows by outside his window, the poem can be read as depoliticized. For the political side of the poem to emerge, however, it is enough to consider the poem's gesture as the fundamentally provocative one of superimposing the natural space dedicated to the eclogue onto the city space, so that nature is taken as the other side of a duality imposed by ideology. References will henceforth appear in the text.

11. Beyond the naive interpretation that would make "Versailles" a diatribe against the Jacobins, one could interpret the poem in terms of the problem of instituting law where the king no longer guarantees it. The poem's destiny, where it might be going once language has been emptied of meaning by the fall of an old regime, is the problem the poem gives itself in its title: Vers-ailles, which looks like a commanding or wishful send off of the poem (*que le vers aille*—let these lines go forth).

12. Cf. Derrida, *Politics of Friendship* for a modern treatment of the classical topos.

13. Derrida, *Dissémination*, p. 225.

14. Kamuf's interest is in the way this division affects the institution of literature, but the cleavage, as she is very well aware, can also be found in the literary object itself.

15. In "Essai sur les causes." In an ironic text, Chénier depicts the courtier who borrows vanity from the looks of his master, and whose looks in turn transmit to the poet a gleam of that borrowed glory: "The moon receives its light from the sun and comes to earth to reflect it in a mud-pit" (p. 639).

16. See, for instance, Derrida, "Declarations of Independence."

17. I quote from the English translation by Chris Turner, p. 14. References will henceforth appear in the text. In context, as the astute reader will object, Lacoue-Labarthe means something else by the tag. He is quoting Habermas (himself quoting Heidegger on Nietzsche), in order to disagree with Habermas over the possibility of making a thoroughgoing critique of Heideggerian philosophy. We cannot think with Heidegger against Heidegger, because the position "outside" that would be required to do so is lacking. However, Lacoue-Labarthe does insist that he wants to have a discussion with Heidegger in the domain of poetics and politics, where he admits to being wary (*méfiant*) of the latter's political attitude. I use the phrase to describe Lacoue-Labarthe's discussion of his wariness of Heidegger in this domain.

18. "Poétique et politique," in *L'Imitation*, p. 199. References will henceforth appear in the text.

19. See Newmark, "*L'absolu littéraire*," p. 916.

20. *Technè*, Lacoue-Labarthe says, is "a mode of *poiein*, to produce" ("Poétique," p. 188).

21. "*Dichtung*... goes beyond 'poetics' as an 'art of speech'" says Lacoue-Labarthe ("Poétique," p. 194).

22. Weber, *Mass Mediauras*, p. 71.

23. Ibid., p. 70.

24. Ibid., p. 71. The first meaning of "nation" quoted by the *Encyclopedia Britannica* is instructive on the effects of setting "boundary" into play:

> NATION, in medieval universities, a group of students from a particular region or country who banded together for mutual protection and cooperation in a strange land. In some universities nations were responsible for educating and examining students. Each one was governed by its own proctor, who was elected for terms varying from one month (at the University of Paris) to a year (University of Bologna). Through participation in elections and meetings, the students—many of whom in later life were to serve on committees and councils of kings and princes—were exposed to the practical workings of constitutional government.
>
> At Bologna, the original site of the division into nations and the model for this development in other universities, there were four nations—Lombard, Tuscan, Roman, and Ultramontane (including French, German, and English). Students who were Bolognese citizens were not admitted to a nation: they did not need the protection afforded foreign students. Also, for a citizen of Bologna there would have been the question of divided loyalties, since members owed their first allegiance to their nation.

The model for the nation arises among students who can only be members because they are "not at home," as a sort of enclave within the country where the university is located. The associations do not respect language boundaries (three divisions are reserved for Italian dialects, and one for a group of students speaking widely different tongues). Finally, encysted as they are in a strange land, the associations cannot be joined by citizens. At every level, the boundary between the inside and the outside is evoked as infracted.

25. Weber, *Mass Mediauras*, p. 72.

26. Some of Jacques Derrida's recent work—for instance, on friendship, the secret, hospitality, testimony—could be read in this direction, as rethinking the political in terms of a place not secured and homogeneous.

27. The themes of the new actor (the people) and a new organization of place run throughout Michelet's *Histoire de la Révolution française*.

28. See *The Old Régime and the French Revolution*, pp. 136–37 for Tocqueville's analysis of the downfall of the House of Cards a.k.a. the House of France. The undoing of a metaphorical system takes place when a metaphor that seems to totalize and unify all the divergent forces of a text is shown to be an illusion. As Tocqueville analyses it, the monarchy was brought down by its

successful policy of overcoming all obstacles to centralization, and thereby reducing to nothing its supports. The analysis is of a necessary fiction that collapses under the weight of its own success.

29. Tocqueville, *Old Régime*, p. 147.

30. As for the critical role Tocqueville accords literature in the events of the
Revolution—it provided abstract political models based on a few general principles leading a generation without practical experience in politics to think that
the government could be reformed according to those principles by its artist-
people into a more perfect work of art—it bears a more than superficial resemblance to the function Lacoue-Labarthe awards fictions of the political in the
abortively modern state. See, among other places, pp. 138–48.

31. Hunt, *Politics, Culture and Class*, p. 16.

32. Ibid., pp. 123–24.

33. See the opening pages of *Sylvie*, in *Oeuvres*, pp. 589–94. In the famous
opening line, Nerval plays on the imperfect tense (which paints either duration
or repetitive action) to establish that the tale narrates a repetitive, incomplete
withdrawal from the representational space of theatre: "Je sortais d'un théâtre
où tous les soirs je paraissais aux avant-scènes en grande tenue de soupirant." (I
quitted [or, was quitting] a theater where every night I appeared at the stage-
boxes in the full costume of a suitor.)

34. On plagiarism and translation see especially Chénier, *Oeuvres complètes*,
p. 159; on the comet or meteor as the light hair of Chénier's Muse, see for examples pp. 126, 392, 427.

35. See Chénier's allegory of poetry, "Creux en profonde coupe, un vaste
diamant, / Lui porta du nectar le breuvage écumant" (Hollow in the form of a
deep cup [or, Hollow of deep cut], a vast diamond / Bore her the foaming
drink of nectar) (p. 3), where the drink is carried by a diamond variously cup or
product of cutting. See also "Le Retour d'Ulysse" where three vignettes show
the suitor Antinous cup in hand, cup at lip, and then, dying from a cutting
blow at the hand of the returned Ulysses in the equivocal line "La coupe de sa
main fuit" (either, Antinous's cup is loosed from the hand, or the cut of the
hand, the force by which Antinous might have parried Ulysses' thrust, flees).
The death of Antinous is followed by a veritable barrage of *cou*-words—*cour-
roux, coups, coupable, coup, avant-coureur, secourir*—in a dispute where Ulysses'
attempts to prevail over the crowd of suitors figure the poet's attempts to prevail over a proliferation taking place around the signifier (pp. 26–27). Or see
p. 524 where the poet satirizes those "Barbarous possessors, furious Procrustes"
who shut nature "into vases of clay, of glass and of bronze." "Et les coupes ser-
vaient d'armes" (And cups served as weapons) reads one fragment (p. 633). In
every case, the transformation of the cup involves questioning the model of
language as container.

36. Mallarmé, *Oeuvres complètes*, p. 74. References will henceforth appear in the text.

37. See Lacoue-Labarthe's *La Poésie*. This motif drives the question of how Celan's poetry situates us with respect to the Extermination (p. 18), and also the reflection on Celan's Judaism (pp. 154–66). See also "Poétique," pp. 199–200.

38. In a poem about poem-making from *Les Contemplations*, "Il faut que le poète," Hugo picks out the caesura as the milieu elected by the poet: "Au milieu de cette humble et haute poésie, / Dans cette paix sacrée où croît la fleur choisie" (In the middle of this humble and high poetry, / In the sacred peace where the chosen flower grows). In *Oeuvres complètes*, 9:111. References will henceforth appear in the text.

39. For a pertinent discussion of names as having the qualities of hieroglyphic writing for Hegel and Baudelaire, see Chase's *Decomposing Figures*, pp. 117–23.

40. Plato, *Dialogues*, para. 607c–d, p. 832.

41. Ibid., para. 607d–e, pp. 832–33.

42. In this context, it would be possible to read the "immemorial" story with which the *Republic* ends not as a founding myth but rather as a parable of election and thus of reading, in which memory and forgetfulness are at stake.

43. See Derrida's "La Double séance" in *Dissémination* as indispensable reading in this context.

44. Derrida, *Dissémination*, p. 213.

45. Prendergast, *Paris*, p. 2.

46. Valéry summarizes the situation of the city as representation in *Fonction de Paris*:

> To be by itself the political, literary, scientific, financial, commercial, pleasure and sumptuary capital of a great country; to represent its whole history; from it to absorb and concentrate the whole thinking substance as well as all the credit and almost all the resources and possible ways to dispose of money, and all this, good and bad for the nation it crowns: this distinguishes the city of Paris, among all the gigantic cities. The consequences, the immense advantages, the disadvantages, the grave dangers of this concentration are easy to imagine. (2: 1008)

47. See Derrida's "My Chances" for an account of luck as attached to literature through its privileging of the proper name, the letter, and the trait.

48. See Prendergast, *Paris and the Nineteenth Century* for a description of Haussmannization:

> It is an intellectual precondition of the idea of the city as pleasure garden and work of art, that it be seen as a "collectively created complex," the product of a common will and the expression of a high degree of homogeneity in the social and political culture. This, ideologically speaking, is pure Haussmann: the vision of the modern city as unified, centred and fully legible, opened up as a safe and regulated space of leisure and pleasure to all its citizens. (p. 8)

Prendergast's discussion of the public park as an Arcadian retreat set aside by city planners for bucolic fraternizing could be extended, almost *tel quel*, to the lyric.

49. On Baudelaire's demons, see Culler's "Baudelaire's Satanic Verses."

50. *Death* is to be read here in the sense Warminski gives it of linguistic death (*Readings in Interpretation*, p. 41).

51. See Pachet for an extended discussion of the role of the first-comer for Baudelairian politics. See Culler, "Baudelaire and Poe," pp. 70–71, for a reading of "Le Mauvais vitrier," and of the flowerpot dropped by the poet.

52. The French *que* is only partially translated by the English *whom*, which here makes the relative refer to a person. The French *que* does not make the distinction, and allows the reading of person as *role*, or linguistic function.

53. In "Baudelaire au féminin" (in *Signature Pieces*) Peggy Kamuf espies an address to woman of the problem of address: its violence, a disjunction between the thematic address *in* and the gesture of address *to*, is of interest for the analysis of "Le Mauvais vitrier" and "Assommons les pauvres!"

54. P. 70. Warminski's discussion of undecidability is incisive. It is particularly helpful in explaining the difference between qualities such as ambiguity and equivocality (which affect the semantic field with richness), and undecidability, where sense-making itself is interrupted by another logic (a syntax).

55. In "Le Mauvais vitrier," the poet says he cannot *say* why he conceives so despotic a hatred toward the glass-seller. If he cannot say it, it is not because he does not have a hypothesis (the poem is about that, after all), but rather because, in saying the cause of the rivalry (the recurrent difference between saying and meaning), he reopens it.

56. "Every big city is an immense gaming house," says Valéry. "But in each, one game dominates. . . . Paris does a bit of everything" (2: 1008).

57. It is significant that Baudelaire should have chosen to remember Andromache mourning over an empty tomb (Virgil in Book Three of the *Aeneid*), rather than to have found a spot in Aeneas's Rome that might have put Paris more squarely in line with the tradition of *translatio imperii*. See Hampton, "Virgil, Baudelaire and Mallarmé."

58. For a discussion of "Le Cygne" in terms of the empty tomb and its implications for a material history in Baudelaire, see Bahti, *Allegories of History*, pp. 224–25. See also Starobinski, *La Mélancholie*, pp. 56–78.

59. De Quincey, *Confessions*, p. 31. Here, I am making the opium eater or addict into the exemplary figure for such a class. De Quincey's text, which was translated by Baudelaire, allows it. The etymology of *addict* (from *ad*, "to" + *dicere, dictus*, "say, pronounce," meaning "assigned, bound over, surrendered by a formal act of swearing") would also permit a linking of addiction to the performative and the placeholder.

60. Sainte-Beuve, *Poésies complètes*, p. 377.

61. His was also a fate puzzlingly predicted by his name: *Chef-nier*, negate the head. His work can thus stand as owing much to a violence and chanciness associated with the letter, and to a catachrestic name that contains a destiny.

62. In the title of one group of essays, *Essais quasi politiques*, collected in *Variété*.

63. As it happens, Valéry was quite aware of the implications of radio technology for a world more and more interconnected, in which it would be all but impossible to isolate and locate events, ascribe responsibility for actions, and so on. See, for example, the Avant-propos to *Regards sur le monde actuel*, in *Oeuvres complètes*, 2: 923–25.

Chapter 1

1. "Fraternel" can refer to the relations between siblings of either sex, and the much rarer "sororal"—particularly in the context of a poem about 1789—would be surprising. But because at this point the poem has allegorized poetry and freedom as feminine, the adjective brings out a discrepancy between the gendered figures (one sister succors the other), and the description of the aid lent as "brotherly."

2. In stanza 14, the poet apostrophizes this new people born by a speech act: "O peuple deux fois né! peuple vieux et nouveau! . . . Phénix sorti vivant des cendres du tombeau!" (Oh twice born people! old and new people! . . . Phoenix come forth living from the ashes of the tomb!) (p. 173).

3. The English translation cannot do justice to the French. What makes the line stand out in French is the clash between the feminine adjective *seule*, which agrees with the gender of the female figure apostrophied, and the masculine noun *man*, a predicate distinguishing Corday from other humans, characterized as eunuchs.

4. In *Death Comes to the Maiden*, Naish quotes from various descriptions by Corday's contemporaries, all of which make gender a means to display an attitude about her action. The portraits range widely, as the following list shows: a blushing convent girl; Carlyle's "Citoyenne who would do France a service"; a polite and decorous prisoner who mended her torn dress and fichu for her trial; a termagent, "hoydenish, with mannish bearing" (the Revolutionary Tribunal's contribution); a red-shirted parricide whose bravery was testified to by the executioner Sanson. Naish also provides two posthumous portraits: An autopsy determined that Corday was a virgin (and not, as some charged, pregnant and mesmerized by some Manson of the time), and her skull was considered by Cesare Lombroso to be "typical of male criminals" (pp. 110–21).

5. There is no doubt that starting from the premise that novels represent ex-

perience has been productive for feminist readings. It has paved the way for a consideration of what might have been left out by the dialectical view: the experience of women occulted before reaching the full light of consciousness; its expression in language silenced or depreciated by various mechanisms and strategies, required to go underground and to find oblique ways to manifest itself by ms-appropriating the discursive strategies available; texts or genres on the margins of the canon that turn out to be deserving of study. It is not in the spirit of returning to the closed canon that I point toward a resistance in poetic language to being thought in dialectical terms. Rather it is with the idea that letting feminist discussion become dominated by concepts like identity, experience, representation, and so forth forecloses on the indeterminacy of language. It is that indeterminacy, language's ability to mean otherwise, that was tapped very productively in the first stages of feminism in the recognition of phallogocentrism and its exclusions. It may still bear questions and lessons worth considering.

6. Johnson, "Gender," pp. 163 and 166. References will henceforth appear in the text.

7. Otherwise it would not be possible to say that "Baudelaire is here enacting male privilege as the right to play femininity" (Johnson, p. 178) or, of the speaker in "*Son Image*," that "*she* 'forgets all' as soon as 'he' falls on his knees and weeps" (my emphasis, p. 173). Johnson places quotation marks around "he," suggesting some reservations about the identity of the referent, but does not frame the voice of the feminine speaker. Johnson knows about the possibility of a difference affecting the voice, but the point she is making is that how we hear the voice *before* its alteration will determine how we understand that alteration.

8. The passage on the altered voice appears in a section where the poet is discussing the seductive effects of "my songs" on "my naïve Camille" (p. 140). That section is part of a longer meditation on the effects of altering the Greek source (the Permesso, which runs through the Valley of the Muses) by French additions: "J'ose, nouveau pontife aux antres du Permesse, / Mêler des chants français dans les choeurs de la Grèce" (New pontif in the caves of the Permesso, / I dare mix French songs into the choruses of Greece) (p. 138).

9. Ovid, Bk. XI, ll.58–59.

10. "Elle est dans ma voix, la criarde," (1: 78) Baudelaire says of irony, by which we have to take it he means more than that he plays at hysteria, since a hysterical voice cannot be put on or taken off like a disguise. It is a voice inhabited by a shrillness that signals an internalized wound to the self, and the impossibility of understanding difference as recuperable self-difference.

11. See Miller-Frank, *The Mechanical Song*, for an interesting study, from a different perspective, of feminine automata in nineteenth-century literature.

12. See Kamuf, *Signature Pieces*, and especially the fine essay "Baudelaire au féminin" that was one point of departure for this study. Starting from a call "(t)o hear the deviation in Baudelaire's voice" (p. 127), Kamuf goes on to speculate on that deviation in terms of the signature and countersignature.

13. The poet is playing on the term *faits* which means (1) finished, done and (2) made, fabricated, produced. The statement can thus be read in terms of the procrastination motif being developed, as making the point that the songs, while unfinished, are in process. But the underlying possibility that he may be concerned with the poem as production or fabrication doesn't go away, since in any case the poet is talking about the poetics behind the fragmentary works.

14. On prosopopeia, see de Man, "Autobiography" in *Rhetoric*.

15. A cursory autopsy can determine the sex of a person now dead. Similarly, the clothes and ornaments found in a tomb can tell us much about the gender structure of the society in which that person once walked. But how are we to understand the attribution of a gendered voice or body to a cadaver whose being is that of a cadaver, or, what comes down to the same thing, known to be a voice box or poem? Does a zombie have sex or gender?

16. P. 635. Besides the narrow definition we are exploring here, the article broadens the definition to make poetic license synonymous with fictional language.

17. Marceline Desbordes-Valmore, in a passage from a letter to Sainte-Beuve quoted by Johnson for another purpose, underscores the origin of her vocation in a rhythmed language: "At age twenty, profound sufferings obliged me to give up singing, because my voice made me cry; but music still rolled about in my fevered head, and regular measures always arranged my ideas, without my thinking about it. I was forced to write them down in order to free myself from this feverish beat, and someone told me I had written an elegy" (Johnson, p. 166). The poet's ideas do not precede her measures but appear organized by them, already scanned as an elegy. The passage itself is elegiac, mourning as it does the loss of voice and song.

18. See Diderot's *Lettre sur les sourds et les muets* for a relevant discussion of inversion. See also Genette, "Blanc Bonnet *versus* Bonnet Blanc" in *Mimologiques*, pp. 183–226.

19. Blanchot, *Faux Pas*, p. 127.

20. Take, for instance, the following passage from Chénier's *Epître à Lebrun*:

> Mais la tendre Elégie et sa grâce touchante
> M'ont séduit: L'Elégie à la voix gémissante,
> Au ris mêlé de pleurs, aux longs cheveux épars;
> Belle, levant au ciel ses humides regards.
> Sur un axe brillant c'est moi qui la promène
> Parmi tous ces palais dont s'enrichit la Seine.

> But tender Elegy and her touching grace
> Have seduced me: Elegy of wailing voice,
> Of laughter mixed with tears, of long, dishevelled hair;
> Beautiful, raising her humid looks to heaven.
> Along a brilliant highway, I take her strolling
> Among all the palaces that enrich the Seine.
>
> *(p. 139)*

What determines Elegy's appearance as a woman in this allegory? One could answer that Elegy shares qualities that are those of a woman: tenderness, grace, weepiness. Gendering Elegy as a woman allows those properties to be brought forth in an extended metaphor, to show Elegy's properties by developing those qualities of her human counterpart. The problem with such a reading is that it is easily stood on its head. If we look at Boileau's take on the same subject in *L'Art poétique* from which Chénier appears to be borrowing, Chénier's procedure looks forced and arbitrary rather than based on a "natural" resemblance. Boileau says:

> D'un ton un peu plus haut, mais pourtant sans audace,
> La plaintive élégie, en longs habits de deuil,
> Sait, les cheveux épars, gémir sur un cercueil.
> Elle peint des amants la joie et la tristesse;
> Flatte, menace, irrite, apaise une maîtresse.

> In a tone a bit more lofty, but still without daring,
> Plaintive elegy, in long mourning dress,
> Hair dishevelled, knows how to wail over a coffin.
> She paints the joy and sadness of lovers;
> Flatters, menaces, irritates, calms a mistress.
>
> *(Oeuvres, p. 166)*

Boileau starts with an attribute shared by humans and poetry, tone, and justifies his personification of elegy as a mourning woman by means of it. Chénier, on the other hand, daringly sets a gendered Elegy before us without preparation or apology, celebrating her hair and so on only after an arbitrary and strained move. We can state the difference thus: Chénier's Elegy is feminine because French nouns are gendered (*belle* is the required form for an adjective agreeing with *la élégie*); Boileau's Elegy is feminine (confining ourselves to this single example) because French nouns reflect the natural order of things.

Nor is it possible to conclude that Chénier tries afterward to smooth things over by naturalizing the structure. Tenderness, grace, weepiness—these properties may be conventionally coded as feminine but it is still a *code* and not a woman that is in question, as could be shown by reference to the poem *Hylas*, where the same attributes cluster around the boy beloved of Hercules (pp. 28–29).

21. Baudelaire, *Oeuvres complètes*, 1: 182.

22. The guillotine, for instance, got its name as a result of a rhyme that stuck. The machine, designed and developed by Dr. Louis and proposed to the National Assembly as a more humanitarian, democratic killing technique by one Dr. Joseph Guillotin, was addressed in a satirical song by one of its victims as La Guillotine, to rhyme with *machine.* The requirements of French prosody—specifically, the need for a feminine rhyme, says Arasse, "married Guillotin to the guillotine forever." Not only the gender of the noun but the name credited with its making were determined by formal poetic requirements. See Arasse, *The Guillotine,* pp. 8–9.

23. See Valéry, in the Avant-propos to *Regards sur le monde actuel,* where he discusses the essays as marked by the occasion, and dedicates the ensemble to those without a system or party (*Oeuvres complètes,* 2: 913). The importance of the occasion for Mallarmé is beginning to be recognized (notably, by Vincent Kaufman in *Le Livre et ses adresses*).

24. In Chénier's *Hermès,* those who give the law are male: "*ces hommes saints,* ces sublimes courages" (*those holy men,* those sublime courages) (my emphasis). So too are those to whom the law is given: "qui . . . vivant pour leurs *frères,* / Les ont soumis au frein des règles salutaires" (those who . . . living for their *brothers,* / Have submitted them to the brake of healthy laws) (my emphasis). A patrilinear law of the proper makes men into citizens: "En leur donnant des lois leur ont donné des biens, / Des forces, des parents, la liberté, la vie; / Enfin . . . d'un pays ont fait une patrie" (In giving them laws have given them goods, / Strength, relatives, freedom, life; / And, . . . from a country have made a fatherland). Most often the God in whose name the law is given is male: "C'est alors qu'il rapporte . . . La voix de Dieu *lui-même* écrite sur la pierre," (Then it is that he brings back . . . The voice of God *himself* written on stone) (my emphasis). Cf., however: "Une Nymphe l'appelle et lui trace des lois . . . un oiseau divin . . . vient lui dicter des oracles" (A Nymph calls out to him and traces laws for him . . . a divine bird . . . dictates oracles to him) (pp. 397–98). Dimoff cites two fragments on oaths where Chénier specifies oaths sworn by women to Ceres and Proserpine (*La Vie,* 2: 281).

25. That is true in, among other poems by Chénier, *Hermès* where Orpheus sings "quelles lois à ce vaste univers / Impriment à la fois des mouvements divers" (Which laws imprint on this vast universe / All at once diverse movements) (p. 396), and in the ode we will discuss, "La Jeune captive," where the poet bends a song "to the sweet laws of verse" (p. 186).

26. Blanchot, *Faux pas,* p. 128.

27. Ibid., p. 128.

28. Irigaray's affirmation in *Je, tu, nous* that "the feminine remains secondary syntactically, not even a norm" (p. 32) confirms that the feminine is used for the singular, although from a very different point of view.

29. See Dimoff in his edition of Chénier, *Oeuvres complètes*, 3: 222.

30. Scarfe, *André Chénier*, pp. 332–34. References will henceforth appear in the text.

31. Or, as Chénier puts it elsewhere: "Je te crie en quel lieu sous la route est caché / Un abîme où déjà mes pas ont trébuchés" (I cry out to you at what point under the road / Is hidden an abyss where my steps have already faltered) (p. 549).

32. For Spitzer ("André Chénier" in *Interpretationen*), the ode is entirely in keeping with Chénier's famous line "Sur des pensers nouveaux faisons des vers antiques." Spitzer translates this line in the light of his interpretation of the ode: "Sur des sentiments éternels faisons des vers naturels" (p. 105).

33. Starobinski, "Leo Spitzer" in *Relation*, p. 46.

34. For Spitzer, "triste et captif" demands a human subject (in the masculine grammatical gender) in the place of the actual inanimate (and feminine) subject of the sentence "ma lyre" (p. 103).

35. Since it seems impossible to reconcile her pastness, as revealed by the *passé simple* of the verb expressing being, *fut*, with the fearful and expectant attitudes of her fellow prisoners described in the future tense by *craindront* and *passeront* (p. 102).

36. Spitzer proposes:

> Ainsi triste et captif, j'écoutais tant de fois
> S'élever près de moi ces plaintes, cette voix,
> Ces voeux d'une jeune captive;
> Et secouant le faix de mes jours languissants
> Ma lyre s'éveilla joyeuse aux doux accents
> De sa bouche aimable et naïve.
>
> So, sad and captive, I many times heard
> Rise up near me these complaints, this voice,
> These wishes of a young captive;
> And shaking off the burden of my languishing days
> My lyre awoke joyous at the sweet accents
> Of her lovable and naive mouth.   *(pp. 103–4)*

37. Spitzer says: "Those who linger near her must fear the end of this life the more, manifestly because they must take leave of so splendid a being (*herrlichen Wesen*); that is, because her presence on the last day of their life makes life seem more beautiful. Certainly that is the meaning of the entire poem: this overturning of the negative into the positive" (p. 102). The poem does not say that. It says that those who dwell nigh her will fear to see their days end. Proximity to this being, a being manifestly of another order, is fear-inducing.

38. See Spitzer, *Interpretationen*, pp. 101–2.

39. For an informed discussion of disavowal in ideological fantasy see, be-

sides Žižek's *The Sublime Object of Ideology* (pp. 11–53), Spackman's reading of fetishism and Medusa in *Fascist Virilities,* esp. pp. 77–113.

40. Hertz, *End of the Line,* p. 167.

41. A poem close in date to "La Jeune captive," the "Ode à Charlotte Corday," explores and reverses Medusa themes. Marat is called a "black serpent," a monster and dismembering tiger, and Corday, whose head was chopped off by a people mistakenly glorifying Marat, is made out a Perseus figure in the startling line quoted earlier: "Seule, tu fus un homme, et vengeas les humains / Et nous eunuques vils" (Alone, you were a man, and avenged humanity / And we, vile eunuchs) (p. 180).

42. Hertz, *End of the Line,* p. 166.

43. Ibid., p. 166.

44. Ibid., p. 179.

45. The line quoted in the heading (Who are these beauties, if they are mortal?) is from "Sujets et ébauches de Bucoliques." Chénier, *Oeuvres complètes,* p. 531.

46. The prosopopeia brings to life a being that seems to exist only so it can be deprived of life again. It brings deprivation to life.

47. The fact that prison conditions in St. Lazare were relatively cushy for the time, according to Walter (*André Chénier,* pp. 287–92), does not affect this destitution which concerns the figure's relation to a present.

The bookish quality of the comparisons derives from the speaker's reliance on memory. We are not to understand that she is seeing or even necessarily once saw the wheat and vine to which she compares herself in the ode. There is not a "fresh" comparison among them. Instead, as various critics have noticed, the voice remembers clichés, revives readings, and patches together a song from various sources—the Bible, Meleager, Pindar, La Fontaine, Gilbert, and popular sayings (the banquet of life, life's road) have all been named. See Scarfe, *André Chénier,* pp. 332–33, and Spitzer, "André Chénier," in *Interpretationen,* p. 100.

48. This persuasion—that it is a human being pleading with her judges—is all that stands in the way of reading the poem allegorically, in terms of the nineteenth-century "rebirth" of the lyric, as an appeal of the sentence of banishment pronounced against poetry in Plato's *Republic.*

49. Benveniste, *Problèmes,* 1: 256.

50. The rest of the passage evokes the need for this process in order to *maintain* the existing universe:

Wolves that eat lambs, lambs devoured by wolves, the strong who sacrifice the weak, the weak the victims of the strong—that is nature, that is her vision, that is her plan; a perpetual action and reaction, a crowd of vices and virtues, a perfect equilibrium, in a word, resulting from the equality of good and evil on the earth; equilibrium necessary for the maintenance of the stars, of vegetation, and without which everything would be immediately destroyed. (Sade, *Justine,* pp. 174–76)

51. A similar movement can be seen in the last lines of the fifth stanza where the topos of a full cup still to be drained at life's banquet, presumably presented as yet another persuasive argument for life, is shadowed by a reverse reading. In a context that has already brought together the scythe (*faux*) and the winepress (*pressoir*) as metonyms for waiting death, lines that state "Un instant seulement mes lèvres ont *pressé* / La coupe en mes mains encor pleine" invite another interpretation. The singer celebrates à la Salomé her loving relation to the slicing action (*la coupe*) of the guillotine's cutting blade (*couperet*). What emerges as the focus for the poem, given this reversibility and given that to argue for life on the grounds of nature is also to argue for one's death, is the attempt to claim or reclaim death as something other than the mere extinction of a natural creature, or a sublimating transcendence. Rather than appealing for a right to life, the captive may be asking for the right to death.

52. It is worth noting that the undoing of nature produces fear and is accompanied by a last-ditch effort to absorb undoing as process into a new ideological formation: a revolutionary Nature that maintains itself by destruction, by devouring its offspring. Sade's libertine is absolutely germane here (as is Arendt's analysis of revolution). A parable about the Terror from Chénier's posthumous *Les Autels de la peur* makes a similar point in the following passage, where the animals trained to aid humans in their struggle to dominate an inhuman "nature" threaten to turn against their supposed masters to devour them: "Chardin reports that the Persians make use of a kind of leopard to chase other beasts; but when the animal misses the prey against which they have sent it, it returns in a fury and its guides, afraid for themselves, always have in reserve some other prey which they throw out to pacify it" (p. 362). The leopard who advances on its trainer is an apt emblem for the conjuncture of two processes that come together without being reducible to one another: On the one side, the trained cat unleashed against a natural prey necessarily misses (since, with the leopard, nature has been revealed as artifice so there is no nature left for it to hunt). On the other side, a process of *renaturalization* is evident, in the leopard disappointed of its prey turning on its guide, but also in the return of nature within the guides themselves, first in their *feeling* of fear that designates them as prey, and then by their act of self-despoiling (throwing another animal to the leopard) through which they deprive themselves of the wealth acquired to distinguish them from nature in the first place. In *Les Autels de la peur* the emblem suggests that the two processes can exist as separate moments in a succession: first the trained leopard is sent out against nature, and then, frustrated of its prey, it returns to its guides. But in "La Jeune captive," they are two ways of looking at the same lack of groundedness to the analogy. Nature deprived of determination is indistinctly process and procession of appearances, indistinctly an ideology known to be past, and a renaturalization.

The processes are inseparable, like an anamorphic painting, two views of the same figure.

53. Chénier's work is a compendium of ruined or unfinished comparisons. This is true of the poems considered fragmentary, where often only a single leg of the comparison is provided. See, for instance, "Comme aux jours de l'été" (p. 592), "Comme aux bords de l'Euxin" (p. 608). Some of the short poems seem elaborated from such "found" fragments. See, for instance, "Comme un dernier rayon" (p. 193), "Tel lorsque, n'ayant plus de traits" (p. 5), "Telle éclate Vénus" (p. 7), "Tel j'étais autrefois" (p. 65). Within the longer poems, the effect is that of self-fracturing. See, besides passages from *Hermès* (pp. 392, 393, 396, 401), the remarkable series of largely unconnected comparisons in section 14 of *L'Amérique* ("Et comme on voit une nation de fourmis . . . Ainsi pour les travaux . . . Ainsi un homme . . . Ainsi le paysan . . . Ainsi le voyageur . . . Comme un chien vigilant . . . Ainsi . . . Ainsi, une génisse . . ." [And as we see a nation of ants . . . Just so for work . . . Just so a man . . . Just so the peasant . . . Just so the traveler . . . As a vigilant hound . . . Just so . . . Just so, a heifer . . .]). The series culminates in a final, unconnected comparison that collects all the rest in the figure of an unstable snowdrift whose self-fracturing causes an avalanche: "Just so [*ainsi*], on a high peak an immense quantity of snow is heaped up and remains suspended and immobile on the mountain's slope. But a single flake detaches and sets the whole in movement; it pulls a second after it, and then another; and soon this enormous mass falls down into the valley with a terrifying crash" (pp. 442–44).

54. The line quoted in the heading (Oh beauty [her name; not the true one?]) (p. 537), comes from a fragmentary study for an elegy (with the address "O Belle" presumably the finished piece, and the parenthesis the author's placeholding reminder to himself), which I am citing as if it were a finished poem. This is a polemical *parti pris*, and many of Chénier's interpreters would take exception to this strategy, insisting that the difference between the finished and the unfinished poems, never mind the sketches for poems, has to be respected. But because the poet published almost no writings and did not himself divide finished pieces from unfinished projects or private memoranda along the axis of the publishable, I would maintain that it is impossible to make that distinction. By attempting to make it, moreover, we deprive the work of the poet's gestures to a problem of the referent and of naming. When Chénier, as we suppose, writes a little memo to himself *not* to use the beauty's name in the work he will be writing about her, we assume he knows the name, but has to remind himself to consider whether or not to use it. But if, as the elegy shows, the poet's point is that the poet keeps erring in thinking he knows beauty's name—she is love, the beaux arts, then specific women he sees, then all of them, then the ambiguously sinister, "the most beautiful of mortals" (*la*

plus belle des mortelles), then undecidably, "a beauty (the name of the beginning)" (*une belle* [*le nom du commencement*]), then the lack of a proper name for beauty and the need to impose one are the scaffolding of the poem. They constitute the significant theoretical problem it can only address in its fragmentary state. It would be a pity to miss it.

55. Nature in "La Jeune captive" is not primarily visible, in sharp contrast to such natural landscapes as that of Valais in *Julie*. Rousseau makes his natural landscapes spectacular in all senses of the term. For instance:

> Add to all this optical illusions, the mountain peaks differently lit, the *clair-obscur* of the sun and the shadows, and all the accidents of light that morning and evening result, and you will have some idea of the continual scenes that never stopped attracting my admiration, and that seemed to me offered in a true theater; for the perspective of mountains, because it is vertical, strikes the eyes all at once, and much more strongly than that of the plains, which can only be seen obliquely, as receding, and with each of its objects hiding another from you. (*Oeuvres complètes*, p. 77)

Whatever Chénier has borrowed from Rousseau, it is not a theatrical nature: his dawn provides dew for the vine to drink; the eyes of the second stanza do not see, they are dry or weeping fountains.

56. In stanzas 4–6. There, she welcomes the day with an aspect reanimating to those who look upon her, her desire to see the harvest is compared to the sun's wish to complete a year, she represents herself as a brilliant heliotrope having glimpsed the fires of morning.

57. Unless one were to take the *captive* of the title as such a prior noun. For two reasons this assumption is not possible. First, for philological reasons: scholars think the title was probably added by someone else. Second, "captive" is itself a nominalized adjective, and might as easily replace an abstract noun, like *la Terreur, la Poésie*, or *la victime*, as refer to a woman, like Aimée de Coigny. The gap between the title and the poem, as abyssal as the one between the two parts of the song, would have to be accounted for in order to justify such a move.

58. Once the mistake is made, the attempt to correct it by providing the relevant information merely helps ensure the tragic outcome. Balzac gives the reader an equivalent occasion for misunderstanding in the *elle* with which the narrator refers to the prima donna, the pronoun demanded by the rules of pronoun replacement but one that lets the reader participate in the plight of the hapless Sarrasine by envisioning the role as a being. A timely reminder to the reader that third person pronouns "either replace or relay material elements of the enunciation" (Benveniste, *Problèmes*, 1: 256) might have prevented the initial misunderstanding. It would, however, have spoiled the story, which by its means inscribes its readers as so many Sarrasines.

59. Arasse cites a satire of Guillotin's speech to the assembly that it is tempting to see as a possible intertext for Chénier's ode:

I have at last invented, with the help of my machinist, the delightful machine you see before you. . . . Under the platform there is a bird-organ, set up to play the jolliest tunes, as for example: "My goodwife when I dance"; or again "Farewell, my Lady of France"; or perhaps "Goodnight to my friends then one and all." The chief protagonist being once mounted on the rostrum, shall stand between the two columns, and shall be requested to place his ear against this stylobate, the better to hear the ravishing sounds that the bird-organ pours forth; and his head shall be so discreetly chopped off, that it will itself, long after its truncation, be in doubt as to this event. Only the applause that shall doubtless resound through the square will suffice to convince it of its state. (*The Guillotine and the Terror*, p. 19)

Arasse makes much of the loss of the spectacular side of capital punishment, owing to the rapidity of the decapitating machine. The satire quoted suggests a way to make up for the lost visibility by organizing the death around sound (the song the prisoner bends to hear, the resounding applause convincing the head of its truncation). The drama is organized in terms of a sense perception that is associated with the phenomenal body of language, with the signifier whose ability to be heard by the ear constitutes one of the elements mobilized by poems to persuade us that, in lieu of ordinary experience, they offer us some more originary experience of the body of language. Over and above the external resemblances between "La Jeune captive" and this satire (the bird-organ, Philomela's song), this centering on the sound of the verbal act is the source of likeness.

60. See Arendt, *On Revolution*, p. 198. In her terms, the American people do not have to stand as source both of power and of law, but receive the law as a writing to be worshiped, in the Constitution. A discussion in the early part of *On Revolution*, where she quotes from Thomas Paine, shows her awareness of the linguistic form to the problem: "The point to remember is that the American Revolution succeeded, and still did not usher in the *novus ordo saeclorum*, that the Constitution could be established 'in fact,' as a 'real existence . . . , in a visible form,' and still did not become 'to Liberty what grammar is to language'" (p. 68).

61. Here, the words of Tocqueville on the first period of the Revolution, when "war has not yet broken out among the classes (and) the language of the nobility is in every respect similar to that of other classes, unless it be to go further and take a loftier tone," are worth recalling: "In the ardor with which they attacked power, they armed themselves against it with whatever weapons they found, even those that were least suited to their hands. One would have thought that the *aim of the revolution being prepared was not the destruction of the old regime, but its restoration*" (my emphasis; Tocqueville, *L'Ancien Régime*, 2: 69–72).

62. P. 687. As Chénier uses it, *belle* is often little more than a rhyme word or honorific epithet, rather than a descriptive term. Even a cursory skimming of his work shows the term appearing consistently in the rhyming position. It is often accompanied by internal rhyming as well, as if wherever poetic language thrusts itself forward in its formal aspect, and the signifier puts in an appear-

ance as determining, the term imposes itself. See, for example, "Mais c*elle* qui partout fait conquête nouv*elle*, / C*elle* qu'on ne voit point sans dire: 'Oh! qu'*elle* est *belle!*'" (But she who everywhere makes new conquests, / She whom one never sees without saying: "Oh! How beautiful she is!") (p. 111).

63. In *Hymne à la justice*, an address to poetry identifies an aesthetic based on the signifier's plasticity with a decay linked to the monarchy: "belle vierge à la touchante voix, / Nymphe ailée, aimable sirène / Ta langue s'amollit dans le palais des rois" (beautiful virgin with touching voice, / Winged nymph, lovable siren / Your tongue grows soft in the palaces [or, palates] of kings) (p. 167). In "La Jeune captive" aesthetic play is linked to the Revolutionary interregnum as maintaining a formalism that still relies on the old idealism.

64. Arendt, *On Revolution*, p. 183. See also, for a language and analysis very close to Chénier's, her discussion of Robespierre's halfhearted attempt to shore up virtue by proposing a cult of the Supreme Being. It was an opportunistic improvisation, a decision by the "god of philosophers" to "disclose himself in the guise of a circus clown" (p. 184).

65. See Arendt, *On Revolution*, p. 183.

66. Baudelaire, *Oeuvres complètes*, 2: 110.

67. Just so, in a fragment previously cited, Minerva arrives "*secouant* le glaive et le casque guerrier / Et l'horrible Gorgone à l'aspect meurtrier" (shaking the sword and the warrior's helmet / And the horrible Gorgon of murderous aspect) (p. 131), and one of the Maenads in a fragmentary bucolic is glimpsed "agitant le thyrse environné de lierre" (shaking the ivy-wrapped thyrsus) (p. 528). The theme is constant enough to allow us to affirm that for Chénier, the literary model afforded by the play of the signifier is in certain situations apotropaic. See on this de Man, *Romanticism and Contemporary Criticism*, pp. 171–74.

68. Hugo, *Littérature*, in *Oeuvres complètes*, vol. 5, bk. 1, pp. 78–79.

69. Compare, for a normal construction, "Le jeune Thurien aussi beau qu'elle est belle" (The young Thurian as handsome as she is beautiful) (p. 13).

70. Grevisse, *Le Bon usage*, p. 403.

71. *Comme lui belle* is a stumbling block; it calls attention to the order of the line as untranslatable. It is not untranslatable simply because one cannot get across the harmonious echoes and sounds of French. On the contrary, what would be lost through translation is Chénier's advertisement of grammar struggling to break with incomplete symbolization and imitative harmony. The poem indicates a point where its grammar, before conceived as ultimately reconcilable with figure, stands forth as inalterably disjunct. The order is to be construed as more than simply a particular disposition of terms. It is at once a poetic law (and a case), an order to (be) dispose(d) in such a manner as to show the language "armed with rebellious obstacles" (Chénier, p. 132).

72. Grevisse, *Le Bon usage*, p. 226.

73. Ibid., p. 226

74. Ibid., p. 403. Grevisse remarks that

When the adjective has endings in the masculine and the feminine that do not differ to the ear, although they may do so to the eye, the immediate proximity of the masculine plural adjective and the feminine noun is plausible. . . . But if the adjective in the feminine has an ending clearly different for the ear from that of the masculine, the proximity just mentioned has something shocking about it. . . . When one or several words are placed between the masculine plural adjective and the feminine noun, the ear has scarcely reason any longer to find itself offended. (p. 403)

75. In the metaphor of *Epître sur ses ouvrages*, the poet works as a transplanter and grafter:

> Des antiques vergers ces rameaux empruntés
> Croissent sur mon terrain mollement transplantés.
> Aux troncs de mon verger ma main avec adresse
> Les attache; et bientôt même écorce les presse.

> From antique orchards these borrowed branches
> Gently transplanted, grow in my ground.
> To the trunks of the orchard trees my adroit hand
> Attaches them; and soon a same bark presses them.
> *(p. 159)*

In *Hermès* the poet sutures and re-members languages into a startling combination "Souvent mon vol, armé des ailes de Buffon" (Often my flight, armed with the wings of Buffon) (p. 399); in the *Epître*, the persona recalls the work as dismembered and fragmentary (p. 158). The most finished of Chénier's poems aim to show this suturing of wings-and-arms, the heteroclite, dismembered pile of parts in the most integral and harmonious-looking body.

76. See "Iamb IX," where the poet envisages leaving unfinished verses ("Before of its two halves / This line [*vers*] that I am beginning has reached the last. . . . The messenger of death, black recruiter of shades. . . . On my lips will suddenly suspend the rhyme"), and requests life to fight with his pen ("In ink and bitterness another arm soaked / Can still serve humanity") against "Those executioners scribblers of laws! / Cadaverous worms [*vers cadavéreux*] of enslaved France," those "perverse ones" (*pervers*). The fight for justice appears to be taking place on the terrain of the interpretation of the poetic line (*le vers*), with the perverse ones being those who read "verse" in perverse, and the poet's final address to virtue as an advertisement that, for the poet, virtue (*vertu*) is a matter both of stifling the clamorous signifier (*le vers tu*) *and* of setting things down for history and memory (pp. 193–95).

77. I take it that Chénier's critique of partisan spirit, his claim that he belongs to no party, are both possible only because he recognizes no other "maître

que la volonté nationale, *connue et rédigée* en loi" (master than the national will, *known as such and written* into law) (p. 227).

78. For Arendt, Jefferson proves a better reader of Rousseau than was Robespierre; his deity is clement with the people and severe with the legislator.

79. The voice compares itself to that of an escaped Philomela (or Philomena, as Chénier calls her), the sister of Procne, who was stolen away and raped by Procne's husband Tereus. The latter ripped her tongue out so she could not tell her tale except by weaving it into a tapestry. A creature in a situation so dire—destitute not only of her legal property and her name, but also, beyond what the law could allow, destitute of her natural rights and voice—owns nothing anymore of humanity and owes nothing to it. Philomela and Procne cooked Procne's children by Tereus into a stew, feeding the unsuspecting father on the limbs of his progeny.

80. According to Bell, *Women of Classical Mythology*, p. 317.

81. See Chénier, p. 192, "Quand au mouton bêlant," for the poet's recommendation to friends to live, even if it means pastoralizing and forgetting about the actual situation of the sheep, who are bleating in the sheepfold as they await slaughter.

82. The reference is to Althusser's "Ideology and Ideological State Apparatuses" in *Lenin and Philosophy*.

83. See also "Iamb VIII," where Chénier treats prison life as a melting pot that divides the prisoner's time into a time of enforced leisure, and roll call, when one by one the "citizens" get called up to enable the machine to function (p. 192).

Chapter 2

1. Publication was deferred until the issue could be definitively settled in the editor's favor by the poet's death. See Yves-Alain Favre's Introduction in Mallarmé's *Oeuvres* (pp. 3–6), for a short account of the Deman edition. See also, for example, *Correspondance*, 8: 203–4 where, after long hesitation (*Correspondance*, 4: 219, 295), Mallarmé rejects italics as too similar to handwriting.

2. For Harold Bloom, writing in the Introduction to *Mallarmé*, "Baudelaire, Rimbaud, and Mallarmé were the crucial continuators of Hugo and French Romanticism" (p. 3). Bloom finds overblown the claims made for Mallarmé as a belated poet of discontinuity, but that is because, for him, "in literary France . . . everything has been belated at least from Romanticism on" (p. 3).

3. In "Situation de Baudelaire" Valéry says: "Baudelaire's problem could then—must then—be posed as follows: to be a great poet, but to be not Lamartine, nor Hugo, nor Musset. I am not saying that this was a conscious resolution, but it was necessarily in Baudelaire,—and was even essentially Baudelaire. It was his reason of state" (1: 600). Later, he comments in specifically economic

terms on the situation of a belated poet faced with Hugo's powerful and precise material, his vastness of register, diversity of rhythms, and superabundance of gifts. Baudelaire, he imagines, notes Hugo's impurities and imprudences as so many possibilities or chances of life for his own poems (1: 602).

4. *Correspondance*, 1: 222. It should be noted that the correspondence of the "crisis" years presents the crisis as a drama of renunciation, which has led critics to understand Mallarmé as having undergone a spiritual transformation dividing his poetic production into two rather neat packages or periods. But the disappearance in later letters of spiritual dramatics, the giving up of a language of giving up, can be analyzed as entirely consonant with the early letters. Traces of an ongoing crisis, in other words, may still be found in the later works. As for the shape given the crisis in the early letters, it was in keeping with Mallarmé's foray into lyric drama with *Igitur* and *Hérodiade*; the letters await the critical treatment owed texts.

5. A few early examples of the tendency can be found in the very disparate writings of Cohn, Jean-Pierre Richard, and Karlheinz Stierle. Despite their many differences, all of these critics consider Mallarmean economies of the signifier as a source of meaning that supplements or even substitutes for the failure of poetic language to represent. Among more recent criticism in this vein, the remarkably patient and astute analyses of Frey foreground the free play of the signifier as the source of potential meaning as the self: "what we playingly create as ourselves . . . in as through music" (*Studies in Poetic Discourse*, pp. 57–58).

6. "This is the procedure of ALLITERATION, procedure inherent to the septentrional genius, and much exemplified in many famous lines. So masterly an effort on the part of the Imagination, desirous not only of satisfying itself through a symbol glittering forth in the world's spectacles, but also of establishing a link between those spectacles and the word charged with expressing them, touches on one of the sacred or perilous mysteries of language, and one that it would be prudent to analyze only on that day that Science, possessing the vast repertory of all the idioms ever spoken on earth, will write the history of the letters of the alphabet through the ages and what was almost their absolute meaning, sometimes guessed at, sometimes unrecognized by men, creators of words: but at that time there will no longer be either Science to summarize or person to say it. Chimera, for the moment let us be content with the flashes that some magnificent writers have thrown out on this subject" (p. 921). See de Man, "Roland Barthes and the Limits of Structuralism" in *Romanticism and Contemporary Criticism*, pp. 164–77, for a discussion of the dream of a semiological science associated with the liberated signifier.

7. Bénichou, *Selon Mallarmé*, p. 19.

8. See Derrida, *Le Monolinguisme*, for an eloquent and incisive account of the other's language.

9. Blanchot, *Le Livre*, p. 341.

10. "Enigme," p. 5 and, for the translation, which has been modified, p. 8. The difficulties, grammatically speaking, are, first, that the antecedent of *elle* may be *la littérature* or *l'exigence d'écrire* and, second, that there are two constructions in French being played on around the preposition *à*: (1) *en appeler* (meaning "to appeal a judgment in front of a superior court"), with *à sa disparition* then taking the role of a temporal modifier and meaning "until its disappearance"; and (2) *en appeler à* (meaning "to submit the case to, to appeal to"), so that literature's appeal is for literature to disappear.

11. Literature is not a life form or a fire; it does not get extinguished. Instead, when it disappears it may either be because it ceases to be recognized as literature (perhaps because it has been incorporated into everyday life, as cultural forms and symbolic practices that are inextricable from it, or as fundamental myths shoring up our social structures) or because it has disappeared from a certain scene and has migrated elsewhere. Thus, says Mallarmé, "poetry, I believe, respectfully waited until the giant [Hugo] who identified it with his tenacious and ever firmer smith's hand went missing, for itself to break asunder. The whole language, adapted to meter and finding there its vital pauses, escapes, according to a free disjunction into a thousand simple elements" (p. 361). Here, Mallarmé identifies the moment where the lyric breaks up with the dissemination of meter into the whole of the language. As for the whole of the language, which is no longer a totality grasped by a hand, it too becomes fragmented and partial. In such a view, the disappearance of the lyric per se is equated with its dissemination into other branches of literature.

12. A passage from Blanchot's "La Poésie de Mallarmé est-il obscur?" is the point of reference here:

> The first reflex, faced with some lines of poetry that discursive reason wants to elucidate, is to give them another form. But its resistance allows for no metamorphosis. One has to understand without feint or detour, and exchanging the poem only against the poem. . . . [Poetic signification] is good for one time only, and it makes unavailable the system of images, figures and consonances indissolubly associated to it. It belongs to the category of the Unique. (*Faux pas*, p. 128)

13. See Mondor, *Vie de Mallarmé*, p. 502.

14. What language does a cook understand? Is it ordinary language, the language that—as the fiction goes—serves the subject who speaks it? Such a language would be a language, so goes the fiction, natural to cooks, whose role is not to think but to serve. Perhaps then, if it is natural in the fiction, this ordinary language is in point of fact a language that *hides* from the cook her servitude to ideological structures. Perhaps the fear is that a cook might understand too well the chance provided by a language that obeys other rules than those of ordinary language.

15. We may consider Mallarmé as a modern "encyclopedist," who seeks to provide samples of the modes of literature of the time (the essay, the poem, the fashion magazine, the newspaper survey, the tale, the translation, the album verse, the letter's address).

16. Hölderin, "Brot und Wein," in *Sämtliche Werke und Briefe*, p. 313.

17. The reference is to Avital Ronell's *Telephone Book*.

18. What matters is the recognition of another speaking in what is said. Another speaking: *allos* + *agoreuein*, allegory. The brush of the feather/pen (*la plume*) is felt at the moment that the most public, ordinary language possible is heard to whisper something else, here, a question concerning language as action.

19. Because we are always faced with texts undecidably documents and fictions, the question of literature is an urgent political question, since where it disappears, for instance, would be where undecidable texts are getting archived as if their documentary status were not questionable. If Mallarmé recollects writing "the supplementary mark" and the "white space that allows for the mark" (Derrida, *La Dissémination*, pp. 283, 285), it is in part as a reminder that a veiled or forgotten fiction is involved in the determination of writing as accessory and belated.

20. The passage that starts off this reflection is on p. 369.

> Cette pratique entend deux façons; ou, par une volonté, à l'insu, qui dure une vie, jusqu'à l'éclat multiple—penser, cela: sinon, les déversoirs à portée maintenant dans une prévoyance, journaux et leur tourbillon, y déterminer une force en un sens, quelconque de divers contrariée, avec l'immunité du résultat nul.

> (This practice implies two modes: either, without knowledge, by a will that lasts a lifetime, up to a multiple outburst—that is thinking: or else, with foresight, the overflow channels now at hand, newspapers and their whirlwind, to determine in them a force in a direction, whichever, thwarted by diverse others, with the immunity of a zero result.)

21. See also "Le Livre, instrument spirituel," in *Oeuvres complètes*, for a discussion of the two economies of newspaper and book.

22. Mallarmé, *Oeuvres*, ed. C. Barbier and C. Millan, pp. 740–41. The edition as planned was to have been even more luxurious: the autograph manuscripts of the poet were to be reproduced by photolithograph on genuine parchment. No more than 25 copies were to be printed; the designs on the stones were to be crossed out, and a last proof was to be printed from the barred stone. The cost was to have been 200 francs. When the number of copies almost doubled (and parchment was abandoned for a less expensive paper), the cost dropped to 100 francs.

23. I am taking the poem and the book as interchangeable. See p. 375, where Mallarmé states the relation as follows: "the poetic line, dispenser, arranger of the game of pages, master of the Book."

24. That is established, among other places, in "Le Livre, instrument spirituel," where Mallarmé is less concerned with capitalizing (finding advantages or displaying the disadvantages of the newspaper or the book) than in analyzing the system in which they occupy specific places. Here, for example, is what he says about the newspaper:

> Journal, la feuille étalée, pleine, emprunte à l'impression un résultat indu, de simple maculature; nul doute que l'éclatant et vulgaire avantage soit, au vu de tous, la multiplication de l'exemplaire et, gise dans le tirage. Un miracle prime ce bienfait, au sens haut ou les mots, originellement, se réduisent à l'emploi, doué d'infinité jusqu'à sacrer une langue, des quelque vingt lettres—leur devenir, tout y rentre pour tantôt soudre, principe—approchant d'un rite la composition typographique.

> (Newspaper, the sheet spread out, copious, borrows the undue result from printing of simple maculature; no question that the glaring and vulgar advantage is, to everyone's eyes, the multiplication of the example and rests in the number printed. A miracle surpasses this benefit, in the lofty sense, or words, originarily, are reduced to the employment, gifted with infinity to the point of consecrating the language, of some twenty letters—their becoming, everything is recovered by it only to well up, principle—bringing typographical composition close to a rite.) (p. 380)

The surprise result of printing—the ink-stained sheets of the newspaper appear blotted against bushes, spread out like laundry—occasions the reflection on print. The writer discusses the sacred of a culture (the infinity of combinations made possible by letters and that make its language sacred), its priest-celebrants (the typesetters), its vulgar interpreters (those who see the advantages and good to be reaped from reproduction); these are set off against the newspaper's inky newsprint, its soiled sheets spread around everywhere (a thrown-away paper has blown off to cover a rose bush, in an earlier passage of the text). The whole of the system is considered—from the throwaway, stained broadsheet, the abjected page, to the sacred, fresh print at the top of the heap. Any discussion of the writer's obligations and investments with respect to this system can only be undertaken with the analysis of what Marcel Mauss, writing in *Essai sur le don*, would have called "le fait total social" in mind.

25. Stanguennec, *Mallarmé*, p. 113.

26. A case in point could be found by considering the 1887 lithographed edition of *Poésies*. Walter Benjamin's comments on lithography as a means of reproducing the graphic arts whose speed approximated that of printing are worth bearing in mind. Mallarmé's decision for the lithograph meant, among other things, that he would be adopting a technology that was slower and more expensive than print, but that, in terms of the reproduction of pictorial arts, was faster and more efficient than copperplate or woodblock (if not so rapid as the photograph was to become). The edition intervenes with respect to the means. It *slows* circulation of the poems as written traces and rarefies them in

that aspect; it *speeds* up circulation of the poems as representation of writing, and dissipates the aura attached to them (the image of the manuscript, the author's authentic hand).

Mallarmé's final decision against italics in the projected Deman edition provides another instance of incisive intervention. His chief objection to italics ("the font appears to me charmless,—without life") is that it is too close to handwriting: "Too close to writing, especially after the Dujardin manuscript edition" (*Correspondance* 8: 203–4). The objection is in keeping with his earlier decision, if we consider that by this decision he is not elevating or idealizing an original as what is to be reproduced, but is making a distinction in writing itself, between writing as iterable inscription and the print as representation of some more original writing (italics as a way of representing handwriting). His preference for a more common roman type, or better yet, "some ordinary Simon Raçon" (ibid., 204) is suggestive of the deliberate foregrounding of the trace over the fetishized hand. See Benjamin's "The Work of Art in the Age of Mechanical Reproduction," in *Illuminations,* esp. pp. 218–20. See also Mallarmé's text on graphology, where he distinguishes the writer by profession as never writing an original. Instead, he "recopies, or sees first in the mirror of his thought, then transcribes in a writing once made forever, as if invariable" (p. 878).

27. See, for instance, Foucault's *Discipline and Punish.*

28. See Althusser's "Ideology" in *Lenin and Philosophy,* pp. 127–86.

29. In French, "l'exception confirme la règle pour les cas non-exceptés."

30. A recourse to a discourse of common sense can be justified if we consider that the passage has some of the marks of a Cartesian situation: its concern with the idea and the body; its positing of an extravagant body akin to the extravagance of Cartesian doubt in positing the *malin génie*; the quotation of the Cartesian trademark term, *certes* (to be sure).

31. Stanguennec, *Mallarmé,* p. 111.

32. The condensation that makes the vocabulary of the Sunday bicycle rider overlap with that of the train rider is enough of a constant to be worth noting. See the short text, "Sur le costume féminin à bicyclette," where Mallarmé designates women on bicycles as "straddlers (or, riders [*chevaucheuses*]) of steel" and calls himself a "passerby who pulls to the side" (*un passant qui se gare*). Both the term *cheval* and the term *gare*, and its verbal form, *se garer*, underwent extensions in the early part of the century, with the development of the railroad and other technical advances. The English term *horsepower*, for instance, was translated into French as *cheval vapeur* (with the "Iron Horse" in the background). As for the archaic meaning of *chevaucher* (to ride on horseback), it was briefly revived by the Romantics in novels about the Middle Ages. In its meaning of "straddle," it not only retains its liveliness in the nineteenth century, but is given various extensions in technical terms (*chevauchement*—the

position of two objects overlapping one another, including letters or signs; *chevauchage*—a technical term in printing for such overlap). *Gare* (etymologically related to *garde*), earlier a basin where boats could cross one another safely or be placed in shelter, was extended by 1831 to mean the portion of track where trains crossed, and then by 1835 to mean the train station. *Se garer* was used by 1865 to mean "take a vehicle out of circulation to allow another to pass it." We can characterize Mallarmé's art as one of *chevauchement* or straddling, where signs and images are made to overlap one another—here, the image of the bicyclist overlaps that of a train rider. The Mallarmean strategy of giving momentary priority to a means of mass transport (like the train or newspaper), while temporarily "parking" a means for transporting single individuals (like the bicycle or poem) also finds a convenient metaphor here.

33. This is according to the empirical observation that most accidents—whether happy or unhappy—happen near home.

34. Notice that the technology of the railroad overlaid on the old roadmap (*sur la chaussée*) gets a double reading from Mallarmé. It rides on an unbroken rail and has to be ridden until it stops, unlike the bicycle, from which a rider can dismount at will. If it stands for progress, it is only by an aestheticizing blindness that overlooks this increased regulation of time and space in the mass transport system to admire the unbroken form. On the other hand, always in allegorical terms, Mallarmé's railroad is as celestial as that of Hawthorne. For instance, a *rail continu*, in the context of a text concerned with the ironies of the letter, is a pretty good translation for Schlegel's permanent parabasis or Baudelaire's *divine ironie*. It suggests that the letter and the techniques for deploying it bear the permanent possibility of derailing of narratives of progress (*raillerie continue*). In a text that, as will be shown, speaks to English, there is a definite (nonsubjective) irony in centering things on the Iron Horse.

35. Derrida, *La Dissémination*, p. 234. See de Man, "The Concept of Irony," in *Aesthetic Ideology*, especially p. 179, for a discussion of Schlegel's definition of poetry as permanent parabasis. See Frey's discussion of Mallarmé's "A la nue accablante tu" in *Studies in Poetic Discourse*. See Newmark on "Mallarmé and the Foundation of Letters" in *Beyond Symbolism*.

36. Drama is not to be understood as a script to be represented on the stage; it is rather closer to what Peter Szondi says of lyric drama, in his discussion of what makes *Hérodiade* contrary to the laws of theater. He notes that the actions of Mallarmé's lyric drama consist, on the one hand, in the decomposition of the main character Hérodiade into organic and anorganic parts and on the other hand, in the metamorphosis and elevation of her hair to the status of symbol. Neither of these actions could successfully appear on stage (the stage presence of the actress would bely her decomposing; the transformation of her hair into an ethereal symbol would be ridiculous to the spectator viewing her heavy tresses),

from which Szondi concludes that "the poetic drama does not find its reality on stage but in the reality of the imagination, evoked by language" (pp. 86–87).

37. The key to reading this passage as about the futures of the text as held by the letter is *entrelacs*, with its connotations of interweaving, and also its typographical meaning: it is the term used to denote the intertwined letters of a monogram, or the overlapping letters of a ligature (like *æ*). See also the comment at the end of the text about the "unknowing flank of the hour" (p. 373).

38. "GARTER, THE MOST NOBLE ORDER OF THE. English order of knighthood founded by King Edward III in 1348, considered to be the highest British civil and military honour obtainable. Because the earliest records of the order were destroyed by fire, it is difficult for historians to reconstruct its original purposes, the significance of its emblem, and the origin of the order's motto. One theory is that Edward III wished to revive the Round Table of Arthurian legend, thereby creating a fraternity of knights, and that the garter perhaps symbolized the homage paid by knights to ladies.

"According to the most picturesque legend, it was established to commemorate an incident in which Edward was dancing with Joan of Kent . . . when one of her blue garters dropped to the floor. As bystanders snickered, Edward gallantly picked up the garter and put it on his own leg, admonishing the courtiers in French with the phrase that remains as the order's motto 'Honi soit qui mal y pense.'" From the *Encyclopedia Britannica*.

39. A long excursus into *Les Mots anglais* would be possible here. On the importance of foreign terms, see Theodor Adorno, "On the Use of Foreign Words," in *Notes to Literature*, vol. 2. Adorno is interested in unleashing a certain explosive force associated with the foreign term. He says that "historically, foreign words are the points at which a knowing consciousness and an illuminated truth break into the undifferentiated growth of the aspect of language that is mere nature: the incursion of freedom" (p. 289).

Chapter 3

1. The unfinished state of the poems has tempted more than one critic to bring scissors or pen to bear on them. Gérard Walter reproaches Chénier's first editor, Henri de Latouche, for "suppressing passages deemed 'subversive' and indecent" (Introduction to *Oeuvres complètes*, p. xxxv). No less a critic than Leo Spitzer rewrites a stanza of "La Jeune captive," claiming that the poet himself would have done so "had he lived longer" (p. 103).

2. See Furet, *Interpreting the French Revolution*, pp. 3–14, for a discussion of the Revolution as the site of a conflict over national identity. Chénier's work has served as one focus in the game of capture the flag played out in interpretations of the Revolutionary period.

3. See, for representative views, the Introduction to the Pléiade edition by Chénier's twentieth-century Marxist editor, Gérard Walter (pp. vii–xxxvi), as well as Walter's biography, *André Chénier*, Francis Scarfe's *André Chénier*, and Paul Dimoff's *La Vie*, pp. 117–73.

4. Jean Starobinski, in "André Chénier and the Allegory of Poetry," finds Chénier to take a crucial turn away from political allegory, expressive of "the triumphal situation, where the voice of the poet-soldier or the poet-prophet gives voice to the authority that the entire community will make use of" (p. 59), to a Romantic poetry of the self, written in incarceration, "where the *self* can make use in solitude only of the authority it discovers within itself, in the hope of a justice which will be granted to it, beyond humiliation and death, by other generations" (p. 59). For Starobinski, it is Chénier's poetry of lyric expression that has a future. With a Giordano or a Brasillach, by means of a reduction of the issue from one concerning the poem's shape to that of the poet's legend, this situation gets turned into a romantic story about a misunderstood genius, caught up in political turmoil, misjudged and sacrificed by a short-sighted people.

5. At various moments in the *Essai* literature is defined to harmonize with political action:

> Two things, being more than others the fruit of genius and of courage, and ordinarily of both, lead most surely to true glory: these are great actions that uphold the commonweal [*la chose publique*], and good writings that enlighten it. To do well may most make a man great; to speak well is not to be disdained either; and often a good book is itself a good action; and often a wise and sublime author, being the slow cause of healthy revolutions in customs and ideas, may seem to have done himself all the good that he makes others do. (p. 622)

In other passages from the *Essai*, Chénier distinguishes literature from the political, with which it nonetheless lives in harmony, because it provides knowledge of corruption in the state. For a corrupt republic, letters are a salutory reminder of antique institutions and are far removed from the avarice and pragmatic economies governing power relations in the state (p. 623). In tyrannies, however, he diagnoses letters as frivolous and sees them as actively propagating ills in the public domain (p. 624). In this case, literature has to retreat, in the person of the poet, from the neighborhood of political action (pp. 624–25).

6. In *Avis au peuple français sur ses véritables ennemis*, for example, Chénier justifies his examination of an enemy "party" of writers by the claim that the Revolution is intimately bound up with writing: "All the good and evil that has been done in this revolution is owed to writings; it will perhaps be there also that we will find the source of evils that threaten us" (p. 206). In *Réflexions sur l'esprit de parti*, previous to a critique of the metaphors and chaotic organiza-

tion of Burke's *Reflections on the French Revolution*, he finds one of the characteristic marks of the Revolution to be good writing (p. 242).

7. Valéry, 1: 1148.

8. Chénier's famous lines on the birth of the poet ought to be considered in this context: "... a Greek, in her young springtime, / Beautiful, from the bed of a spouse nursling of France / Bore me French in the heart of Byzantium" (p. 72). The French poet is born in an Eastern cradle rocked by a Greek hand.

9. See Dimoff's Préface to *Oeuvres complètes* (pp. vii–xxv) for a discussion of the manuscripts. Chénier's writing practices contribute to the difficulty facing editors. He worked on many poems at once, noting down randomly isolated lines, long fragments, prose synopses, or critical reminders to himself; he added to apparently finished poems, inserted short poems in longer poems, or developed, out of the single image of a longer poem, a shorter poem. The poems themselves comment on their composition. See for example the unfinished *Epître* to the chevalier de Pange: "You know how vagabond my muses are. . . . They cannot finish promptly a single project; they make one hundred advance together. . . . Often you think me occupied in making discoveries in America and you see me arrive with a pastoral flute on my lips; you expect a piece of *Hermès*, and instead it is some extravagant Elegy" (p. 563). See also, *Epître sur ses ouvrages* (p. 158).

10. Examples of this kind of speculation are too frequent to be enumerated. In *La Vie* Dimoff provides one of the most fully developed of the fictions attempting to overcome all the disjunctions of the work and life. On the one hand, he dismisses Chénier's fragmentary poems, telling us that if Chénier, "preserved by miracle from the perils of the Revolution, had traversed that agitated and tragic period without his ambitions or his earlier dreams having been modified in any way . . . the chances are entirely minimal that he would have ever realized his literary projects as he had conceived them" (p. 432). On the other hand, he spins a narrative about how the political thinker, faced with the events and personages of the early nineteenth century would have greeted, and been greeted by, them (pp. 434–37).

11. Did the work remain unfinished because there was a defect in Chénier's poetic conception? A whole school of Chénier criticism concentrates on his transitional position between the long didactic poems of the eighteenth century and the emerging lyric of Romanticism, to find in Chénier's incomplete recognition that the future lay with the lyric the explanation for the fragmentariness of the long narrative poems. Similarly, the brittleness of some of the *Odes* and *Bucoliques* derives, or so the theory goes, from a neoclassicism in which too much attention is paid to the respectful recycling of old clichés, and not enough to the expressive originality of the lyrical subject. See, for examples, Scarfe and Starobinski.

12. In a passage from the *Essai*, Chénier talks about an epic on America projected as unfinished:

> As for Mr.———, it is a pity that with such great talents he has not carried through so beautiful an enterprise. We would have a poem to oppose to the ancients. But, as we have heard him say several times, his design, in beginning, was not to finish this work. He was already old and had not yet finished several writings that have placed him in the first rank among our poets. His project was only to show by this sample what road had to be followed and that he alone was capable of holding to it. He aspired to take possession of this land without conquering it, and that his flag planted on the shore should intimidate and make flee whoever might desire to approach it. He wanted the short and precious fragment that he has published to be like the painting that Apelles left imperfect and that no other hand dared take upon itself the charge of finishing. (p. 686)

Paul Van Tieghem has convincingly demonstrated that the "Mr.———" in question is Chénier himself and the poem, his epic *L'Amérique*.

13. Scarfe, *André Chénier*, p. 94.

14. Ibid., p. 94.

15. Ibid., p. 96.

16. Van Tieghem, "Un 'Monsieur . . .' mystérieux," p. 96.

17. For Van Tieghem, the new thoughts are those of a critical Enlightenment thinker, and "antique verse" can be glossed as meaning perfect formal treatment: "It is not easy, when one is very hard to please over the quality of verse and very ambitious as to that of ideas, to make *antique verse* on *new thoughts*, to be at once the thinker and the artist, the Rabelais drunk with modern culture and the Ronsard in love with antique and perfect poetry" ("Un 'Monsieur . . .' mystérieux," p. 97). *Antique* is not, however, a synonym for *formally perfect*. Nor is it certain, in Chénier's vocabulary, that both of the terms in the formula are positively weighted. "New thoughts" are not to be swallowed *tel quel* by a pleasure-seeking wine drinker. In a fragment to *Hermès*, speaking of the discovery of the new world, Chénier evaluates discovery in two entirely contradictory ways: "Speak at the end prophetically of the discovery of the new world. Oh destinies, hasten to bring this *great* day which . . . which . . . But . . . no, destinies, defer this *fatal* day, and, if possible, let it never arrive, this day which . . . which . . . etc." (my emphasis, p. 415). See also the fragment from the *Essai* quoted in note 12, where the poet plants a flag in a New World from which all will flee.

18. There is some evidence for this position. In *Hermès*, Chénier explains it to be the concern of modern science: "Not content with admiring the form and the work, science wants to know the material and to see the hand act" (p. 407). The poet would be seeking to figure the critical posture of modern science with respect to the action of the hand on the material that "to their

(Greek) eyes is yet too veiled" (p. 125). Chénier, who compares the path of the poet with that of the wandering comet, and the poet with Mercury, is perfectly capable of adopting—temporarily—the scientist's position. However, it would be a mistake to think that he confuses his alchemy with the experiments of Newton or Descartes.

19. De Man, "'Conclusions,'" in *Resistance*, p. 76.

20. Van Tieghem, "Un 'Monsieur . . .' mystérieux," p. 98.

21. Lacoue-Labarthe and Nancy, *L'Absolu littéraire*, p. 69.

22. Ibid., p. 67.

23. Ibid., p. 71.

24. It might seem absurd to search, in a poem of epic inspiration, for traces of a lyrical voice, and outright silly to wonder at not finding them. But *Hermès* is not just any epic. It purports to be the epic of a poet "client of nature, . . . Seeking far from our walls the temples and palaces where the divinity reveals its features" (p. 391). He is led by blind Homer to take Lucretius's *De natura rerum* and Buffon's *Histoire naturelle* as helps in his task. He asks us to listen to "these songs depositaries of Hermes, / Where ancient man, wandering along his first roads, / Makes the imprint of his steps live again to your eyes" (p. 392). All of these indices suggest that the poem has at least one foot in the natural world where the lyric takes its origin. Moreover, the father-poet claims his dear poem-child, while in his father's house, gave "free flight [*libre essor*] to his native tongue" (p. 404), the implication being that the poem's language was of lyric origin.

25. The passage insists on the natural landscape as testifying to these covenants, and then goes on to describe the development of portable symbols:

> Quand des premiers traités la fraternelle chaîne
> Commença d'approcher, d'unir la race humaine,
> La terre, et de hauts monts, des fleuves, des forêts,
> Des contrats attestés garants sûrs et muets,
> Furent le livre auguste et les lettres sacrées
> Qui faisaient lire aux yeux les promesses jurées.
> Dans la suite peut-être ils voulurent sur soi
> L'un de l'autre emporter la parole et la foi;
> Ils surent donc, broyant de liquides matières,
> L'un sur l'autre imprimer leurs images grossières,
> Ou celle du témoin, homme, plante ou rocher,
> Qui vit jurer leur bouche et leurs mains se toucher.

> When the fraternal chain of the first treaties
> Began to approach, to unite the human race,
> The earth, high mountains, rivers, forests,
> Sure and mute guarantors of attested contracts,
> Were the august book and the sacred letters
> That made eyes read sworn promises.

Afterward perhaps they wanted to carry away
The one from the other, on their persons, the word and the faith;
They knew then, grinding liquid materials,
How to imprint one on the other their crude images,
Or that of the witness, man, plant or rock,
Which saw their mouth swear and their hands touch.

(pp. 394–95)

26. In the space of 75 lines, the vocable *main* appears no fewer than eight times (aux hu*mains*; une *main* éloquente; la race hu*maine*; leurs *mains* se toucher; les *mains* politiques; l'esprit des hu*mains*; le conduit par la *main*).

27. This is consonant with Warburton's insight, in the section from *The Divine Legation of Moses Demonstrated* that Chénier might have read in a 1744 translation under the title *Essai sur les hiéroglyphes des Egyptiens*, that the Egyptians sought to transmit a science by their hieroglyphs. I quote from the readily available French edition based on that translation.

28. For a discussion of the law of *usure* in Warburton's discussion of the development of Egyptian writing, see Jacques Derrida, "Scribble," in Warburton's *Essai sur les hiéroglyphes des Egyptiens*, pp. 7–43.

29. See Chénier's discussion of the challenge French poses to the poet at the end of *L'Invention* for another twist on the same theme. French is described as having twin sources: the barbarous, rusty, proud, and indocile Frankish tongue and the polished, civilizing, seductive, easily modeled wax of Latin (pp. 131–32).

30. Warburton, *Essai*, p. 160.

31. See Warburton, who explains that epistolic writing—a code at once unambiguous and, at first, secret—was made possible by the invention of an alphabet by a secretary to the king of Egypt (*Essai*, p. 160). For Chénier, the development of the state itself, with its mechanisms, its secrets, its publicity, is indissociably linked with the alphabet.

32. Ibid., p. 219.

33. For Warburton, there are four sorts of Egyptian writing: (1) the Hieroglyphic, divided into curiological and tropic; (2) the Symbolic, divided into the tropic and the allegorical; (3) the Epistolic; and (4) the Hierogrammatic. The last sorts were alphabetical, and stood for words, whereas the first two sorts were symbolic and stood for things (p. 136). Chénier has telescoped these four kinds into two.

34. *Etonner*, besides meaning "to cause a violent moral commotion by admiration or fear" also has a more literal meaning in French. It can mean "to produce a violent commotion, a trembling" of the sort that sometimes rocks Californian buildings. By the nineteenth century, it will have taken on the very technical meaning of "cracking something" (*étonner un diamant*). The *Petit Robert* provides as synonyms *fêler*, *lézarder*: to crack, to split. The lizard is not a

salamander at all. It is a fissure, an interval produced within an apparently seamless surface.

35. For example, in trying to determine what "child of the airs" modifies, one is faced with a dizzying number of possibilities: Does it modify the eagle alone? Does it modify the woman's body with (or on) the forehead of an eagle, or at war with the eagle over territory at the front? Does it modify any *thing* at all, or, deserted child (*enfant désert*), dropped here to complete the line, does it only have the air of being a modifier? It might be a commentary on the poetic imagination, "child of airy fancy," or a commentary on the need for an artifice to fill out the rhyme, the "child of a musical air." "Child of (multiple) airs," it surely also reunites all these possibilities. "Desert child," it comments on its sterility and emptiness. A confusion of tongues can be heard in the very modifier that strikes the most satisfyingly harmonizing of notes.

36. In the next fragment of the poem, Chénier praises Moses for the "great and holy lie! glorious imposture" (p. 398) by which he claims the world and nature as testimony of a God-given law. Again, he appears in agreement with Warburton's central thesis in *The Divine Legation* (that the state and civil society are impossible without established religion). The title of Bishop Warburton's book tells us how unlikely he is to concur with Chénier in calling Moses' claim of divine legation a lie.

37. The point could be supported by the analysis of various political articles, among which the aforementioned *Les Autels de la peur, Avis au peuple français sur ses véritables ennemis,* and *Réflexions sur l'esprit de parti. De la cause des désordres qui troublent la France et arrêtent l'établissement de la liberté* states the problem to be one of misinterpretation. By an anthropomorphism with distinctly religious overtones, the people (defined as a public space or legal system of relations) are viewed as a *body*:

> This Society [of Jacobins] has produced an infinity of others: towns, boroughs, villages, are full of them. Almost all obey the orders of the mother Society, and entertain with her a very active correspondence. She is a body in Paris, and she is the head of a vaster body spread over France. It is thus that the Church of Rome *planted the faith* and governed the world by congregations of monks. . . .
>
> A simple ambiguity was enough for everything. The constitution being founded on the eternal truth, *the sovereignty of the people,* all that had to be done was to persuade the forums [*tribunes*] of clubs that they are *the people.* (my emphasis, pp. 273–74)

In Chénier's poems, a finger is placed on a similar anthropomorphism humanizing the inhuman. The "warlike" (p. 187) "Iambs" in particular are illuminating of the mechanical aspect masked by the appeal to the body of the people. For example, in "Voûtes du Panthéon, quel mort" the personified guillotine weeps, seeks consolation and justice, tries to save France by calling its vassals to it by name. The machinery of decapitation is greased by the personification. In the name of humanity, of patriotism, and so forth, it starts to decapitate those who once made it function. Nor ought one to think that Chénier sees in the axe turned against its wielders a "just" solution. The guillotine is impartial. It does not stop calling roll. Whoever wields it in the name of justice becomes subject to its justice:

> . . . You will save France.
> For your arms la Montagne . . .
> Le Gendre . . . / Collot d'Herbois . . .
> More than one Robespierre, and Danton
> Thuriot, and Chabot; at last the whole band;
> And club, commune, tribunal;
> *But who can count them?* I recommend them to you.
> You will call the roll.　　　　　　　　　　*(p. 188)*

Chapter 4

1. A classic example of the way that language's undecidability can operate at a greater level of complexity than that of a mere option between fiction or history can be found in Rousseau's dialogued preface to *Julie*. In *Allegories of Reading*, Paul de Man discusses the insistent assertion by one of the two interlocutors, "R," who says he really does not know whether he is the author of a tableau, a fiction of man, or the editor of documents portraying particular men and women. De Man shows a reemergence—at the very moment when the question seems resolved in favor of the self-signifying tableau—of a referential moment: "The more the text denies the actual existence of a referent, real or ideal, and the more fantastically fictional it becomes, the more it becomes the representation of its own pathos. . . . In the terminology of the text, the 'tableau' has become a 'portrait' after all, not the portrait of universal man but of the deconstructive passion of a subject" (pp. 198–99).

2. Cited as it appeared in *Representations* 7, pp. 59–86. References will henceforth appear in the text.

3. Fineman explains the effect aimed at:

> Language thus speaks *for* its own gainsaying. The result is a new kind of Cratylism, a second degree of Cratylism, that, like the Liar's Paradox Shakespeare often flirts with in his sonnets—"Those lines that I before have writ do lie" (Sonnet 115), "When my love swears that she is made of truth" (Sonnet 138)—is proof of its own paradoxicality. In this gainsaying way—a speech acquired on condition that it speak against itself—Shakespeare accomplishes a limit case of the correspondence of signifier to signified. (p. 77)

The choice of the term *gainsaying* reveals that Fineman's text translates the problem of literary language into a set of oppositions ultimately governed by a dialectic. To gainsay is to say against, to deny or refute. It is not to speak in a language that, neither true nor false, operates along another axis, as fiction. This translation ultimately, as it were, gains saying for truth ("a speech *acquired* on condition that it speak against itself") by establishing it as a sort of philosopher's stone for testing truth's limits.

4. As another, more recent instance of a similar tack, see Alan Liu's *Wordsworth*, which starts by suggesting the pastoral to be an anti- or prehistorical mode: "The purpose of the mirror of georgic nature is to hide history in order, finally, to reflect the self" (p. 19). The thesis about poetry's ahistoricism is then refined by a turn: "The denials of history are also the deepest realizations of history" (p. 32). This turn, Liu suggests, is the one by which the self-referential language of poetry ends by referring to the ideology of its age: "The very scheme of differences that allows certain ages to define a 'literary text' separate from historical event (for example, as representation rather than action, aesthetic object rather than utilitarian artifact, medium of the cultured rather than of popular culture) is a reference to, or mimesis of, the scheme of differences that divides and organizes the historical context of that culture" (p. 47). Liu's notion that each age has its ideology of literature follows Fineman's idea of a shift in Shakespearean subjectivity taking place around a more sophisticated understanding of language's deceitfulness. Both share the further assumption that a literary text and a historical event are two distinct objects for study and that texts in no way tend to interfere with that distinction. Whereas Liu merely asserts the distinction, however, Fineman finds a basis for it in the Liar's Paradox.

5. Hugo agreed with this view. He credited Paris, the critical center of the Revolution, with being "the city-pivot around which, on a given day, history turned" (*Paris*, in *Oeuvres complètes*, 13, bk. 1: 586).

6. "La Révolution" (10, bk. 1: 217–47). The passage with which I will be working can be found on pp. 220–21. References will henceforth appear in the text. See the Présentation by Jean Massin (10, bk. 1: 199–216) for details of the poem's composition and publication.

Only published in 1881, the poem might very well serve as a reflection on the major revolutions of the nineteenth century (1830, 1848, 1870) in which Hugo was more or less closely an implicated participant. Hugo was very much the historian of his own shift in partisan politics. The interested reader is referred to the autobiographical *Les Contemplations* (especially "Réponse à un acte d'accusation," "Suite," "Ecrit en 1846," "Ecrit en 1855") as also, among various journals and political texts, to *Littérature et philosophie mêlées* and the various journals and notebooks grouped by Hubert Juin under the title *Choses vues*.

7. The definite article, *la*, is a first indicator of the poem's hesitation between signification and reference. The definite article may modify a noun that

designates a unique and well-known thing. *The* revolution, for a Frenchman, is, of course, the French Revolution. On the other hand, *la* may modify a generic noun about which something is predicated, in a usage roughly synonymous with the English suppression of the article, as in the phrase "*Revolution* consists in a radical break with past forms of government." In the first case, the article suggests a referential language use; in the second, it introduces a meaningful fiction, positing a definition of what revolution is.

8. The choice of Hugo's *Révolution* to pursue the argument with Fineman is not purely arbitrary, both on account of its use of phantasm and on account of literary influence. As will be shown, the centrality of hallucination marks the poem out as the sort of text that someone engaging in Foucauldian-style analysis would find interesting. Author of a study called *William Shakespeare*, an admirer in particular of the dramatist to whose plays he often referred, Hugo explicitly mentions Shakespeare in *La Révolution* in the series of unconscious geniuses with whom the poetic voice is identified. Furthermore, the play that scholars generally agree to have been Shakespeare's last, *The Tempest*, shows at least one important parallel to this poem: the court is driven mad by a series of hallucinations, as the invisible is rendered visible by Ariel's agency. The dark lady's deceptions are a relatively mild form of a problem that surfaces in Hugo's poem as a paralyzing terror and in Shakespeare's play as insanity.

9. Riffaterre, "La Vision hallucinatoire chez Victor Hugo," in *Essais*, pp. 222–41.

10. The tendency to psychologize the Revolution, to make of it a kind of Racinian tragedy in which is represented a conflict of forces within a single personality, is very strong. In *Interpreting the French Revolution*, Furet warns against the 200-year-old interpretation by historians that perpetuates the notion of the Revolution as a mythic tale of new beginnings and thus of the formation of a self. Historians tend, claims Furet, to identify with the actors, commemorate the founders, and execrate the deviants, as if compelled to reenact the dramatic conflict they are writing about. In that, they do a disservice to an analytical understanding of the event (which is not a tale of self-constitution), as well as to Leftist political thought. The latter has become imprisoned, Furet suggests, by thinking in terms of a promise of unity that has failed, in lieu of thinking new political alternatives (p. 11).

11. Foucault, *Language*, p. 172.

12. Ibid., p. 155.

13. Ibid., p. 155.

14. See Foucault's discussion of the event and the phantasm (Ibid., pp. 172–81). The phantasm is not to be equated with the lost event. It is defined rather "as the play of the (missing) event" (p. 177).

15. Ibid., p. 99. See, for an example of a figure become object of experience,

"Pasteurs et troupeaux," a rewriting of one of the earliest poems figuring in *Les Contemplations*, "Le firmament est plein" (9: 69). Riffaterre explains that in Hugo's hallucinatory poems "metaphor disappears from style" (*Essais*, p. 239), and the figure is treated as a "literal reality" (*Essais*, p. 239). The most frequently commented-upon lines in "Pasteurs et troupeaux"—"Le pâtre promontoire au chapeau de nuées / S'accoude et rêve au bruit de tous les infinis" (The promontory shepherd with hat of clouds / Leans on elbows and dreams to the noise of all infinities) (9: 287)—contain such a figure treated literally. "Pâtre promontoire" does not compare shepherd and rock, but rather treats the rock as if it really were the ocean's shepherd.

16. Hugo, *Promontorium somnii*, in *Oeuvres complètes*, 12, bk. 1: 464. Cited in James, "Hallucination," p. 1034, which see for an account of nineteenth-century medical beliefs about hallucination that might have influenced Hugo.

17. Riffaterre defines this giving of movement to the immutable as hallucinatory:

> Not the movement of life which a good writer knows how to give his creations, and without which certain of Hugo's myths would be only allegories, rebuses telling stories, but an abnormal movement that transforms the reality to which we are accustomed. Not the movement of what we know to be living, but the movement of what ought to be immutable. That is what alarms the imagination and suggests hallucination. (*Essais*, p. 226)

18. See de Man, "Time and History," in *Romanticism and Contemporary Criticism*, p. 202, n. 11.

19. See Poulet's "Hugo," pp. 194–230, for a fine account of Hugo as seeking to image the conditions of thought, Kant's a priori forms of human perception.

20. A little later in *La Révolution*, the collapse of time is registered in the collapse of narration. It is impossible, claims the poet, to narrate the reign of Louis XV (10, bk. 1: 239).

21. In *Choses vues*, Hugo remarks à propos of the death of the son of Louis-Philippe, then king of France, that the law of history has for some time gone against the law of patrilinear descent. This leads him to speculate not only about the failure of human attempts to foresee and regulate the succession of rulers, but also, more generally, about the failure of the teleological model and of linear progression to account for history's laws. The laws of history, he suggests, do not operate as rational, human schemes, but are as necessary and undeviating as the laws that regulate "material facts." The passage is worth quoting:

> When one meditates on the history of the past one hundred and fifty years, a remark comes to mind. Louis XIV reigned, his son did not reign; Louis XV reigned, his son did not reign; Louis XVI reigned, his son did not reign; Napoleon reigned, his son did not reign; Charles X reigned, his son did not reign; Louis-Philippe reigns, his son will not reign. Extraordinary fact! Six times in a row human foresight has picked out from

a whole people the head that is to reign, and it is precisely that head that does not reign. Six times in a row human foresight is caught lacking. The fact persists with a redoubtable and mysterious obstinancy. A revolution arrives, a universal earthquake in ideas that swallows in a few years a past of ten centuries and the whole social life of a great nation; that huge commotion overturns everything, except the fact we have just signaled; it makes it leap out, on the contrary, from the midst of everything that it makes crumble; a great empire is established, a Charlemagne appears, a new world rises up, the fact persists; it seems that things are the same in the new world as they were in the old. The empire falls, the old races come back, the Charlemagne dissolves, exile takes the conqueror and gives back the exiled; revolutions reform themselves and break out, dynasties change three times, events wash over events, floods wash over floods—and always again the fact bobs up, whole, without discontinuity, without modification, without rupture. So long as monarchies have existed, the law states: *The eldest son of the king will always reign,* and look here, for the past one hundred and forty years, the fact answers: *The eldest son of the king never reigns.* Doesn't it seem as though a law were being revealed, and were being revealed in the inexplicable order of human doings [*faits*], with the same degree of persistence and precision that up to the present had belonged only to material facts [*faits*]? Isn't it time for providence to intervene to upset this, and wouldn't it be terrifying if certain laws of history were to manifest themselves to men with the same exactness, the same rigidity, and so to speak the same harshness, as the great laws of nature? (*Choses vues,* 1: 234–36)

22. The two time schemes suspended are both associated with the interpretation of the French Revolution. Hannah Arendt, in her discussion of "The Meaning of Revolution" (in *On Revolution,* pp. 21–58), suggests that the modern concept of revolution involves linear time: it is "inextricably bound up with the notion that the course of history suddenly begins anew, that an entirely new story, a story never known or told before is about to unfold" (p. 28). "It is obvious," she states, "that only under the conditions of a rectilinear time concept are such phenomena as novelty, uniqueness of events, and the like conceivable at all" (p. 27).

Arendt also reminds us of the persistence of an earlier meaning, carried over from the time when *revolution* was an astronomical term "designating the regular, lawfully revolving motion of the stars, which . . . was certainly characterized neither by newness nor by violence. On the contrary, the word clearly indicates a recurring, cyclical movement" (p. 42). Carrying the term over into the political domain gives a distinctly restorative flavor to revolution, as revolutionaries "pleaded in all sincerity that they wanted to revolve back to old times when things had been as they ought to be" (p. 44).

We can correlate Arendt's problematic to the one raised by Hugo's stupefied clock because in both cases it is the correspondence of an ideal, rational model to a perceptual experience by way of a mediating sign—clock, or narrative construct—that is at stake.

23. In 1841, describing the Invalides where Napoleon's casket is provisionally

lying upon its return to France, Hugo comes upon three statues off their pedestals and develops their allegory:

> There in the shadows, I found three more lead statues, descended from I know not where, that I recall having seen as a small child in the same place, in 1815, during the mutilations of buildings, dynasties and nations that were occurring at the time. Those three statues, in the worst of Empire style, cold like whatever is allegorical, dreary like whatever is mediocre, are there upright the length of the wall, in the grass, amidst a heap of capitals, with I know not what false air of tragedies hissed at. One of them holds a lion attached to a chain and represents Force. Nothing looks so disoriented as a statue positioned feet on the ground, without a pedestal; one might say a horse without a rider or a king without a throne. There are only two attitudes for the soldier, battle or death; there are only two for the king, the empire or the tomb; there are only two for the statue, to be upright in the heavens, or lying down on the earth.
>
> A statue on foot astonishes the spirit and bothers the eye. One forgets it is made of plaster or bronze and that bronze walks no more than plaster, and one is tempted to say to the poor persona with a human face, so maladroit and unhappy in its posture of display: "All right! Go then! Go! Walk on! Continue on your way! Bestir yourself! The earth is beneath your feet. Who is holding you back? Who is hindering you?" At least a pedestal explains immobility. For statues as for men, a pedestal is a small, confined and honorable space, with four precipices around it. (*Choses vues*, 1: 213–14)

24. See Nerval, *Sylvie*, in *Oeuvres*, p. 598, where the narrator affirms that he does not have a watch (*une montre*) to *show* the hour. His unwound clock, with its allegorical figure of Time, its "historic Diana," is annotated by the editor Henri Lemaître for the role it plays in evoking memories of lost Nervalian loves.

25. *Notre-Dame*, in *Oeuvres complètes*, 4, bk. 1: 251.

26. To name just a few of those that show up in the parallel passage in *Notre-Dame de Paris*, where Frollo—after watching the sun set behind the Tour de Nesle—has a hallucination (the word is Hugo's) in which the illuminated houses along the river bank appear a sort of recumbent bell-tower between the two dark voids of the heavens and the river. This tower is compared to the *clocher de Strasbourg*, to all cathedral steeples, to the Tower of Babel, and finally, called Hell's own tower (*le clocher de l'enfer*) (4, bk. 1: 252–53).

27. *Choses vues*, 2: 311.

28. See Paul de Man's "Hypogram and Inscription," in *Resistance*, pp. 27–53. De Man explains that the relationship between the carillon and time "is analogous to the relationship between signifier and signified that constitutes the sign. The ringing of the bells . . . is the material sign of an event (the passage of time) of which the phenomenality lacks certainty" (p. 48). He further explains that "the phenomenality of experience cannot be established *a priori*, it can only occur by a process of signification" (p. 48). I have drawn heavily on de Man's analysis of prosopopeia and hallucination in this essay.

29. See on this point Alexis de Tocqueville, *L'Ancien Régime*, 2: 56, 80. Toc-

queville attributes a revolutionary force to the transfer onto a new stage, in
front of an audience unfamiliar with such usage, of the exaggerated language
by which Parlement traditionally remonstrated with the king. The violence
with which the Parlement addressed the king was a conventionalized figure,
whose decoding was not problematic for Parlement and king. To those unfamiliar with the convention, however, the clichéd figures and forms of address
appeared a literal, referential use of language. Tocqueville is then describing as a
precondition for revolutionary violence the conflation of language's two functions into its single referential function.

30. In "Bièvre," from *Feuilles d'automne*, the poet turns away from the pastoral vision he has been describing to remember the nearby city as recumbent
colossus:

> Et l'on ne songe plus, tout notre âme saisie
> Se perd dans la nature et dans la poésie
> Que tout près, par les bois et les ravins caché,
> Derrière le ruban de ces collines bleues,
> A quatre de ces pas que nous nommons des lieues,
> *Le géant Paris est couché.*

> And we no longer dream, our whole soul transported
> Loses itself in nature and poetry
> That very near, hidden by the woods and the ravines,
> Behind the ribbon of these blue hills,
> Four of those steps we call leagues away,
> Lies the giant Paris.   *(4: 439)*

31. The construction is not, strictly speaking, grammatical (since *horse* is part
of the modifier). It is in the spirit of Hugolian constructions to provide such seductive possibilities to the unwary eye, however. In one famous line from "Mes
deux filles," a similar effect of positioning joins a modifier to another modifier,
and makes it seem as though the poet were asserting that the marble of an urn
is agitated, instead of discussing the movement of the bouquet the urn contains: "Un bouquet d'oeillets blancs aux longues tiges frêles, / Dans une urne
de marbre agité par le vent" (A bouquet of white carnations with long, frail
stems, / In a marble urn, agitated by the wind) (*Les Contemplations*, in *Oeuvres
complètes*, 9, bk. 1: 68). The detail calls attention away from the poem's supposed representation of a natural scene, to its allegory of its own production.

In *La Révolution*, the play is prepared by an earlier part of the passage where
the city's corners can be thought as eyes: *mirer*, in "Les mille toits mirant leurs angles dans la Seine," can mean either "to reflect, to mirror" or "to sight, to look
at." The roofs reflect or look at their angles, that is, depending on the perspective,
at their corners or at their eyes. The placement of a signifier, the angles it makes
with other strategically-located signifiers are, so to speak, the eyes of the text.

32. For an instance where the disruption of an enumeration from within transforms an orderly, lyric celebration of the universe addressed to "God, the father of the day," into a more disquieting dissemination poured into Satan's ear, see the fourth poem of Book I of *Les Contemplations*, "Le Firmament est plein," in *Oeuvres complètes*, 9, bk. 1: 69.

33. James, "Hallucination," p. 1027.

34. *Choses vues*, 1: 213–14.

35. The engendering of a text by way of a play with the signifier takes place at various moments in the poem. In the discussion of the reigns of Henri IV, Louis XIII, Louis XIV, and Louis XV, the most referential of signs, the proper name, is treated as if it were a signifier devoid of meaning or reference which motivates the other elements in the passage by assonance. Of Henri, we are told "Il fit tout en *ri*ant / Il *ri*ait à la guerre, il *ri*ait en pri*ant*" (He did everything while laughing / He laughed at war, he laughed while praying) (10: 233). His wind of inspiration is a "b*rise*" (breeze), and what puts his reign into question, "non loin de ces jeux et de ces *ris*" (not far from these games and this laughter) are the "b*ruits*" (noise) and debris of skeletons, "b*risés* / Nus" (broken / Naked) (10: 234). Similarly, Louis XIV, whose "was the conquering name proclaimed by thunder," shines, "*luit*" at Versailles, but his crimes "*Lui* firent dans son *Lou*vre un colossal trophée / De r*uine*" (In his Louvre made him a colossal trophy / Of ruin) (10: 235–36). As for Louis XV, his nickname "Le Bien-Aimé" (the Well-Loved) is earned not only ironically, by his misdeeds, but by a cascade of *m*'s, that make him very "well-*m*'ed" (Bien-*m*'é) indeed:

> Infâ*me*; soulevant des é*m*eutes de *m*ères;
> Froid regard, pied sali, front hautain, coeur fer*mé*;
> Co*mm*ent no*mm*er ce roi, sinon le Bien-Ai*mé*?
>   . . .
> On le *m*éprise tant, ce *m*alheureux, qu'on pleure.
> *M*onstre! . . . O *m*isérable!"
>
> Infamous; provoking insurrections by mothers;
> Cold look, dirtied foot, high forehead, closed heart;
> How to name this king, except the Well-Loved?
>   . . .
> He is so despised, this unhappy man, that people weep.
> Monster! . . . O miserable man!   *(10: 240)*

Again, Hugo considers this model a game with serious consequences. Henri IV, the ruler of an aesthetic kingdom of laughter where the play of signifiers is the rule, is undone, broken, because he is blind to a dimension of language—"not far from these games and this laughter"—that makes it escape the phenomenalization on which such play is based.

36. Laplanche and Pontalis, "Fantasy and the Origins of Sexuality," p. 15.

37. De Man, "Hypogram," in *Resistance*, p. 49.

38. Ibid., p. 49.

39. In thematic terms, this healthy thought about reason's demise provides Frollo with two images: one of Esmeralda, called the Egyptian; the other of undecidability, the gallows (4: 251).

40. Foucault, *Language*, p. 177.

41. Ibid., p. 103.

42. Laplanche and Pontalis suggest that by means of the phenomenalization of the sign the subject gets a glimpse of its own original fantasy, and thus of its origin. Further, by way of the sense of hearing, the subject inserts itself into "the history or the legends of parents, grandparents and the ancestors: the family *sounds* or *sayings*, this spoken or secret discourse, going on prior to the subject's arrival, within which he must find his way. Insofar as it can serve retroactively to summon up the discourse, the noise—or any other discrete sensorial element that has meaning—can acquire this value" ("Fantasy and the Origins of Sexuality," p. 11). For Laplanche and Pontalis, the noise of the signifier, which often appears in a fantasy and is in fact the starting point for its elaboration, is eminently historical. It gives the subject its origins as subject, and inserts it as well into a family history.

43. Hugo thought the revolutions of the nineteenth century, particularly the 1848 Revolution, largely in terms of a parody of a repetition at work in the French Revolution. The parody of the Revolution by the nineteenth century, for Hugo, does not constitute a genuine historical move. He returns over and over again in his writings on the 1848 Revolution to lament its plagiaristic bent: "O parodistes de 93! . . . Quoi la Terreur parodie! Quoi la guillotine plagiaire! . . . 93 a eu ses hommes, il y a de cela cinquante-cinq ans, et maintenant il aurait ses singes" (Oh parodists of 93! . . . What, the Terror a parody! What, the guillotine a plagiarist! . . . 93 had its men, fifty-five years ago, and now it will have its monkeys) (*Choses vues*, 2: 315). What is parodic about 1848 is not simply the fact that it repeats 1793. Rather 1848 is parodic because it transforms the mechanical repetition of the Terror and the guillotine in 1793, and gives it the friendlier and more familiar shape of a humanoid aping. Aping *masks* repetition, but it does not stop its recurrence—'93 will have its monkeys in the same way it once had its men: by execution or exile.

44. The text can be found as it has been reconstructed by Pierre Albouy in *Oeuvres complètes*, 10, bk. 1: 261–87.

45. A reader of Baudelaire's *Tableaux parisiens* cannot help but notice an affinity between this passage and "A une passante" with its "jambe de statue," its hurricane's eye, and so on (Baudelaire, *Oeuvres complètes*, 1: 92–93).

46. Hugo, *Notre-Dame*, in *Oeuvres complètes*, 4, bk. 1: 100.

47. These four *pas* give meaning to the lines from "Bièvre" quoted previ-

ously: "A quatre de ces pas que nous nommons des lieues / Le géant Paris" (Four of those steps we call leagues away / The giant Paris) (4, bk. 1: 439). The four steps necessary to reach Paris are not necessarily all steps (one could be a step, one a negation, one a pace, one a footprint). They are rather to be called poetic topoi, places (in French, *lieux*), and may well correspond to the four winds of the title from which the poem *La Révolution* is taken.

48. See *Paris* for an account of affirmation and negation, and for a discussion of the function of Paris as sower (13, bk. 1: 592, 597).

Chapter 5

1. The decision was made possible by a law passed in 1946 allowing a judgment on a book to be appealed after twenty years had passed.

2. Flaubert, *Correspondance*, p. 214.

3. The popular rhymster Béranger was successfully prosecuted in 1821, for instance. According to Jean Pommier, although Béranger was pursued for "offense against public and religious morality," his aim was "political provocation." The first attacks in the press came from the Ultras, who noted the greater freedom of expression enjoyed by verse: "Here we must admire the marvelous privilege of rhyme: it is doubtless as powerful as the letters of inviolacy enjoyed by our Deputies, for an unprotected citizen who had said *in prose* what M. Béranger has said in verse would certainly have had a bone to pick with the King's Prosecutor." Cited in Pommier, *Autour de l'édition*, pp. 7, 9.

In his work *Obscenity and the Law*, which draws heavily on English cases, Norman St. John-Stevas remarks on violent attacks in the press against Keats, Byron, Shelley, Tennyson, and Swinburne. As a rule, these attacks did not lead to legal problems. St. John-Stevas cites only a pirated edition of *Queen Mab* as prosecuted for blasphemy. Indeed, while deploring the attacks, St. John-Stevas nonetheless finds reason to take heart in the fact that to attack poetry is to acknowledge it as an important social force. "Critical excesses are indefensible," he writes, "but the assumption of the value and relevance of poetry to the life of the community which determined their approach was sound" (p. 49).

4. Walter Benjamin comments on the small likelihood of the work's popular success in "On Some Motifs in Baudelaire," in *Illuminations*, p. 155.

5. In Baudelaire, *Oeuvres complètes*, 1: 1208. I have drawn heavily on Claude Pichois's account of the trial reproduced in the notes of this edition. Because the laws of the time forbade the reporting of trials, the statements of the prosecution and the defense were not published until 1885. Evidence suggests that they may well not have been written out until near the later date.

Pinard explains that the government does not lose its freedom to pursue a given work because it has not pursued others equally offensive. If the government is reserved in some cases, it is because it judges that the work will have "no chance of being read or understood" and that "to bring it to justice would be to indicate it to the public and perhaps assure to it the day's success it would not have had without that" (1: 1208–9).

6. It is this paradoxical situation of poems whose style removes them from ordinary experience the better to make them represent modern experience that is the point of departure for Walter Benjamin's analysis in "On Some Motifs in Baudelaire."

7. Quoted in St. John-Stevas, *Obscenity and the Law*, p. 249.

8. The two charges brought against the total of eleven poems were "offense to public morality" and "offense to religious morality." Only the first charge was upheld in the condemnation of six of these poems.

9. "The Aesthetic Dignity of 'Les Fleurs du Mal'" is the title of an essay by Erich Auerbach that is roughly contemporaneous with the 1949 decision. In *Scenes*, pp. 201–26.

10. There is a resemblance to be noted between the critic and Baudelaire's figure for the reader in "Au lecteur," the monstrous Ennui who dreams of dramatically violent deeds while yawning and smoking his dope (1: 5–6).

11. This is somewhat the scene as Pinard paints it. He is acutely aware that he is cast in the role of persecutor by the world of letters, and he boasts of his (anti)heroism in laboring for the good of the public nonetheless.

12. Benjamin, *Illuminations*, p. 160.

13. Quoted in Ibid., p. 160.

14. In Post, *Censorship and Silencing*, p. 68.

15. A recent *New York Times* article, describing billboards plastered with sexually explicit imagery and lone artists (Mapplethorpe, Alpern) targeted for censorship, supports the point that it is the medium and not the message that is the lightning rod here. Vicki Goldberg writes: "The sensationalistic images that flood the visual environment appear far more frequently and get immeasurably greater distribution in the popular culture than they ever do in art. Yet art bears the brunt of public attacks" ("Testing the Limits," p. 40). The show of Merry Alpern's photos that is the occasion of the article bears the Baudelairean title "Dirty Windows." Speculating from the title and the single photograph that is shown in the *Times*, we can ask whether Alpern is not breaking the rule that in art we view things through colored windows (roseate or not), whereas in ordinary commerce we see through clear windows, that is, transparent language. What Alpern does in giving us *dirtied* windows is note the presence of "color" in the apparently transparent windows of sexshop bathrooms. This is subversive, and makes the show a worthy successor to Baudelaire's "Mauvais vitrier."

16. Strauss, "Persecution," in *Persecution*, p. 24. Cited henceforth in the text.

17. This is the source of Gadamer's interest in Strauss (see Gadamer, *Truth*,

pp. 482–91). See also de Man (*Resistance,* pp. 106–14), for a discussion of Strauss and Bakhtin.

18. I am extending Strauss's argument by suggesting its consequences for the liberal state.

19. All this is well known; discussion of silencing and hate speech—concentrated as it is on the discursive situation as on the exclusion of certain groups and speech acts from the scene of "friendly" dialogue—can only take place because the foregoing points have been acquired. If I rehearse them here, it is as the background necessary to raise two points. The first is that the Straussian liberal state gains an astonishing flexibility and durability as a result of its disregard of content. Once the state ceases to occupy itself with dictating what can be said, the positive content of its history, the details of a moral education, and so on, it can occupy itself instead with what Judith Butler calls the "formation" of its subjects in "Ruled Out: Vocabularies of the Censor" (in Post, *Censorship and Silencing,* p. 253). For instance, the state produces as normal citizens those who state their opinions freely and explicitly, who say exactly what they mean (although what they mean is never more than mere opinion). As for those who make use of parody or irony to write between the lines, their heterodoxy may be suspect, but it is indulged on account of the inventive energy released in the liberating of the performative aspect. The liberal state goes out of the business of censoring messages; instead it feeds off the energy released by the lifting of such repressions. The second point concerns the limits that Strauss effectively places on writing between the lines by determining it as educational. A writing that appears to state an opinion in order to criticize it is a writing whose use of parody, irony, strategy, and so on has been limited to what can be recuperated as critique, according to a teleology in which the formation of subjects is the end. It can be asked, however, whether this limitation on the subversiveness of writing between the lines does not, as it were, leave out leaving out—censor its own censorship—and, in doing so, lose sight of aspects of writing that do not lead to education, construed positively.

20. Strauss mentions Homer, but it is only to quote the cliché "even Homer nods from time to time" (p. 26). Milton is also mentioned, but as the author of the *Areopagitica.* Literary works do not figure as instances of texts persecuted.

21. Strauss is actively repressive of one aspect of language, figurative language. He remarks, for instance, that persecution teaches good writers to avoid flowery utterances when uttering the hidden doctrine ("he would silently drop all the *foolish excrescences* of the liberal creed" [p. 25]), and on the contrary to display a flowery style when uttering the orthodoxy being criticized ("The attack, the bulk of the work, would consist of *virulent expansions* of the most *virulent utterances*" [p. 25]).

22. Baudelaire, "La Fanfarlo," in *Oeuvres complètes,* 1: 555.

23. In Joyce, *Ulysses*, p. ix. Since 1934, Woolsey's remarks have been published as part of the prefatory material in the Modern Library edition. References will henceforth appear in the text.

24. Morris Ernst and Alan Schwartz cite a case lost when the defense lawyer felt unable to "mention in court or print in his brief an Anglo-Saxon word used in the novel several times by one of the characters" (*Censorship*, p. 95). The lawyer's inability to mention the term showed the term to be censorable. At the other extreme, the defense attorney for Baudelaire spent most of his time reading long quotations from various literary sources, with the aim of defusing the effect made by the abbreviated textual "clippings" of Pinard. The length or brevity of quotations is a recognized ploy of argument.

25. That is true of expletives, for instance, where the names for the sexual organs or functions are not used as names, but as meaningless signifiers allowing the speaker to vent feeling in language freed from referential constraints. A "motherfucking verb paradigm" is an abusive use of terms properly used to describe an Oedipal situation carried over instead to express the speaker's frustration at having to learn a difficult Latin verb. Obscene language shocks by virtue of an abusive transfer of a term valued as a name, to express the pleasure or anger the speaker feels (among other things, at language being so unanchored). It is as though by taking a name in vain one *made* naming in vain. It is obscene to persist in substitution where metaphor as an exchange of names between entities on the basis of an observable resemblance is no longer possible.

26. In lieu of quotation marks, which are of course literally absent from *Ulysses*, Joyce has made use of a multitude of techniques for marking (and blurring) the distinctions between what characters say and their accompanying thoughts, hesitations, automatic actions, and so forth. He is a master at wielding dashes, paragraphs, italics, parentheses, blanks, and spaces, as well as at standing standard English syntax and spelling on its head. One effect is that the language appears defamiliarized and at the center of the action. Woolsey appears to have picked up on these techniques that frame Joyce's language as slightly foreign, the language of another, or, as we are asserting, as quoted.

27. Woolsey says: "Each word of the book contributes like a bit of mosaic to the detail of the picture which Joyce is seeking to construct for his readers" (p. xii).

28. Ernst and Schwartz, *Censorship*, p. 94.

29. Ibid., p. 94.

30. A somewhat similar view, reported in St. John-Stevas as that of Havelock Ellis, is the theory that obscene books are not aphrodisiacs but "safety valves protecting society from crime and outrage" (p. 189).

31. They have also to judge the extent to which the work is successful at transforming custom. It was twenty years after *Ulysses* was published that Woolsey decided to let it into the United States. It took 90, and a new law al-

lowing cases of "offense against morality" to be reheard, for the *Fleurs du mal* to be acquitted. These cases merely dramatize the time lag that is a necessary feature of obscenity cases, where one cannot know until after publication whether an offense is felt, and until long afterward whether custom has been effectively transformed. Writers on the subject of obscenity laws in America and in England consistently deplore the fact that the shock the artist must deliver in order to be true to her art opens her to accusation by any reader, however untutored, who happens to pick up the work, and equally to the unjust verdicts of fearful or unknowing judges: "Any private person can start (a prosecution), any old lady who unluckily picks out of a twopenny library a book which shocks her" (Alan Herbert, Introduction to *Obscenity and the Law*, by St. John-Stevas, p. xiii). Another writer, discussing the situation in America in 1976, deplores the inability of most judges to discriminate between works allowable to artistic license and hard-core pornography (Lewis, *Literature*, p. 247).

32. The American Supreme Court Justice Stewart once said, for instance, that he knew hard-core pornography when he saw it, but he could not define it. This is a recurrent theme. Ernst and Schwartz ironically entitle one chapter "The Word Obscenity 'Defies Misunderstanding,'" and they cite the dictionary to show that the terms *lewd, lascivious, indecent*, and *obscene* are synonyms that do not help determine the concept, but repeat it.

33. Ernst and Schwartz state the problem:

> Not all law is as untidy as the Law of the Obscene. Lawyers and jurists have always had trouble defining in a courtroom words such as "negligence" or "reckless," or drawing a picture of "The Reasonable Man." But even "reckless," for example, has some objective definable outlines. "Reckless" driving can be described in terms of speedometer reading, condition of the road, density of population in the area and traffic on the road, infirmities of the driver, condition of the vehicle, and hundreds of factors on which factual testimony might be taken. Not so with censorship of the obscene. . . . When man has had fears of such concepts as blasphemy, impiety, or obscenity, law attempts avoidance rather than solution. (pp. 244–45)

34. Woolsey's bon mot gets cited and recited, on both sides of the Atlantic, as if it were a definition. See, for instance, St. John-Stevas, *Obscenity and the Law*, p. xiv.

35. See Richard Sieburth's very interesting Foucauldian analysis in "Obscenity in Baudelaire and Swinburne," pp. 464–71.

36. It is a picture not without its irony, since the peculiar exposure of the work to accusation from the public offended is such as also to make censorship laws protect individual authors from discrepant readings.

37. The translation is by James McGowan. From Baudelaire's *Flowers of Evil*, pp. 47–49. As a representation of a sensuous nude beauty, McGowan's translation works very well. Among other indications of such an interpretation, one

could notice that he has sought to produce an acceptable *rhymed* translation of
this poem. Moreover, he has replaced the poem in the position it had in the
original edition, prior to its excision, as a transitional poem between the songs
about beauty in the abstract, and the songs of the Jeanne Duval cycle (devoted
to a particular beauty).

Notwithstanding the success of McGowan's translation in rendering the
scene of seduction, I will be arguing against it, seeking to restore to the poem
its status among the censored texts that Baudelaire published in 1866 under the
title *Les Epaves* (Flotsam). My contention is that, by the time the ban had been
lifted on the poem and it had theoretically become possible to reintegrate it
into the collection and publish the *Fleurs* in a new "original" edition, it was no
longer possible to do so for two reasons: "Les Bijoux" had become redundant,
its place as bridging poem in the collection having been taken by the two poems Baudelaire wrote to replace it; "Les Bijoux" had been collected by its author as wreckage belonging to another group of poems. The poem must be
read in terms of its redundancy and its status as wreckage, for it has become
unclaimable as a poem celebrating the triumph of an aesthetics.

38. This a consistent theme in Baudelaire. Women are always flashing clothing. We could cite "A une passante" and "Avec ses vêtements ondoyants et
nacrés." Even the poem "A une mendiante rousse" spends more time looking at
the holes in her dress as signs of her poverty and beauty, than peering through
them for a glimpse of skin. As for "Le Serpent qui danse," the snake's very skin
is a shimmering fabric, not just because of its light, but presumably because it
can be discarded like a dress. For Baudelaire, nudes are clothed. In this he follows André Chénier: "C'est par ses vêtements qu'elle est nue à tes yeux" ("By
her clothing she is nude/cloud to your eyes") (p. 459).

39. At the end of *Mon coeur mis à nu* Baudelaire cites a sonnet by Théophile
de Viau that rhymes *nue* with *nue.* De Viau's homonym explains a state of error, in which a dreamer takes as an airy illusion what is actually a substantial
shadow: "Je songeais . . . que Philis revenue . . . Voulait que son fantôme encore fît l'amour, / Et que, comme Ixion, j'embrassasse une nue. // Son ombre
dans mon lit se glisse toute nue." (I dreamt . . . that Philis returned . . .
Wanted her phantom to make love again, / And that, like Ixion, I should embrace a cloud. // Her shadow slides into my bed all naked) (1: 708).

40. Leconte de Lisle, in a poem much appreciated by Baudelaire, "Le
Manchy," roughly contemporaneous with the *Fleurs du mal,* starts out his description of the approaching Muse as follows:

> Sous un nuage frais de claire mousseline
> Tous les dimanches au matin,
> Tu venais a la ville en manchy de rotin,
> Par les rampes de la colline.
>
> La cloche de l'église tintait.

Beneath a fresh cloud of clear muslin
Every Sunday morning,
You came to the town in a rattan palanquin,
Down the slopes of the hill.

The church bell rang out.

(Oeuvres, p. 164)

The approach in a swirling cloud of muslin, with a poetic fanfare of exotic terms like *palanquin* (*manchy*) and *rattan* (*rotin*), the attention called to sound, makes "Le Manchy" a near cousin of Baudelaire's "Bijoux" with its sonorous jewelry, enveloped woman, and exotic Moorish detail.

See also *La Fanfarlo*, which contains a description of a deity in a "ravishing hovel, that owed at once to the place of ill-repute and the sanctuary." The "radiant and sacred splendor of her nudity" is rejected by the poet, who wants her back as Colombine "with her fantastic get-up and her clown's blouse" (1: 576–77).

41. In the first edition, the poem occupied the transitional position between the cycle of idealized representations of Beauty and the Jeanne Duval cycle. The two poems which Baudelaire writes to replace "Les Bijoux" both insist on the double face of Beauty. In "Le Masque," the statue turns out to be wearing a mask, and is called a "bicephalous monster." As for the Beauty of "Hymne à la beauté," a series of questions states her origin to be undecidably divine or satanic, her nature that of "Angel or Siren." Both poems help us read "Les Bijoux" as concerned with a redoubled face, as the execrable pun, *bi-joues*, supports.

42. That is the itinerary followed in "Le Voyage" (1: 129–34), which starts out in a natural landscape, and relies on a perceivable resemblance between the forms of cloud and woman. It is also the course taken by Gautier, the poet to whom Baudelaire dedicated *Les Fleurs du mal*, in a poem inserted into the 1872 edition of *Emaux et camées* called "La Nue," a poem about a cloud shaped by the natural forces of wind and sun into the undulating postures of a torso. The poem bears enough features in common with "Les Bijoux" (the pun, the postures of a body, a reference to Corregio's painting of Antiope) to suggest that Gautier's poem is a response to Baudelaire's. The response takes the form of asserting that the relation between woman and cloud is that of a visible resemblance (and not based on the homonym and its reading, as in Baudelaire).

43. It is against the argument that the *Fleurs du mal* is redeemed by way of an allegorical intention of this sort that the prosecutor Pinard directed his heaviest fire in the 1857 trial. Without naming allegory as such, he took it upon himself to refute the claim that the work teaches by way of a counterexample. Certain argument would have it, states Pinard, that the "author wanted to depict evil and its deceitful caresses, for the sake of preserving against them" (1: 1207).

44. De Man, *Allegories*, p. 74.

45. It is presumably this sort of rapid degradation that so shocks the prosecutor in this poem that he claims, against the argument that the poem provides a didactic allegory, that it makes grown (male) readers "pick up easily a taste for lascivious frivolities" (1: 1208).

46. In the essay on Tassaert in the *Salon de 1846*, Baudelaire comments on the tendency of obscene literature toward degrading the divine. "Genius sanctifies everything, and if these subjects were treated with all the care and self-collection necessary, they would not be soiled by that revolting obscenity that is rather a *flourish of trumpets* than a truth." In an aside, "revolting obscenity," already identified with sound ("flourish of trumpets") rather than ideas, is associated with the miserable drawings we find hanging above the "pots fêlés et les consoles branlantes" (broken pots and shaky tables) of a prostitute's room. The double entendre of *branlantes* ("shaky," but also the slang for "masturbating"), particularly right next to *console* ("a table," but etymologically from "to console"), provides another example of the way that the excessiveness of the signifier interferes with the meaning production (2: 443). Baudelaire identifies puns, tautology, expletives—whatever draws attention to the signifier as it interferes with meaning—as the obscenity in need of sanctification by genius.

47. In "Avant-propos à la connaissance de la déesse," Valéry defines symbolism as "the intention common to several families of poets . . . 'to take back their belongings from Music'." In evaluating this intention doubly, like Baudelaire, Valéry insists on both a sensuous and what he calls a "quasi-intellectual" pleasure to be derived from taking over the resources of music. He insists that the final impression left is "of omnipotence and of lying" (1: 1271–72).

48. Baudelaire's observation in *Mon coeur mis à nu* about the trial, as about the reading of the *Fleurs du mal*, is apposite: "Histoire des *Fleurs du mal*, humiliation par le malentendu, et mon procès" (The story of the *Flowers of Evil*, humiliation by misunderstanding, and my trial) (2: 682). *Malentendu* means "misunderstanding," but it is the sort of misunderstanding to which the ear exposes one (*mal-entendre—mis-hear*).

49. Once again the *Salon de 1846* has a parallel. Baudelaire tells us that melancholy is the proper attitude in front of erotic drawings: "Has it happened to you, as it has to me, to fall into great melancholy after having spent long hours leafing through erotic engravings?" (2: 443). In other places, Baudelaire mimes noise-making the better to discuss the seduction that consists in giving voice to what has none. For instance, in *Fusées* he says: "Do you hear these sighs . . . these wails, these cries, these death rattles?" (2: 651). He thus draws attention to the lack of any such lively sound and to the figural means by which the poet can make the mute text appear as speaking.

50. Note that the poem spends a good deal of time collecting *b*'s and *d*'s, as if to draw attention to the crucial missing letters.

51. Mallarmé writes the line in the 1887 revision of the 1868 sonnet we know as "Sonnet en -yx." The 1868 version had no *nue* (pp. 68–69).

52. Chénier, *Hermès*, in *Oeuvres complètes*, p. 405.

53. For instance, having told us that philosophers and poets will enjoy this museum as much as the curious, Baudelaire deftly describes a lithograph of a boudoir scene taking place between two lovers in travesty on "un *sopha*—le sopha que vous savez, le sopha de l'hôtel garni et du cabinet particulier" (the sofa—the sofa you know, the sofa of furnished apartments and private rooms) (2: 444). The repetition of the term *sopha*, especially in its archaic spelling and with the modifier "que vous savez" winking in the direction of knowing, pulls the discussion away from the love scene to the furnishings, which furnishings are designated by a word of Turkish origin that coincidentally is a near rhyme for the very thing that a philosopher loves—*Sophe, Sophie*, wisdom, knowledge. If this is a good example of the pictures to be found in the museum Baudelaire contemplates, then it would be made up of reminders of a fracturing affecting the presumed unity of the language.

54. See Jean Starobinski, *La Mélancholie*, for a discussion of the poet as melancholic. See especially p. 90 n. 22 for a link—suggestive in the context of a discussion of obscenity—of melancholy to excrement, "black poison," and "the corrupt element."

55. In "A une passante," the fascinating widow is afflicted with a statue's leg; here, the "dear one" displays a museum full of polished members.

56. The poem is written in the past tense, and stands out from the poems in the Jeanne Duval cycle, which are mainly in the present tense, and from the poems of the cycle on beauty, which are also in the present tense. The commentators have not known what to make of the historical vision implied. F. W. Leakey speaks of the poem as "the recollection of a privileged moment of deep intimacy" (in *Baudelaire*, p. 388), but gives no account of the rather terrifying "Passaient devant mes yeux clairvoyants et sereins," with its suggestion that the poet is watching a pageant of transitory forms passing before and vanishing.

57. Michael Riffaterre is certainly right when he reproaches Claude Lévi-Strauss and Roman Jakobson for noting too many formal patterns, many of them insignificant, in their classic analysis of "Les Chats." However, with a poet like Baudelaire so insistent on the effects of the *labor* of poetry on the poem, one has to take into account the possibility that he may have considered the potential interference of readable as well as perceptible poetic patterns on the meaning of the poem. See "La Description," in *Essais*, pp. 305–64.

58. The first chapter of the King James version of Genesis contains striking cases of the English *and* with this force: "And the Spirit of God moved upon the face of the waters. And God said, Let there be light: and there was light." Each phrase translates the disruptiveness of God's creative positing.

59. The reading is all the more plausible because Baudelaire has a habit of using the vocative "my soul" as a term of ironic endearment, so that the problem would be that of a Galathea coming to life to disturb the poet's earlier tranquil assumption of the idol's immobility and his own agility. See "Une Charogne" (1: 31).

60. Pinard's recommendation of indulgence for Baudelaire "who is a troubled and unbalanced nature" (1: 1209) and of condemnation for a work that tries to "paint everything, describe everything, say everything" (1: 1209) confirms this point.

61. See Levinson, "The Tutelary State," in *Censorship and Silencing*, ed. Robert Post, for a discussion of the state's role as educator with respect to memory.

62. See Derrida's discussion in "Declarations of Independence" (pp. 7–15), specifically of the wild performative bringing into legal existence "the good people" that did not exist before its positing.

63. On trauma and history see Caruth's "Unclaimed Experience."

64. Genuine creation (as opposed to the spontaneous inventiveness the mind shows as we make our way through daily life) takes place through the mind's attempt to establish a dike against the chaotic nature of spontaneous productions. Logic, he claims, is the obstacle invented to parry the vicious circles and contradictions of everyday language production (1: 1470).

65. On chance, see Derrida's "My Chances."

Bibliography

Adorno, Theodor. *Notes to Literature.* Trans. Shierry Weber Nicholsen. Vol. 2. New York: Columbia University Press, 1992.

Althusser, Louis. *Lenin and Philosophy; and Other Essays.* Trans. Ben Brewster. New York: Monthly Review Press, 1971.

Arasse, Daniel. *The Guillotine and the Terror.* Trans. Christopher Miller. London: A. Lane, 1989.

Arendt, Hannah. *On Revolution.* Harmondsworth, England: Penguin Books Ltd., 1973.

Auerbach, Erich. *Scenes from the Drama of European Literature.* Minneapolis: University of Minnesota Press, 1984.

Bahti, Timothy. *Allegories of History: Literary Historiography after Hegel.* Baltimore: The Johns Hopkins University Press, 1992.

Baudelaire, Charles. *Oeuvres complètes.* Ed. Claude Pichois. 2 vols. Paris: Gallimard, 1975–76.

———. *Correspondance générale.* Ed. Jacques Crépet. 6 vols. Paris: Conard, 1947–53.

———. *The Flowers of Evil.* Trans. James McGowan. World's Classics. Oxford: Oxford University Press, 1993.

Bell, Robert. *Women of Classical Mythology.* Oxford: Oxford University Press, 1991.

Bénichou, Paul. *Selon Mallarmé.* Paris: Gallimard, 1995.

Benjamin, Walter. *Illuminations.* Trans. Harry Zohn. New York: Harcourt, Brace and World, Inc., 1968.

Benveniste, Emile. *Problèmes de linguistique générale.* Vol 1. Paris: Gallimard, 1966.

Blanchot, Maurice. "Enigme." *Yale French Studies* 79 (January 1991): 5–10.

———. *Faux pas.* Paris: Gallimard, 1943.

———. *Le Livre à venir.* Paris: Gallimard, 1959.

Bloom, Harold, ed. *Modern Critical Views: Stéphane Mallarmé.* New York: Chelsea House, 1987.

Boileau, Nicolas. *Oeuvres.* Ed. Gidel. Paris: Garnier frères, 1961.

Brasillach, Robert. *Chénier.* Paris: Les Sept Couleurs, 1947.

Caruth, Cathy. "Unclaimed Experience: Trauma and the Possibility of History." *Yale French Studies* 79 (January 1991): 181–92.

Chase, Cynthia. *Decomposing Figures: Rhetorical Readings in the Romantic Tradition.* Baltimore: The Johns Hopkins University Press, 1986.

Chénier, André. *Oeuvres complètes.* Ed. Gérard Walter. Paris: Gallimard, 1958.

———. *Oeuvres complètes.* Ed. Paul Dimoff. 3 vols. Paris: Librairie Delagrave, 1908–19.

Cohn, Robert Greer. *Toward the Poems of Mallarmé,* expanded ed. Berkeley: University of California Press, 1980.

Culler, Jonathan. *"Baudelaire's Satanic Verses."* The Cassal Lecture (6 October 1994), University of London.

———. "Baudelaire and Poe," *Zeitschrift für französische Sprache und Literatur.* Band C (1990): 61–73.

De Man, Paul. *Aesthetic Ideology.* Minneapolis: University of Minnesota Press, 1996.

———. *Allegories of Reading: Figural Language in Rousseau, Nietzsche, Rilke, and Proust.* New Haven: Yale University Press, 1979.

———. *The Resistance to Theory.* Minneapolis: University of Minnesota Press, 1986.

———. *The Rhetoric of Romanticism.* New York: Columbia University Press, 1984.

———. *Romanticism and Contemporary Criticism: The Gauss Seminar and Other Papers.* Baltimore: The Johns Hopkins University Press, 1993.

De Quincey, Thomas. *Confessions of an English Opium Eater.* Ed. Alethea Hayter. Harmondsworth, England: Penguin, 1971.

Derrida, Jacques. "Che cos' è la poesia." In *Points de suspension.* Comp. Elisabeth Weber. Paris: Galilée, 1992: 303–8.

———. "Declarations of Independence." *New Political Science* 15 (1986): 7–15.

———. *La Dissémination.* Paris: Seuil, 1972.

———. *Le Monolinguisme de l'autre.* Paris: Galilée, 1996.

———. "Mes Chances / My Chances." In *Taking Chances: Derrida, Psychoanalysis, and Literature,* ed. Joseph H. Smith and William Kerrigan, 1–32. Baltimore: The Johns Hopkins University Press, 1984.

———. *Politics of Friendship.* Trans. George Collins. London: Verso, 1997.

Diderot, Denis. *Lettre sur les sourds et les muets.* In vol. 2 of *Oeuvres complètes,* ed. Roger Lewinter. Paris: Club français du livre, 1969.

Dimoff, Paul. *La Vie et l'oeuvre d'André Chénier jusqu'à la Révolution française: 1762–1790.* 2 vols. Geneva: Droz, 1936.

Ernst, Morris, and Alan Schwartz. *Censorship: The Search for the Obscene.* New York: Macmillan, 1964.

Fineman, Joel. "Shakespeare's Perjur'd Eye," *Representations* 7 (summer 1984): 59–86; rpt. in *Shakespeare's Perjured Eye: The Invention of Poetic Subjectivity in the Sonnets.* Berkeley: University of California Press, 1986.

Flaubert, Gustave. *Correspondance,* 4th series (1854–1861). Paris: Louis Conard, 1927.

Foucault, Michel. *Discipline and Punish: The Birth of the Prison.* Trans. Alan Sheridan. New York: Pantheon Books, 1977.

———. *Language, Counter-memory, Practice.* Trans. and ed. Donald F. Bouchard. Ithaca: Cornell University Press, 1977.

Frey, Hans-Jost. *Studies in Poetic Discourse: Mallarmé, Baudelaire, Rimbaud, Hölderlin.* Trans. William Whobrey. Stanford: Stanford University Press, 1996.

Furet, François. *Interpreting the French Revolution.* Trans. Elborg Forster. Cambridge: Cambridge University Press, 1981.

Gadamer, Hans-Georg. *Truth and Method.* New York: Crossroad Publishing, 1975.

Genette, Gérard. *Mimologiques; Voyage en Cratylie.* Paris: Seuil, 1976.

Goldberg, Vicki. "Testing the Limits in a Culture of Excess," *New York Times,* Sunday, 29 October 1995, Arts section.

Grevisse, Maurice. *Le Bon usage: Grammaire française avec des remarques sur la langue française d'aujourd'hui.* 11th ed. Paris-Gembloux: Editions. Duculot, 1980.

Hampton, Timothy. "Virgil, Baudelaire and Mallarmé at the Sign of the Swan: Poetic Translation and Historical Allegory." *Romanic Review* 73, no. 4 (1984): 438–51.

Heidegger, Martin. *An Introduction to Metaphysics.* Trans. Ralph Manheim. New York: Doubleday, 1961.

Hertz, Neil. *The End of the Line: Essays on Psychoanalysis and the Sublime.* New York: Columbia University Press, 1985.

Hölderlin, Friedrich. *Sämtliche Werke und Briefe.* Vol. 1. München: Carl Hanser Verlag, 1970.

Hugo, Victor. *Choses vues.* 4 vols. Ed. Hubert Juin. Paris: Gallimard, 1972.

———. *Oeuvres complètes.* 18 vols. Ed. Jean Massin. Paris: Club français du livre, 1967–70.

Hunt, Lynn. *Politics, Culture and Class in the French Revolution.* Berkeley: University of California Press, 1984.

Irigaray, Luce. *Je, tu, nous. Toward a Culture of Difference.* Trans. Alison Martin. London: Routledge, 1993.

James, Anthony R. W. "L'Hallucination simple"? *Revue d'histoire littéraire de la France* 86, no. 6 (Nov.–Dec. 1986): 1026–37.

Johnson, Barbara. "Gender and Poetry: Charles Baudelaire and Marceline Desbordes-Valmore." In *Displacements: Women, Tradition, Literatures in French*, ed. Joan DeJean and Nancy Miller, 163–81. Baltimore: The Johns Hopkins University Press, 1991.

Kamuf, Peggy. *The Division of Literature, or the University in Deconstruction.* Chicago: University of Chicago Press, 1997.

———. *Signature Pieces: On the Institution of Authorship.* Ithaca, N.Y.: Cornell University Press, 1988.

Kaplan, Alice. *French Lessons: A Memoir.* Chicago: University of Chicago Press, 1983.

Kaufmann, Vincent. *Le Livre et ses adresses: Mallarmé, Ponge, Valéry, Blanchot.* Paris: Meridiens Klincksieck, 1986.

Lacoue-Labarthe, Philippe and Jean-Luc Nancy. *L'Absolu littéraire: Théorie de la littérature du romantisme allemand.* Paris: Seuil, 1978.

Lacoue-Labarthe, Philippe. *Heidegger, Art and Politics: The Fiction of the Political.* Trans. Chris Turner. Oxford: Basil Blackwell, 1990.

———. *La Poésie comme expérience.* Paris: C. Bourgois, 1986.

———. *L'Imitation des modernes: Typographies II.* Paris: Galilée, 1986.

Laplanche, Jean, and J.-B. Pontalis. "Fantasy and the Origins of Sexuality." *The International Journal of Psychoanalysis* 49, part 1 (1968): 1–18.

Leakey, F. W. *Baudelaire: Collected Essays, 1953–1988.* Cambridge: Cambridge University Press, 1990.

Leconte de Lisle, Charles. *Oeuvres.* Ed. Edgard Pich. Vol. 2. Paris: Les Belles Lettres, 1976.

Lewis, Felice Flanery. *Literature, Obscenity, and Law.* Carbondale: Southern Illinois Univerity Press, 1976.

Liu, Alan. *Wordsworth: The Sense of History.* Stanford: Stanford University Press, 1989.

Macherey, Pierre. *The Object of Literature.* Trans. David Macey. Cambridge: Cambridge University Press, 1995.

Mallarmé, Stéphane. *Oeuvres.* Ed. C. Barbier and C. Millan. Vol. 1. Paris: Flammarion, 1983.

———. *Oeuvres complètes.* Ed. Henri Mondor. Paris: Gallimard, 1945.

———. *Correspondance.* Ed. Henri Mondor and Lloyd Austin. 11 vols. Paris: Gallimard, 1959–85.

Michelet, Jules. *Histoire de la Révolution française.* 2 vols. Paris: Robert Laffont, 1979.

Miller-Frank, Felicia. *The Mechanical Song: Women, Voice, and the Artificial in*

Nineteenth-Century French Narrative. Stanford: Stanford University Press, 1995.

Mondor, Henri. *Vie de Mallarmé*. Paris: Gallimard, 1950.

Naish, Camille. *Death Comes to the Maiden: Sex and Execution 1431–1933*. London: Routledge, 1991.

Nancy, Jean-Luc. *The Inoperative Community*. Ed. Peter Connor. Minneapolis: University of Minnesota Press, 1991.

Nerval, Gérard de. *Oeuvres*. Ed. Henri Lemaître. Paris: Garnier, 1966.

Newmark, Kevin. *"L'absolu littéraire*: Friedrich Schlegel and the Myth of Irony," *MLN* 107, no. 5 (Dec. 1992): 905–30.

———. *Beyond Symbolism: Textual History and the Future of Reading*. Ithaca, N.Y.: Cornell University Press, 1991.

Ovid. *Metamorphoses*. Trans. Mary Innis. London: Penguin, 1955.

Pachet, Pierre. *Le Premier venu: Essai sur la politique baudelairienne*. Paris: Editions Denoël, 1976.

Plato. *The Collected Dialogues*. Ed. E. Hamilton and H. Cairns. Princeton: Princeton University Press, 1961.

Pommier, Jean. *Autour de l'édition originale des "Fleurs du mal."* Geneva: Slatkine Reprints, 1968.

Post, Robert, ed. *Censorship and Silencing: Practices of Cultural Regulation*. Los Angeles: The Getty Research Institute, 1997.

Poulet, Georges. "Hugo." *Etudes sure le temps humain II. La Distance intérieure*. Paris: Plon, 1952: pp. 194–230.

Prendergast, Christopher. *Paris and the Nineteenth Century*. Oxford: Blackwell, 1992.

Riffaterre, Michael. *Essais de stylistique structurale*. Paris: Flammarion, 1971.

Ronell, Avital. *The Telephone Book: Technology-Schizophrenia-Electric Speech*. Lincoln: University of Nebraska Press, 1989.

Rousseau, Jean-Jacques. *Oeuvres complètes*. Ed. B. Gagnebin and M. Raymond. Vol. 2. Paris: Gallimard, 1964.

Sade, D.-A.-F. de. *Justine, ou les malheurs de la vertu*. Paris: Union Générale d'éditions, 1969.

St. John-Stevas, Norman. *Obscenity and the Law*. London: Secker and Warburg, 1956.

Sainte-Beuve, Charles. *Poésies complètes*. Paris: Bibliothèque-Charpentier, 1910.

Scarfe, Francis. *André Chénier: His Life and Work, 1762–1794*. Oxford: Oxford University Press, 1965.

Sieburth, Richard. "Poetry and Obscenity: Baudelaire and Swinburne." In *Proceedings of the XXth International Congress of Comparative Literature*, ed. Anna Balakian, 464–71. New York: Garland, 1985–87.

Spackman, Barbara. *Fascist Virilities: Rhetoric, Ideology and Social Fantasy in Italy*. Minneapolis: University of Minnesota Press, 1996.

Spitzer, Leo. *Interpretationen zur Geschichte der Französischen Lyrik*. Heidelberg: Selbstverlag des Romanischen Seminars, 1961.

Stanguennec, André. *Mallarmé et l'éthique de la poésie*. Paris: Librairie J. Vrin, 1992.

Starobinski, Jean. "André Chénier et le mythe de la régénération." In *Savoir, faire, espérer: les limites de la raison*, 577–91. Bruxelles: Facultés Universitaires Saint-Louis, 1976.

————. "André Chénier and the Allegory of Poetry." In *Images of Romanticism: Verbal and Visual Affinities*, ed. K. Kroeber and W. Walling, 39–60. New Haven: Yale University Press, 1978.

————. *La Relation critique*. Paris: Gallimard, 1970.

————. *La Mélancholie au miroir: Trois lectures de Baudelaire*. Conférences, essais et leçons du Collège de France. Paris: Julliard, 1989.

Strauss, Leo. *Persecution and the Art of Writing*. Glencoe, Ill.: Free Press, 1952.

Szondi, Peter. *Das Lyrische Drama des Fin de Siècle*. Frankfurt-am-Main: Suhrkamp, 1975.

Tocqueville, Alexis de. *The Old Régime and the French Revolution*. Trans. Stuart Gilbert. Garden City, N.Y.: Doubleday, 1955.

————. *L'Ancien Régime et la Révolution*. Vol. 2. Paris: Gallimard, 1953.

Valéry, Paul. *Oeuvres complètes*. Ed. Jean Hytier. 2 vols. Paris: Gallimard, 1957.

Van Tieghem, Paul. "Un 'Monsieur . . .' mystérieux: André Chénier." *Revue d'histoire littéraire de la France* 35 (1928): 92–98.

Walter, Gérard. *André Chénier: Son milieu et son temps*. Paris: Robert Laffont, 1947.

Warburton, William. *Essai sur les hiéroglyphes des Egyptiens; Où l'on voit l'origine et le progrès du langage et de l'écriture, l'antiquité des sciences en Egypte, et l'origine du culte des animaux*. Trans. Léonard des Malpeines. Paris: Aubier Flammarion, 1977.

Warminski, Andrzej. *Readings in Interpretation: Hölderlin, Hegel, Heidegger*. Minneapolis: University of Minnesota Press, 1987.

Weber, Samuel. *Mass Mediauras: Form, Technics, Media*. Stanford: Stanford University Press, 1996.

Woolsey, John M. Introduction to *Ulysses*, by James Joyce, vii–xii. New York: Random House, 1961.

Žižek, Slavoj. *The Sublime Object of Ideology*. London: Verso, 1989.

Index

In this index an "f" after a number indicates a separate reference on the next page, and an "ff" indicates separate references on the next two pages. A continuous discussion over two or more pages is indicated by a span of page numbers, e.g., "57–59." *Passim* is used for a cluster of references in close but not consecutive sequence.

MERIDIAN

Crossing Aesthetics

Maurice Blanchot, *The Work of Fire*

Jacques Derrida, *Points ... : Interviews, 1974–1994*

J. Hillis Miller, *Topographies*

Philippe Lacoue-Labarthe, *Musica Ficta (Figures of Wagner)*

Jacques Derrida, *Aporias*

Emmanuel Levinas, *Outside the Subject*

Jean-François Lyotard, *Lessons on the Analytic Sublime*

Peter Fenves, *"Chatter": Language and History in Kierkegaard*

Jean-Luc Nancy, *The Experience of Freedom*

Jean-Joseph Goux, *Oedipus, Philosopher*

Haun Saussy, *The Problem of a Chinese Aesthetic*

Jean-Luc Nancy, *The Birth to Presence*

Library of Congress Cataloging-in-Publication Data

Burt, E. S.
   Poetry's appeal : nineteenth-century french lyric and the political
space / E. S. Burt.
      p.   cm. — (Meridian)
   Includes bibliographical references and index.
   ISBN 0-8047-3490-9. — ISBN 0-8047-3873-4 (pbk.)
    1. French poetry—19th century—History and criticism.
2. Political poetry, French—History and criticism.   I. Title.
II. Series: Meridian (Stanford, Calif.)
PQ433.B87   1999
841'.709358—dc21   99-39452

⊗ This book is printed on acid-free, archival quality paper.

Original printing 1999
Last figure below indicates the year of this printing:
08 07 06 05 04 03 02 01 00 99

Typeset by James P. Brommer in 10.9/13 Garamond
and Lithos display